Inequality and Industrial Change

This book presents a global analysis of the distribution of pay, deploying systematic new measurements on a large scale. Contributions cover the U.S. wage structure back to 1920 and up to 1998, pay inequality and unemployment in Europe since 1970, and the evolution of inequality alongside industrial growth, liberalization, financial crisis, state violence, and industrial policy in more than fifty developing countries. The chapters evaluate the major debates over rising inequality and support the emerging view that there exists a powerful macrodynamics of pay inequality in both rich and poor countries – a view whose origins go back to Keynes and Kuznets. Several chapters present detailed descriptions of a new global pay inequality data set based on Theil's T statistic. The chapters on theory and methodology provide students and specialists with full access to the measurements and the nonparametric statistical techniques underlying these studies.

James K. Galbraith is Professor in the Lyndon B. Johnson School of Public Affairs and in the Department of Government, University of Texas at Austin. He is also a Senior Scholar with the Jerome Levy Economics Institute and National Chairman of Economists Allied for Arms Reduction. Professor Galbraith is the author of *Created Unequal: The Crisis in American Pay*, sponsored by the Century Foundation and published by the Free Press in 1998, and *Balancing Acts: Technology, Finance, and the American Future* (1989). He served as Executive Director of the U.S. Congress's Joint Economic Committee in 1981–1982 and was a Guest Scholar at the Brookings Institution in 1985. Professor Galbraith is the coauthor of two textbooks on economics, *The Economic Problem* with Robert Heilbroner and *Macroeconomics* with William Darity, jr.

Maureen Berner is Assistant Professor in the Institute of Government, University of North Carolina at Chapel Hill. She is the recipient of the University of Texas Excellence in Teaching Award (1996–1997), taught at the Public Service Academy of Southwest Texas State University, and served on the staff of the Accounting and Information Management Division of the U.S. General Accounting Office. Professor Berner has published articles in a number of research and policy journals, including an analysis of welfare reform in *Spectrum: The Journal of State and Local Government*. Her Ph.D. dissertation received the 1999 Best Dissertation award of the National Association of Schools of Public Affairs and Administration.

Praise for *Inequality and Industrial Change*

"This well documented book pulls together evidence on the evolution of inequality in ORCD and developing countries and presents an innovative and wide ranging analysis of a crucial set of issues. It also reaches some controversial conclusions, and is therefore sure to become an important component of the international debate."

—Lars Osberg, *Dalhouse University, Canada*

"The book by Galbraith and Berner is a superb collection of papers on how inequality and growth are in fact correlated in both developed and developing countries. Galbraith and his students have produced a group of studies that all illustrate how modern econometric methods can be synthesized with insightful economic analysis to give us a better understanding of the inequality/growth relationship. Jamie Galbraith is one of the best applied economists around, and this collection of papers proves it. . . ."

—Daniel Slottje, *Southern Methodist University*

Inequality and Industrial Change
A Global View

Edited by

JAMES K. GALBRAITH
University of Texas at Austin

MAUREEN BERNER
*University of North Carolina
at Chapel Hill*

CAMBRIDGE
UNIVERSITY PRESS

PUBLISHED BY THE PRESS SYNDICATE OF THE UNIVERSITY OF CAMBRIDGE
The Pitt Building, Trumpington Street, Cambridge, United Kingdom

CAMBRIDGE UNIVERSITY PRESS
The Edinburgh Building, Cambridge CB2 2RU, UK
40 West 20th Street, New York, NY 10011-4211, USA
10 Stamford Road, Oakleigh, VIC 3166, Australia
Ruiz de Alarcón 13, 28014 Madrid, Spain
Dock House, The Waterfront, Cape Town 8001, South Africa

http://www.cambridge.org.

© James K. Galbraith and Maureen Berner   2001

First published 2001

Printed in the United States of America

Typeface Times Roman 10/12 pt.   *System* QuarkXPress [BTS]

A catalog record for this book is available from the British Library.

Library of Congress Cataloging in Publication Data
Inequality and industrial change: a global view / edited by James K. Galbraith,
Maureen Berner.
p. cm.
Includes bibliographical references and index.
ISBN 0-521-66274-5
1. Income distribution.   2. Wages.   I. Galbraith, James K.   II. Berner, Maureen.
HC79.I5 I494 2001   339.2′2–dc21   00-052887

ISBN   0 521 66274 5   hardback
ISBN   0 521 00993 6   paperback

For Peter S. Albin

Contents

vii

Contributors

Maureen Berner is Assistant Professor of Government and Public Administration, University of North Carolina at Chapel Hill.

Amy D. Calistri is a former Program Director at IBM and a consultant at the Applied Economic Consulting Group in Austin, Texas.

Paulo Du Pin Calmon is Professor at the Institute of Political Science and International Relations and Executive Director of the Center for Public Policy Research at the University of Brasilia, Brazil.

Pedro Filipe Teixeira da Conceição is Lecturer at the Center for Innovation, Technology, and Policy Research, Institut Superior Tecnico, Lisbon.

Thomas Ferguson is Senior Associate Provost at the University of Massachusetts, Boston.

Pedro Ferreira is a Research Assistant at the Internet and Telecommunications Convergence Consortium at MIT and is affiliated with the Center for Innovation, Technology, and Policy Research, Institut Superior Tecnico, Lisbon.

James K. Galbraith is Professor at the Lyndon B. Johnson School of Public Affairs, the University of Texas at Austin, and Senior Scholar at the Jerome Levy Economics Institute. He is Director of the University of Texas Inequality Project. His previous book is *Created Unequal: The Crisis in American Pay.*

Vidal Garza Cantú is Director of the Center for the Improvement of Public Function and Assistant Professor of Economics and Public Policy at the Instituto Tecnológico y de Estudios Superiores de Monterrey, Mexico.

Abel Hibert Sanchez is Chief Economist at Grupo Pulsar Internacional, Monterrey, Mexico.

Junmo Kim is a Senior Researcher at the Korea Institute of Public Administration, Seoul, Korea.

Jiaqing Lu is a Senior Consultant at the Applied Economic Consulting Group in Austin, Texas.

George Purcell is a Ph.D. candidate in Government at the University of Texas at Austin.

Maureen Berner, Jiaqing Lu, and Junmo Kim hold Ph.D. degrees in Public Policy from the Lyndon B. Johnson School of Public Affairs, the University of Texas at Austin. Amy Calistri, Vidal Garza Cantú, and Pedro Conceição are currently completing dissertations in the same program.

Permissions

Pedro Filipe Teixeira da Conceição and James K. Galbraith, "Constructing Long and Dense Time Series of Inequality Using the Theil Statistic," *Eastern Economic Journal*, 26(1), June 2000, 61–74. Copyright © 2000, Eastern Economic Association.

Paulo Du Pin Calmon, Pedro Filipe Teixeira da Conceição, James K. Galbraith, Vidal Garza Cantú, and Abel Hibert, "The Evolution of Industrial Wage Inequality in Mexico and Brazil," *Review of Development Economics*, 4(2), June 2000, 194–203. Copyright © 2000, Review of Development Economics.

James K. Galbraith, Pedro Conceição and Pedro Ferreira: "Inequality and Unemployment in Europe: The American Cure," *New Left Review*, No. 237, September–October 1999, 28–51. Copyright © 1999, New Left Review.

Thomas Ferguson and James K. Galbraith, "The American Wage Structure, 1920–1947," *Research in Economic History*, Vol. 19, 1999, 205–257. Copyright © 1999, Research in Economic History.

James K. Galbraith and Vidal Garza Cantú, "Inequality in American Manufacturing Wages, 1920–1998: A Revised Estimate," *Journal of Economic Issues*, Summer 1999, 735–743. Copyright © 1999, Journal of Economic Issues.

James K. Galbraith and Junmo Kim, "The Legacy of the HCI: An Empirical Analysis of Korean Industrial Policy," *Journal of Economic Development*, '23 (1), June 1998, 1–20. Copyright © 1998, Journal of Economic Development.

xi

Acknowledgments

This book is the work of the University of Texas Inequality Project, an enterprise that consists essentially of ourselves, a small office, and a handful of computers, based intellectually at the LBJ School of Public Affairs and located in the Government Department of the University of Texas at Austin. We have received strong financial support from the Ford Foundation, from the Jerome Levy Economics Institute of Bard College, and from two centers at the University of Texas: the Policy Research Institute and the Center for the Study of Western Hemispheric Trade. We thank especially Lance Lindblom of Ford, Dimitri Papadimitriou of Levy, Peter Ward of the PRI, and William Glade of the CSWHT for their unflagging and generous support. I also thank the Dean of the LBJ School, Edwin Dorn, for his support and encouragement and particularly for providing leave in the fall of 1999 so that this work could be finished.

The work as a whole draws heavily on my book *Created Unequal: The Crisis in American Pay*, a Twentieth Century Fund Book published by the Free Press in 1998. It may be viewed in part as a companion volume to that book.

A version of Chapter 1 is forthcoming in a *New Guide to Post Keynesian Economics*, edited by Steve Pressman and Ric Holt. I thank Paul Davidson and Steve Pressman for valuable comments on an earlier version of this chapter, and I thank Pressman and Holt for permission to use the work here.

Chapter 3 is adapted from an article that appeared in the 1999 issue of *Research in Economic History*. Thomas Ferguson and I thank the editor of that journal, Alexander Field, and two anonymous referees for comments over the three years that this article was in preparation. One of the referees in particular deserves our thanks for repeated and extended comments, corrections, and suggestions of exceptional value.

We also note the important contribution of Maureen Berner, who served as research assistant on this article.

Chapter 4 is adapted in part from an article in the *Journal of Economic Issues*. Chapter 6 first appeared in *New Left Review*. Chapter 8 was prepared first for a project on global capital markets under the direction of Lance Taylor and John Eatwell. A version of this chapter has appeared as a working paper of the Center for Economic Policy Analysis at the New School University.

Chapter 12 is adapted from an article published in the *Review of Development Economics*, and Chapter 13 is republished from the *Journal of Economic Development*. Chapter 15 first appeared in the *Eastern Economic Journal*. We thank the editors and referees of these journals, and especially Pan A. Yotopoulos of the *JED* for his encouragement.

Maureen Berner has served this project as my coeditor with great energy and distinction, despite the burdens of finishing her own Ph.D. dissertation and moving to the University of North Carolina with her young family. Together, we are deeply indebted to Scott Parris of Cambridge University Press for his early and strong support of this project and to three anonymous referees for Cambridge. We thank Ms. Helen Greenberg and Mr. Ernie Haim for meticulous editing of the manuscript.

We are all deeply in debt to our Webmaster, Wang Qifei, whose technical wizardry and artistry with the computer have provided us with our principal means of communicating among ourselves and with the outside world. Readers of this book should look for his work at *http://utip.gov.utexas.edu*. It is wonderful, and it is also the source of an electronic version of much of the data displayed on these pages. We are also indebted to Liu Xioali (Maggie Liu), who built and maintained our paper archive of articles on inequality during the 1998–1999 academic year. And we thank Peter P. S. Bradford, whose other commitments kept him from participating as fully as he might have liked. Finally, we thank Mr. Jack Dangermond, Environmental Systems Research Institute, Inc., for the gift of mapping software employed here in Figures 9.1 to 9.4.

Our larger intellectual debts are too numerous and diffuse to acknowledge in full. However, we would like to single out seven colleagues who have played important encouraging roles over the years. They are Professors Chandler Stolp and Robert Wilson of the LBJ School; Professor Michael Marder and Dr. Ping Chen of the Center for Non-Linear Dynamics and Professor Ed George of the Business School and Department of Statistics at the University of Texas at Austin; Professor Daniel Slottje of Southern Methodist University; and Professor William (Sandy) Darity of the University of North Carolina at Chapel Hill. Readers will have no difficulty identifying our weightiest intellectual debt. It is to Henri Theil, a man none of us has ever met, though he has encouraged us in occasional correspondence. Without Theil's work, this book could not have been conceived of.

We have another debt, entirely hidden. It is to Peter Albin, an economist of the greatest brilliance, who very early on, as much as fifteen years ago, saw the importance of this work and encouraged me to pursue it. Which I, and we, have done. To him we dedicate this book.

Finally, we thank our spouses and, in one case, fiancée: Andrew Berner, Eric Calistri, Katya Calmon, Eliza Garza, Marta da Cruz Vilaça, Hyeree Kim, Ann Macauley, Kirsten Mullen, Tang Ying, and Wei Chunyan. And we acknowledge a very special group that includes Will Berner, Viviana and Daniela Garza, Eve (Tang Ye) Galbraith, Ah-Young and Gyu-Young Kim, and Ray (Tao-Tao) Lu. These are all the children who did not yet exist when our group got underway.

James K. Galbraith
Austin, Texas
May 16, 2000

PART I

INTRODUCTION TO THEORY
AND METHOD

CHAPTER 1

The Macroeconomics of Income Distribution

James K. Galbraith

Inequality has become perhaps the foremost preoccupation of modern empirical economics. Yet the conventional theoretical explanations of changing inequality rest on premises long ago demolished on logical grounds. This chapter summarizes a Keynesian theory of income distribution. The theory integrates macroeconomic and distributive phenomena and so accounts for the empirical relationship between the changing shape of the distribution and major macroeconomic events.

1.1 Introduction

Income inequality is surely "the prevailing social issue of our time."[1] But the development is recent. The rise in income inequality in postwar America dates only to 1970 and the reemergence of inequality as a social issue only to the late 1980s. It took the spur of Reaganism, with its celebration of conspicuous differentiation, to reawaken class consciousness in American political life. Before that time, attention had been on other issues for nearly sixty years.

The original submergence of class was a liberal achievement. It was perhaps John Maynard Keynes's greatest service to capitalism that he focused attention on jobs, that unemployment and not equality was the great issue of the Great Depression. In the Keynesian period – from 1945 to 1970 – income inequalities received scant scholarly attention. The great leveling achieved during World War II seemed to have become a fact of nature, and attention shifted to *poverty* as the organizing principle for social action. As early as 1957, John Kenneth Galbraith observed that "few things are more evident in modern social history than the decline of interest in inequality as an economic issue."[2] Michael

---

[1] Michael Lind, "It Takes a Nation," *The Washington Monthly*, November 1998, pp. 39–41.
[2] *The Affluent Society*, Boston: Houghton Mifflin, 1958, p. 82.

3

Harrington's *The Other America* (1963/1971) is widely credited with mobilizing opinion on poverty. In a world that saw itself as prosperous, egalitarian, and fully employed, the poor were "other." Poverty became defined as separation from the capitalist system rather than as an extension of it.

And so the theory of income distribution passed into the domain of *microeconomics*. Textbooks taught neoclassical marginal productivity theory, loosely rooted in two-factor production functions, according to which profits are the reward of capital and wages are proportional to personal productivities, as duly adjusted by stocks of human capital. The theory nicely explained the stability of income shares – as between profits and wages – as reflecting the slow unfolding and neutral character of technological change.[3]

The theory also predicted a smooth relationship between the rate of interest and the capital intensity of technique. An evolution toward greater capital intensity and a correspondingly lower marginal productivity of the capital stock implied a declining rate of profit and interest – not unlike that heralded by Marx and fretted over by Mill – as sure as heat death in the thermodynamic long run. And in the international setting, meanwhile, the theory predicted the flow of capital from wealthy to developing lands, reflecting the capital scarcity and high marginal productivities of the latter. The microfoundations had optimistic macroimplications: convergence of incomes within countries and of development processes between them.

This is the context of the uprising that became known as the *Cambridge capital critique*. It began in the 1950s with the observation by Joan Robinson that there were difficulties in assuming a unit of measure for the capital stock. Under simple alternative specifications that admitted the heterogeneity of capital goods, the smooth inverse relationship between interest rates and capital intensity would not hold. This was "reswitching." It would lay waste to the optimistic macroimplications of the simple two-factor distributional story.[4]

Already by 1960, Joan Robinson and Piero Sraffa had raised lethal objections to the idea that the distribution of factor income could logically be interpreted as a set of factor returns related to marginal pro-

---

[3] And it provided a universal, irrefutable, empty rationalization for existing wage differentials, because human capital cannot, by its nature, be observed or measured with any useful degree of precision.

[4] Jan Kregel's essay on "Income Distribution" in the 1978 *Guide to Post Keynesian Economics* remains a classic introduction to the work of Kalecki, Robinson, Kaldor, Sraffa, Pasinetti, Harcourt, and others in the tradition of Keynes on this issue.

ductivities under constant returns to scale. Robinson had presented the "special theory" of this critique, namely, that the concept of aggregate capital as a *physical quantity* was incoherent. Capital goods cannot be aggregated into a common measure of the capital stock without first assigning a value to each physical capital item. But treatment of the capital stock as a *value aggregate* requires prior knowledge of the rate of interest. The value of a particular capital good depends on the future net revenue stream attributable to the acquisition of that good, *discounted at a rate of interest*; capital goods will be acquired up to the point where their internal rate of return (marginal efficiency) just *equals* that rate of interest. How then can the neoclassical rate of interest be itself precisely the "marginal productivity" of capital that the theory was supposed to determine? Robinson had identified an indeterminacy at the heart of the paradigm.

Sraffa's contribution was to generalize Robinson's position and to render the concept of marginal productivity redundant. In *Production of Commodities by Means of Commodities* (1960), Sraffa showed that short-period production prices can be derived purely from dated physical quantities of embodied labor input (and an exogenous discount or interest rate), as indeed Marx had postulated long before, but without satisfactory proof. Relative prices, and for that matter relative wages, therefore do not depend on marginal productivities. Meanwhile, Keynes supplied a theory of the interest rate built on liquidity preference and so eliminated the need for a marginal physical productivity of the aggregate capital stock to underpin the theory of the rate of interest.

We are now four decades after Sraffa. Yet for reasons psychological and political rather than logical and mathematical, the capital critique has not penetrated mainstream economics and it never will. Today, only a handful of economists seem even aware of it. Applications of aggregate production-function methodology run rampant in studies of economic growth (new-growth theory), of development and convergence, and of international trade (e.g., factor-price equalization and other applications of Heckscher-Ohlin). Ostensible liberals are not exempt: Arguments for higher public infrastructure investment based on its alleged marginal productivity are of precisely this type, as are arguments for increased investment in education based on the higher marginal productivity of human skill.[5] To mainstream economics, Keynesianism

---

[5] Aggregation of human capital – heterogeneous education acquired at different moments in time – faces exactly the same problems as aggregation of physical capital. The

has been reduced to a narrow doctrine relating sticky wages, public spending, and employment. The fact that there exists a Keynesian interest rate theory, still less the reasons for it, seems to have been forgotten; new generations of economists are not taught liquidity preference.

Thus, when inequality resurfaced as a social, political, and economic issue in the 1980s, economists responded with a flood of new studies founded on microeconomics. It is perhaps a mark of the capital controversies that these studies rarely, if ever, refer baldly to nonlabor income or attempt to rationalize the vast rise of profits in the early 1990s as a response to the "rising marginal productivity of capital." But otherwise, the debate over increasing inequality has been conducted almost exclusively in pre-Sraffian, anti-Keynesian terms, that is, in terms of the pricing of underlying factors of production, of their marginal productivities. The idiom is of competitive supply-and-demand models operating under conditions of diminishing marginal returns.

The fault line in these inequality debates has been a question of demand or supply. Is rising inequality due to an increase in the relative demand for (read: a rise in the marginal physical productivity of) highly skilled workers? Or is it due to an increase in the effective supply of low-skilled workers, through immigration or trade, driving down the wage (e.g., along a fixed marginal productivity schedule)? Either way, the arguments entirely respect the marginal productivity paradigm and the market mechanism.

The empirical literature has many points of interest and merit. Juhn, Murphy, and Pierce (1993) show, for example, how rising inequality in the United States in the 1970s was mainly due to the falling position of the bottom half of the wage distribution; it is only in the 1980s that the top half also spreads out, with a corresponding increase in the estimated value of years of schooling. Krueger (1993) has shown how higher wage differentials are associated with the use of computers at the workplace, though as Krueger and others in this area now acknowledge, the direction of causation in this relationship is far from certain. Carnoy (1994), Howell and Gittleman (1993), and others have noted that skill differentials and wage differentials do not always move together: For African Americans, the former have narrowed but the latter have increased. In a new paper, Thurow (1998), citing a study by Houseman, points out that while the wage gap between high school and college grads increased, real

(needless to say, ludicrous) response of the literature is to treat all moments in school as identical and timeless, so that they can be added and compared, once and for all, for each worker.

wages in both groups declined; what sort of technological progress is this?

In practice, the mainstream analysts generally downplay supply factors, leaving a plurality for the hypothesis of *skill bias* in technological change. Yet the impression left by surveys (Danziger and Gottschalk, 1995; Lawrence 1996) is that of an evidentiary impasse, with the final result dominated by the power of conventional thinking. It may be that the core empirical issues will never be resolved to the entire satisfaction of the contestants. It is even more unlikely that this work will evolve into a satisfactory examination of the underlying theoretical questions.

At the same time, the literature is vulnerable to a Keynesian critique. But to make such a critique persuasive, it needs a clear theoretical restatement, going beyond the usual appeal to "institutions," "politics," and "history." But it also needs empirical substantiation capable of accounting in detail for the movement of inequality through time and in different national settings. Keynesians need to show that the personal distribution of income is linked to the flow of economic profits as a share of national income and therefore to the spending decisions of capitalists and their *macroeconomic* ramifications.

For this, we need more and better data, particularly a substantial expansion in the volume and improvement in the quality of measures of the movement of economic inequality through time, so that the relationship between such movements and measured macroeconomic phenomena can be tracked. A macroeconomic theory of distribution requires macroeconomic measures of distribution. Fortunately, this condition can be met. The requisite data are available on the historical record, for long time spans and in many countries, though their potential for this particular purpose has rarely been recognized and almost never exploited.

1.2   Toward a Macroeconomic Theory of Personal Income Distribution

If the marginal productivity theory is to be thoroughly discarded, it follows that aggregate income distribution, the division of national product between wages and profits, has to be determined by some mechanism other than the marginal rate of return on an alleged capital stock. But what mechanism?

Keynes, Kalecki, and Kaldor presented a Keynesian position on this question: "Capitalists get what they spend." Aggregate profits are determined by the spending decisions of the capitalist class. Businesspeople, motivated by animal spirits, receive back as profit income what they lay out as capital investment and luxury consumption. Aggregate wages, on the other hand, are determined merely by the aggregate stock of consumption goods produced. They are a function of effective demand for output; average wages are this value divided by the total number of workers.

Where workers save, as Pasinetti showed, the flow of profit income runs partly to workers. But, other things equal, the aggregate volume of profit income is unaffected. In other words, total profits depend entirely on business and government spending decisions and not on the distribution of claims to profit income as between workers and capitalists. Nor do gross profits depend on the quality or type of spending. So far as the gross flow of profits is concerned, it does not matter what the spending is for: "Paint the Black Forest white!" Joan Robinson declared. "If you can't pay men to do something sensible, pay them to do something silly."

The ratio between aggregate wages and gross profits is the *national* distribution of income. It has a close association with the business cycle. After a slump, exhilaration takes over and investment soars. An investment-and-profits boom leads back to full employment. In times of full employment, with consumption and wages high, there is a profit squeeze and business gets "boom tired." Artificial booms are possible, for the government can provide a stimulus to spending if private businesses are unwilling to do so. But initiatives of this kind are met with ambivalence by business leaders because they deprive them of their controlling position in the political economy.

In all of this, the *personal* distribution of wage income, or the shape of the wage structure, is left entirely up in the air, to be settled by further assumptions or by political, institutional, and historical forces. Galbraith (1998a) offers a linkage between the Keynesian macroeconomic forces and the wage structure along the following lines.

Consider a simple setting: an economy with one production factor, labor, alongside firms with identical rising marginal production costs but distinct markets. One firm faces a competitive, perfectly elastic demand curve and therefore prices at marginal cost. Another faces a downward-sloping demand curve and therefore sets output so that marginal revenue equals marginal cost, with a price taken from the corresponding point on the demand function – as first stipulated by Joan Robinson. The second firm thus enjoys a degree of monopoly equal to the inverse of the elasticity of the demand function, per Abba Lerner, and a monopoly return per unit equal to the difference between price and marginal cost. However, because in this model there is no "capital," there is no profit either, and the monopoly return must be distributed to the sole factor of production, namely, labor: It is a firm-specific labor rent. The distribution of income therefore depends entirely on the relative degree of monopoly power.

This is the simple theory of personal income distribution that best corresponds to the post-Keynesian view of pricing. Sraffa's pricing scheme, though worked out for the competitive setting, does not exclude monopoly power. Rather, it rules out the notion of a separate return to capital and therefore a coherent idea of profit as a factor return. Rent and quasi-rent, on the other hand, remain viable. And there is no reason why certain classes of labor cannot earn scarcity premiums, just as much as can certain grades of land. The premium commanded by the purveyor of a new machine, so often referred to as a return to capital or to technological innovation, is simply the scarcity rent commanded by the labor that produced it. Remove the patent protection or veil of secrecy surrounding the technique embodied in the machine, and the return will collapse even though marginal productivity in a technical sense is unaffected.

Now consider the effect of an equal proportionate upward shift in the demand function facing the two firms. In the competitive case, prices (and wage rates, which by assumption make up the marginal cost) rise along the marginal cost function. But in the monopolistic case, the slope of the marginal revenue function ensures that the rise in price will not be to the full extent of the shift in demand. Furthermore, because the wage rate in the monopolistic case already includes a substantial element of quasi-rent, the *proportionate* shift in the wage must be lower for the identical shift in the demand function. For these reasons, an upward shift in demand will raise the wage of the competitive sector relative to that of the monopolistic sector, reducing the difference between the two and therefore the degree of inequality in the system as a whole. A downward shift will have the opposite effect.

From this simple argument, two hypotheses emerge. First, because of rent sharing, firms facing less elastic demand functions should pay higher wages than firms facing more elastic demand functions. Second, the degree of dispersion in the wage structure should vary with macroeconomic conditions: falling in booms and rising in slumps. In other words, most countries should be found on the downward-sloping portion of an inverted Kuznets U curve, such that economic growth is equalizing and recession is not. These predictions differ from the neoclassical view, according to which monopoly rents flow to capitalists rather than to workers, and according to which there should be no connection between the microeconomically determined interpersonal distribution of wages and the business cycle.

This is a reasonable beginning, but it is not enough. One needs a ratio-
nale for the existence of monopoly power, of downward-sloping demand
curves facing the firm. This is to be found in the existence of machines,
which are the embodiment of past labor frozen for current and future
use. It is the machinery used in production, and nothing else, that permits
one final product to be distinguished from another, making possible the
differentiation of individual firm demand curves. Once title to machinery is vested in the capitalist, some of the monopoly rent (as well as, and
distinct from, the transferable title to the firm itself) may be paid to that
person. And a larger portion of the monopoly rent also flows downward,
through the salary and wage structure, reaching managers and even production workers in the form of efficiency wages. Everyone connected
with machinery enjoys some leverage as a result and a corresponding
advantage over those not so connected.[6]

Our two firms can be reinterpreted as representing two sectors in the
economy. One of them works entirely with current labor, supplied com-
petitively, and prices output at a conventional but small markup over a
socially determined minimum wage. We might call this the *S sector*; it
resembles the largest parts of the services sector in real life. The other
sector – we may call it the *C sector* – produces ordinary machinery and
consumption goods from current labor and existing machines, which is
to say, from current labor plus a potpourri of embodied past labor over
which the firm holds ownership rights. Because each such potpourri is in
some respects unique, the essence of monopoly power is right there; it
lies in the particularity of manufactured output and the corresponding
differentiation of consumer demand.[7]

The still missing element is a central one in capitalist economic life,
the defining characteristic of advanced industrial countries as opposed
to developing ones. This is the creation and production of *new* products,
machinery, and means of production. This is, in large part, the function
of a separate, specialized sector that we may call the *K sector*: the producers of knowledge goods.

From the standpoint of distribution theory, the income of the K sector
corresponds to the Keynes-Kalecki-Kaldor flow of profits. It is deter-

---

[6] The salary paid to the owner-executive may be difficult to distinguish in accounting
terms from other employee compensation. But the important distinction is between
pay derived from the flow of current rents and the capital value of ownership rights.
The latter are typically much larger but do not represent a drain on the cash flow of
the firm.

[7] There is, of course, a certain amount of monopoly rent in human talent, the winner-take-
all phenomenon of sports stars and divas admirably dealt with by Cook and Frank (1997).
But in comparison with product differentiation, this phenomenon is minor.

mined by capitalists' spending. Because capitalists spend on investment goods, a swing in the flow of gross investment corresponds to a swing in the income of the K sector. The Keynes-Kalecki proposition that capitalist consumption also enhances the flow of profits (like the widow's cruse, which cannot be emptied no matter how much is poured from it) has its material counterpart in the observation that nonwage goods, or capitalists' consumption goods, are merely and for the most part advanced-technology investment goods adapted for personal enjoyment. In a cyclical economy, the K sector will be a strongly cyclical performer. The cycle itself is above all a cycle of capitalist spending.

Production in the K sector is not based primarily on an accumulation of past labor inputs, organized as a specific stock of machines, but rather on an accumulation of people and their skills. Like the C sector, the K sector *is* monopolistic, but in an unstable way. Monopoly power in this sector is inherently transient and depends on the fabrication of new markets and the extraction of maximal revenue from them while they last. The K sector is Schumpeterian. It is the sphere of creative destruction, a winner-take-all proposition, a lottery, in which the purpose of competition is to beat the competition with new products and better processes. Wages in the K sector are necessarily high, both because the prizes are great and because there is nothing to be gained from second-rate talent.

But on the other hand, employment in the K sector is radically dependent on the flow of investment demand. The K sector is the central producer of new capital equipment. It therefore depends for its prosperity entirely on a high rate of acquisition of such equipment. It also depends on a periodically high rate of destruction of old capital equipment. The K sector therefore benefits, as the C sector does not, from a strong cycle in investment spending, both from the downturn that wipes out the old and obsolescent and again from the upturn when new plants and processes move into the vacuum left by the old.

In the advanced industrial countries, a rise in business investment, such as occurs with the burst of growth at the start of expansions, increases employment among high-wage groups, such as construction and technology workers and especially among their nonproduction workers – the designers, marketers, managers, and so on. At first, high rates of growth will increase both inequality and the average real wage on that account. It is only as the expansion proceeds, as higher incomes are paid to production workers and as demand shifts to consumer products and services, that the normal income-compressing effects of prosperity will be felt. In short: *Investment demand is unequalizing, while consumption demand is equalizing.*

Extension to the foreign sector is simple. In an advanced economy, K-sector goods dominate exports and C-sector goods dominate the competition with imports. Because the K sector is hypermonopolistic, it has few developing-country competitors. Changes in the (North-South) exchange rate do not greatly affect it. But such changes do undercut the relative wage position of C-sector workers by adjusting, in effect, the relative wages of their direct competition. Because K-sector workers sit at the top of the wage structure, currency appreciations therefore tend to increase inequality in advanced countries and currency depreciations to decrease it. Also, export booms in an advanced country tend to raise inequality in the wage structure, as do the corresponding increases in imports. In countries lacking a K sector, investment demand leads to imports and economic growth is equalizing insofar as the domestic economy is concerned. Depreciations in developing countries have an effect on inequality opposite to that in advanced ones. Because they raise import prices and force the reallocation of spending away from domestic products (Yotopolous, 1996), they are macrocontractionary and inequality-increasing. Thus, a North–South appreciation/depreciation raises inequality both within each region and between the regions.

1.3   Evidence on the Macrotheory of Income Distribution

To evaluate a macroeconomic theory of personal income distribution, one needs dense time series information on the evolution of inequality in many countries. This requirement has been a major limitation. Very few nations have conducted consistent annual household surveys from which inequality measures can be computed over long time horizons. The measures that do exist for the countries that have conducted such surveys tend to focus on income by family or household, measures that can be quite far removed from the structure of hourly wage rates by industry and occupation. Industrial data in household surveys can be sketchy, and, in contrast to information on age or gender or ethnicity, such data are subject to high rates of error in reporting.

But there is an alternative approach to the measurement of the changing dispersion of hourly wage rates, particularly if one is principally interested in the manufacturing sector. This is the generalized entropy approach of Theil (1972), based on information theory. Theil's measure has the virtue that changes in inequality can be estimated from very crude data on wages or earnings and employment grouped by industrial sector. Industrial data sets, organized into standard classification schemes, are available on a consistent annual basis for most countries in the world. While the basic requirements for computing Theil statistics are minimal, these data sets provide a rich and so far largely unexplored source from which estimates of the movement of industrial wage inequality through time can be computed.

Our empirical work in this area (presented throughout this volume) suggests that in the *industrializing* countries there tends to be a negative association between growth and inequality. Rapid growth is equalizing; most countries are on the downward-sloping portion of the Kuznets inverted U curve. This, we argue, is what one would expect when the predominant industrial sector is of the C rather than the K type. Among significant exceptions, we find the United States and the United Kingdom – just those countries where high rates of growth are most driven by domestic investment led by the K sector. After controlling for the effects of unemployment (which raises inequality), inflation, and the exchange rate, growth per se increases inequality to a modest degree. This relationship would appear to reflect the influence of the cycle of profit spending on employment and incomes in the K sector – just as predicted.[8]

At the same time, however, it would be too simple to restrict the study of changes in inequality to the issue of the relationship between inequality and growth. Institutions matter. So do external conditions. We find systematic relationships between certain types of political change and inequality; the arrival of a military government through a coup d'état is generally followed by rising inequality, for instance. We also find systematic relationships between external financial crises and rising inequality in developing countries. And we find evidence of the lasting effect of industrial policies in the case of Korea, which we examine in detail. All of these, we think, illustrate the macrodetermination of changes in the distribution of pay.

1.4   Summary and Plan of the Work to Follow

The Keynesians long ago challenged marginal productivity distribution theory. They also presented the outlines of an alternative, whose major

---

[8] Further research on the U.S. economy has decomposed the sources of between-group variation in industrial performance after establishing a strong relationship between the performance of industries and their wage rates. The four major components of between-industry variation correspond well to the sectoral predictions. The most important component is the flux of investment spending, which differentiates the K sector from the C sector. Second is the flux of consumption spending. Third are the fluctuations of the exchange rate, and fourth are those of the military budget. In this way, a second type of analysis tends to confirm that the major components of flux in the industrial structure are linked in fairly simple ways to the standard Keynesian sectoral structures. Galbraith (1998a) provides details.

elements are the distribution of rents, affected by differing degrees of monopoly power, and the flow of profit spending and therefore of investment, corresponding to the income of the sector producing investment goods. But they did not succeed. What they lacked was a demonstration of the superiority of this theory as the foundation stone for empirical research into the functional and personal distributions of income. In consequence, neoclassical theory has continued to shape the literature.

This book represents our effort to change all this, to demonstrate frankly the advantages of the Keynesian approach. Chapter 2 provides a readers' guide to the key techniques: the use of hierarchical and aggregative data sets, mostly on earnings and employment in manufacturing sectors, to measure the movement of inequality, and the use of cluster and discriminant analysis to pick apart patterns of industrial change. The rest of our work is relentlessly Spartan in its reference to theory. Our aim is instead to demonstrate the usefulness of the evidence itself, to make the point in tables and graphs and maps: Keynesian forces drive the structure of pay and the evolution of industrial structure.

Chapters 3 and 4 take up the case of the United States. Because the post–World War II evolution of industrial wage structures in the United States is explored in Galbraith (1998a), these chapters mainly present evidence on two historical periods not covered in detail in that study: the years from 1920 to 1947 and the years following the end of the *Created Unequal* data set, 1993 to 1999. Chapter 4 also provides some new evidence on changes in inequality in manufacturing earnings for the years 1948 to 1957.

Chapters 5 and 6 move on to Europe and to the larger context of the Organization for Economic Cooperation and Development (OECD), the club of the advanced nations. In Chapter 5, Calistri and Galbraith decompose the patterns of industrial wage change for three major countries – Germany, Italy, and Japan – to show how the behavior of wages or earnings through time can be used to analyze national industrial structures. In Chapter 6, Conceição, Ferreira, and Galbraith extend the measurement of industrial wage inequality to all of Europe and show relationships between inequality and unemployment in Europe that run directly counter to much popular as well as neoclassical thinking. This chapter also presents a direct comparison – we believe it to be the first – between inequality in manufacturing earnings in Europe as a whole, including inequality between as well as within countries, and that in the United States.

Chapter 7 provides a transition between the study of developed and industrial countries by reviewing the large literature related to the Kuznets hypothesis. Chapter 8 presents the core data set against which the experience of the larger world, outside the OECD, can be assessed. Computed from the Industrial Statistics Data Base of the United Nations International Development Organization (UNIDO) and other sources, this now provides annual inequality measures for more than seventy countries covering most of the world's industrial production. We believe it to be a useful addition to the economists' tool kit for the measurement and assessment of inequality in the global setting, particularly because it permits useful assessment of changes in inequality continuously through time, something that is not possible given the intermittent coverage of other data sets. Chapters 9 through 11 provide evidence on the relationship between inequality and financial crises, inequality and various forms of state violence, particularly the coup d'état, inequality and changes in political regimes.

Chapters 12 and 13 present three country studies: on Brazil and Mexico in comparative context and on Korea. Chapter 12 emphasizes the measurement of inequality and shows how our approach can be applied to *monthly* data sets. Increasing the sampling rate in this way, even at the expense of a reduction in the number of categories covered, appears to increase considerably the resolution of the data series. In both the Brazilian and Mexican cases, the results illustrate in even finer detail the relationship between movements of inequality and economic and political events. The chapter on Korea, on the other hand, applies the cluster-and-discriminant analysis technique to the history of Korean industrial development policy.

Today, advances in the measurement of the evolution of inequality, coupled with careful attention to issues of taxonomy in the industrial structure, permit one to demonstrate that in fact the major movements in the inequality of wage structures are traceable to macroeconomic events. They appear to correspond closely to the patterns of performance of the major Keynesian sectors: investment, consumption, and foreign trade. One may hope that the combination of theory and evidence can perhaps change some minds about which theory of income distribution is appropriate to the modern world. Perhaps this approach may enjoy more success than the purely logical critiques of forty years ago.

CHAPTER 2

Measuring Inequality and Industrial Change

Maureen Berner and James K. Galbraith

This chapter introduces in nontechnical terms the principal techniques used in this book: Theil's T statistic, cluster analysis, and discriminant function analysis.

2.1   Introduction

How does one measure whether one society is more equal than another? Or whether an economy is more equal than it had been in the past? Equality is a broad concept with many layers of meaning: There is equality and inequality in legal rights, in social and political standing, and in many matters of culture. And even within the economic dimension, one may focus on inequalities of wealth, of family income, of individual earnings, and of wage rates. Each of these has its own importance, and each is measured from different sources of data and in slightly different ways.

Most of the theoretical literature on economic inequality is concerned with the determinants of pay: with wage rates and employment prospects, which together determine earnings in particular industries and occupations. Pay rates and job openings are a characteristic of the employer and the workplace. Yet most of the empirical work on inequality derives from surveys whose focus is on employees and their households, which are aimed mainly at assessing the distribution of family or household income. This is an important, even vital, issue, obviously: The distribution of household income is a key social fact. Yet data sources based on household surveys of income only indirectly provide information about the distribution of wage rates.

The most widely used measure of inequality in the literature is, of course, the Gini coefficient, derived from the Lorenz curve. The Gini coefficient is measured on a scale from 0 to 1 that is, in principle, well suited to comparing countries with each other or with their own experi-

16

ences through time. To compute the Gini coefficient is, however, quite demanding of data; it requires that the underlying observations (individuals, families, or households) be sorted by rank order of their incomes. This means that the Gini coefficient is best estimated (and typically is estimated) from sample surveys or census-type data. Unfortunately, such surveys are comparatively scarce, and the quality of those that do exist is uneven in many cases.

In this book, we rely on an alternative method based on the work of Henri Theil (1967, 1972), who proposed an entropy-based measure of inequality derived from the theory of information. Theil's T statistic has many interesting properties and, we think, virtues, but the central one is practical. Unlike the Gini, T can be broken, or decomposed, by groups. If information on the underlying observations includes their membership in groups – which may be race, or gender, or age categories, or educational achievement, or any other characteristic – then one can divide the Theil measure of inequality into a component that occurs within each group and a component that occurs between the groups; the sum of these two components will equal Theil's T as a whole.

This elementary fact has a most interesting implication, which Theil himself noted long ago. If one only has grouped data and categorical averages for pay and employment, one can nevertheless compute an estimate of the shape of the distribution as a whole from this information. This is a *lower-bound* estimate: It omits the within-group component.

But under certain circumstances, particularly if the group structure is held constant over time or across countries, the movement of (or difference in) the lower-bound, between-group estimate of Theil's T can yield very useful information about the evolution of inequality in the distribution as a whole. In this book, we exploit this property repeatedly, using a type of grouped data that is widely available for many countries: payroll and employment by industrial category. In this way, we are able to compile detailed annual (and sometimes even monthly) estimates of the change in inequality in manufacturing earnings around the world, usefully supplementing (and, in some cases, contradicting) other sources of information on inequality.

Industrial data sets have another interesting property: They break apart the patterns of change in wages and earnings into a substantial number of discrete components organized by groups of factories – known as *industries* – that are doing reasonably similar things. But to treat each industrial subcategory in some standard classification scheme as a discrete unit of observation is clearly a mistake. In many cases, there may be no material difference between two categories that are distinguished in the data, so that wages and earnings in the manufacture of (say) silk and rayon hosiery march side by side over the years. Trying to work with the original accounting categories in such circumstances needlessly complicates the effort of arriving at a crisp, clear understanding of the economic forces driving changes in relative wage rates.

In this book, we deploy a pair of statistical techniques to reduce the complicated and messy surface patterns of change in industrial data sets to the information that lies buried within them. The first technique is cluster analysis, which permits us to organize patterns of earnings change into small numbers of major groups. In effect, we create for each country a map of its industrial wage structure, of the similarities and differences between the wage behavior of industries over time, which we argue reflects underlying structural similarities and differences of the industries themselves. The second technique is discriminant function analysis, which is a way of sorting out the driving components of changes between the major groups identified in the clustering procedure and of assessing the importance of each component.

Cluster analysis and discriminant function analysis are both established statistical tools; we use a widely available commercial software package for this research (Statistica). What is novel in our work is the combination of these techniques and their application to time series information in the underlying data set – in our case, for the most part, rates of earnings change by industrial category. The beauty of this combination lies in the fact that at the end of the combined process, certain outputs of the discriminant technique are also, themselves, a kind of constructed economic time series, namely, the principal components of earnings variations across groups. This raises the enticing prospect, which we explore in several of the chapters that follow, that the sources of change in relative earnings across large groups of industries can be related directly to measures of macroeconomic performance (such as growth rates) or to quasi-political events (such as strikes) or external circumstances (such as changing exchange rates or commodity prices).

While, say, regression analysis is available for analyzing the effects of multiple independent variables on a single dependent variable, we know of no other effective technique for analyzing the effect of a single independent variable on the differences between the pathways of multiple dependent variables. Therefore, we claim that our innovation opens up a new approach to the analysis of certain important social phenomena.

This chapter introduces our methods: the Theil index, cluster analysis, and discriminant analysis. Our intent here is to avoid a technical presentation, but rather simply to offer an intuitive description and justification for our methods and to try to respond to some of the many questions that readers encountering these techniques for the first time are likely to have. Those with an interest in the more technical aspects of these methods should consult Chapters 15 and 16, the technical appendixes, on which this chapter is based in part.

2.2   Measuring the Evolution of Inequality with Theil's T Statistic

Theil's T statistic originates with information theory. Loosely, if the conditional probability of some event is equal to 1, no information can be gained by the event's actual occurrence. Everything, in that case, was known in advance. If the conditional probabilities of all possible events are equal, on the other hand, no advance predictions can be made; in that case, the information obtained when one possible event actually occurs reaches its maximum value. A measure of the information content of a set of possible events is thus inversely related to the ex ante predictability of any one event. Because probabilities are multiplicative, an information measure that is based on the logarithms of probability values has the nice property that the information in any distinct set of groups of events will sum to the information in the whole set.

Theil turned this observation around, showing that the same general logic could be used to derive a measure of inequality of incomes. To arrive at an appropriate scaling, the measure is inverted: If all incomes are equal, Theil's T measure of inequality is zero. As dispersion grows about the mean, T increases. It has a theoretical maximum given by the logarithm of the number of people in the population; that value is reached when one person has all of the income.

Theil's T statistic satisfies the standard conditions for an acceptable measure of inequality, such as the principle of transfers.[1] But the real beauty of Theil's T statistic lies in its decomposability. If individuals are assigned to groups in a mutually exclusive, exhaustive way, the inequality of the society as a whole can be expressed in terms of a component occurring within each of the groups and a component occurring between the average values of the groups. This is known as the property of *linear decomposability*. And because the measure of within-group inequality for any particular group is simply Theil's T for that group, we can say that Theil's T is even, to that extent, a *fractal*: its formula is self-similar at different scales and levels of observation.

---

[1] This principle requires that a transfer from a poorer person to a richer one increase the index and vice versa.

If the underlying data set is based on observations of individuals – for example, a sample survey or a census – Theil's T statistic can be used to assess the relative importance of inequalities between groups and inequalities within them. Are poor African Americans, say, affected more by the black–white differential on average or more by the degree of inequality that exists among African Americans? This sort of interesting and useful question cannot easily be answered by the method of Gini coefficients.

On the other hand, if individual-level data are available and if the main objective is to make a comparison of the degree of inequality between two societies or two time periods, there is no obvious reason why Theil's T should be used in preference to the more familiar Gini coefficient. While a cross-check with a different index may be useful, differences in the level of or movement in these two measures are not generally likely to be of fundamental importance.

The real advantage of the Theil index arises when there are no adequate or reliable data at the individual level. As a practical matter, household surveys are expensive and censuses are even more so. The latter are actually rare, occurring at most every five years even in rich countries, while the former are truly sporadic. In some countries, decades may pass with only one or two income surveys of doubtful quality having been done. And if a year is missed, the information cannot be re-created, because households do not generally maintain accurate records (or memories) of their income in preceding years (and certainly do not do so uniformly across income classes).

It is also not easy to ensure that household income surveys conducted by different teams, at widely separated intervals in time, proceed with comparable methods and effectiveness. Different regions and countries, moreover, have widely varying cultural practices with respect to the concealment of wealth and income. And so, even surveys conducted in reasonably similar ways in two different places may produce measurements that are not comparable in fact.

In contrast, most governments maintain regular records of the larger manufacturing establishments located within their borders. They keep track of the number of people employed in each such establishment and of the total payroll of each. This is partly for tax and tariff reasons; partly to maintain knowledge of where the industrial base is and of what it consists, for purposes of procurement, war mobilization, and other public missions; partly for policy assessment; and partly as a mere matter of statistical habit. Such data are ubiquitous and voluminous.

As it happens, an industrial classification scheme is a partition of precisely the kind that is useful in the computation of the Theil statistic. One can therefore compute a between-groups component of the Theil statistic, which we call T', from the data for total employment and total payroll by industrial category. In this way, one can obtain a lower-bound estimate of the inequality of manufacturing earnings. It is a lower-bound estimate, of course, because we have no information on inequality that may or may not be prevalent inside each of the industrial groups.

A lower-bound estimate of inequality based on some arbitrary industrial classification scheme might not seem terribly useful. But consider: Every member of the manufacturing labor force is a member of some industrial classification group. The dispersion of group averages is, therefore, a reflection in some sense of the dispersion of the underlying population. And as the classification lines are drawn ever more finely, the number of groups approaches the number of people in the underlying population, until in the limit T' must converge to T, the Theil measure of inequality for the population (in this case, of manufacturing employees) as a whole.

It follows that, if the dispersion of incomes in the underlying population becomes more unequal from one time period to the next, the group average incomes of the various industrial categories will, in general, move further apart. A widening of the distribution in general must almost always mean that a low-wage industry (say, apparel) will lose ground relative to a high-wage industry (say, aerospace). And so, while the between-groups component of Theil's T is not necessarily useful as a measure of the level of inequality as a whole, it is an uncannily good estimate of the movement in the dispersion of earnings through time, so long as classification schemes and employment structures do not change too much. And fortunately, classification schemes generally remain stable over time (thanks to bureaucratic inertia), while changes in the employment structure, which do occur, tend to be sporadic and can also be isolated in the data sets.

A number of transnational data sets now exist, including the Structural Analysis (STAN) database of the Organization for Economic Cooperation and Development (OECD), and the Industrial Statistics Data Base of the United Nations International Development Organization (UNIDO) in Vienna. These data sets now provide, for a few hundred dollars apiece, access to raw material suitable for computing T' for manufacturing earnings for scores of countries around the world – over seventy, in fact – on an annual basis going back at least to 1970 and in many cases to 1963. These calculations form the backbone of the inequality measures in this book, as outlined in Chapter 8. They are supplemented by national annual data sources in a few cases – notably the United States and China – and by monthly data sets in the case of the

United States, Mexico, and Brazil. Generally speaking, we find that the national data sets are more detailed and reliable, and monthly data provide a powerful means of dissecting the political history of inequality in those few countries for which we have developed them (see Chapters 4 and 12). But the availability of inexpensive annual data on so many countries in the transnational data sets is indispensable for making broad comparisons through time and across the entire globe.

One can go further – and we have. The transnational data sets have the appealing property that industrial categories have been standardized, so that one can add up, say, employment in automotive manufacture or inorganic chemicals across countries. But the standardization also means that the level values of T' may be directly comparable across countries, particularly where, as is the case for the OECD, there are not great differences in employment structure across countries. We show in Chapter 6 that a simple comparison of our T' measures for the European countries coincides quite closely with the vastly more complex and detailed work of the Luxembourg Income Studies in the comparison of Gini coefficients. So, we are led to believe that we have developed a shortcut method of considerable power, not only for historical but also for comparative work.

We believe there is little reason to doubt the general accuracy of measures of total payroll and total employment by industrial category, in most cases, on which these calculations rely. To be sure, there will be some biases in the data collection. In country X, establishments with fewer than, say, 50 employees may be excluded; in country Y, the ceiling may be 20 or 100. In country Z, a particular industry may operate partly in secret, and part of its payroll may be excluded from the data set or merged into that of an industry with a different classification code.

These sorts of problems are endemic to our work, but we do not think they are more serious than the standard run of sampling problems in the taking of surveys. Moreover, none of these problems are likely to cause a serious distortion of a measure of *change* in the dispersion of earnings. So long as the degree of bias itself does not vary in some systematic way, the change in a biased measure of T' will closely track the change in an unbiased measure. Other sorts of data problems – such as the misclassification of some industries, missing data, or abrupt changes in the classification scheme – are usually detectable, and we have flagged a few cases.

In sum, we believe that our measure of the change in T' is a useful, reasonably accurate measure of the change in the dispersion of manufacturing earnings in most of the countries for which we make the calculation. A more serious question that one might raise about this work is, so what?

Why be concerned about the dispersion of manufacturing earnings? Manufacturing employment is only a small part of the economically active population in most countries. Services and agriculture are often, even usually, bigger. And a measure of manufacturing earnings excludes of necessity earnings from profits, interest, rent, transfer payments, and other sources of economic income.

To this concern, we offer three replies. First, manufacturing earnings are of interest for many practical and policy purposes. The manufacturing sector, together with agriculture, produces the bulk of traded goods. It is the seat of technological change. And economic theories of wage change have been concerned with the effects of globalization and of technology. If these effects exist and are important, they should be easier to find in manufacturing than in the larger economy as a whole, where they may be buried by events unrelated to technology or to trade.

Second, we think that events that are recorded inside the manufacturing sector are likely to be felt in other sectors as well. The national economy is an integrated entity. Farmers buy from producers of farm machinery and organic chemicals and sell to producers of refined foods and beverages and textiles. If we observe, within manufacturing, a growing gap between the pay of textile workers and chemical workers, it is likely, we believe, that this reflects a growing gap between the pay of high-wage, high-skilled employees outside the manufacturing sector and that of low-wage farm workers, also outside the manufacturing sector. If we have in our room a small window with a fixed frame, we can still usually tell changes in the weather from a glance outside. We do not need, as a rule, to be able to see the entire sky. If we observe that inequality rose in the Chilean manufacturing sector after the coup of September 1973 (see Chapters 10 and 11), we do not feel insecure in arguing that inequality was rising everywhere in Chilean society at that time.

Our third reply is that, in general, *more happens* in the manufacturing sector than outside it. Service workers and farm workers operate with little physical capital and, in the case of the latter, with a largely unchanging supply of land. The manufacturing sector is the scene of Schumpeterian upheaval and Keynesian unemployment. It is the epicenter of newness. The lines of causality, for this reason, generally run from manufacturing outward, and for this reason, too, an analysis focused on manufacturing retains value.

This reply moves us toward our second area of concern. The measurement of changing inequality is all very well, but it provides only an aggregative measure of changing industrial conditions. The same data sets from which we make our inequality calculations, however, also provide the possibility of analyzing the underlying character of industrial and even technological change. But for this, we need to move below the surface measures of inequality and work at the level of the industrial cluster.

2.3   Using Cluster Analysis to Detect Patterns of Industrial Change

Cluster analysis is a taxonomic tool. It finds patterns and group structures. Its usefulness in our research comes from its ability to be applied to the rates of change in wage data through time. In this way, clustering identifies those industries whose wages follow similar paths over long periods of history. We can also use it (and do, in Chapter 9) to group nations according to the similarity of their movements of various macroeconomic variables, including the evolution of inequality itself.

While the use of historical information to classify groups is routine in disciplines such as paleontology and biology, cluster analysis of time series data is relatively new; we have found only a handful of examples in social science and other disciplines. This is in part because the technique is computationally intensive, and became inexpensive only in recent decades, and in part because economists have simply not explored taxonomic issues to the same extent as other disciplines. In this book, clustering is used to build a taxonomy of the American wage structure from 1920 to 1947 (Chapter 3), of OECD wage structures (Chapter 5), of the Asian and European regions (Chapter 9), and of industries in Korea for the purpose of examining Korean industrial policy (Chapter 13).

Cluster analysis holds the promise of revealing a fundamental structure in time series data based on patterns of behavior over time. It is a technique that classifies objects – in this case, detailed wage data – based on the similarities found on a characteristic variable – in this case, average rates of change in wage rates or average annual earnings.

The clustering algorithm we use works in the following way. We start with many groups, each of which represents a particular unit of analysis, such as an industrial category or, in some applications, a country. For each unit, we have a vector of observations, each of them a percentage rate of change, usually of wages or earnings. The vector spans the time frame for which data are available.

One can imagine a multidimensional space, with each dimension representing one annual interval. The axis of each dimension measures a rate of change from one time period to the next. A single point, representing one of the original groups, is placed in a plane according to its growth rate in each of the periods whose axes define that plane. Points for all the original groups are placed in this space, and the Euclidean distance between points can be calculated. Those points with a small distance between them have close comovement; those with a larger distance between them are less interrelated. To cluster data across two or three years, a blackboard is sufficient. To do it across thirty-five years, one would have points located in a thirty-five-dimensional space. This is a bit harder to draw on the blackboard but perfectly easy to program on a computer.

Clustering is a sequential, hierarchical process. We begin with each object in a "group" by itself. In the first step, we find the two objects closest to each other and form them into a new group. In the next step, we follow the same procedure, including now the newly formed group and calculating the distance to and from its center. As we proceed, we link objects together and amalgamate ever larger clusters of increasingly dissimilar elements.

To do this, we need a linkage or amalgamation rule. Ward's method, the amalgamation rule we use in this study, uses an analysis-of-variance approach to evaluate the distances between clusters. Ward's rule is that with each joining, the within-group variance in the new, larger group is minimized and the variance between the new groups is maximized. The result is a clustering that, at each step, produces the most compact clusters available and therefore minimizes the loss of information involved in submerging a previously independent entity into a group.

Clustering can often reveal relationships that are lost when data are aggregated to a higher level. Suppose that one were looking at data for industrial wages over time, with categories as in the Standard Industrial Codes (SICs). Two such codes are for water and air transportation (codes 44 and 45, respectively). But what if one used data at a more detailed level, such as freight water transportation and passenger water transportation and freight airline transportation and passenger airline transportation? The clustering would group together the four disaggregated series according to similarity in wage change over time. It might match up the data according to the SIC coding structure. But alternatively, it might match up passenger water and passenger airline transportation in one group and freight water and freight airline transportation in another. If the latter occurred, one would know that the key lines of difference are not between modes of transportation, but between types of cargo.

Clustering is useful. However, it does have a cost. It inevitably entails a loss of information as the clustering proceeds, and in the final stage (if it goes that far), all the groups are merged into one and all between-group information is lost. The key, therefore, is to know when to stop. One must try to cluster just enough to eliminate redundant entities, but not so much as to lose important information by forcing highly dissimilar objects into a single group. Measures of information lost at each stage of clustering can help resolve this issue, although to some extent it remains a matter of judgment.

The cluster analysis results in a tree diagram in which each branch aligns with the one(s) it most closely resembles, according to the distinguishing characteristic identified by the researcher – in this case, similarity of behavior over time. The tree diagrams reveal a structure based entirely on patterns of behavior over time, exposing the comparative extent of variations in the relative pay performance of the groups. The best number of clusters is sometimes revealed by this diagram. Figure 3.1 in Chapter 3 provides a nice example of very clear group structures in American industry from 1920 to 1947.

Underlying the tree diagram is a matrix of distances between all pairs of observations. If the underlying groups are industries, this matrix maps the similarities and dissimilarities in wage change between every industry and every other. If the underlying groups are countries, the distance matrix that underlies the cluster tree yields a type of global map of the degree of similarity for each country's evolution of the performance variable – which may be a measure of inequality – to that of all the others.

2.4   Using Discriminant Analysis to Identify the Source of Differences

The next step in the analysis is to explore the determinants of the group structure and to ask whether one can actually identify the forces that cause them to behave as they do. Discriminant function analysis is the tool best suited to this challenge.

A discriminant function is simply a vector of weights that the computer assigns to the rows of the original observational matrix in such a way as to separate out, as cleanly as possible, different patterns of movement in (the columns of) the group structure. Imagine that every few years, some outside force – say, a rise in the oil price – cleanly raised the wages in the oil-producing sector and produced a recession that lowered wages everywhere else. If this pattern accounted for a significant amount of the fluctuation in relative wages across industrial groups, then the discriminant function procedure would tend to create a vector with large positive weights assigned to those years when the oil price rose, and perhaps negative weights to those years when oil prices fell and the effect moved in the opposite direction.

Discriminant function analysis simply chooses a set of weighting vectors, such as the hypothetical one described previously, in such a way as to maximize the linear independence of the weighting functions. That is to say, the algorithm ensures the least possible correlation between the various vectors. It also computes the proportion of the total between-group variation in the original data set that can be accounted for by each of the weighting vectors so created.

In this way, the output of a discriminant function analysis is a group of vectors – the maximum number is one less than the number of groups in the analysis – that "capture" in some meaningful sense the principal elements of between-groups variation in the wage structure over time. So much is standard. But now we come to two points of innovation in our analysis.

First, because the inputs to our particular discriminant analysis take the form of industrial groups chosen so as to minimize the within-group variation of their relative wages over time, the between-groups element of the variation is as large as possible for the given number of groups. Thus, the discriminant functions can lay claim to having captured not merely some arbitrary between-group differences, but most of the relevant or interesting sources of variation in the wage structure as a whole. That which is missed – the within-groups variation – has been chosen by construction to be as small and uninteresting as possible.

Second, and even more intriguing, is the fact that the weighting functions (they are known as *eigenvectors* or *canonical roots*) in this special case are vectors whose length is (one less than) the number of years in the original analysis. Indeed, the elements of these vectors are entirely derived from the events of the particular year to which they correspond. Thus, *the weighting functions are themselves a type of time series variable*; they correspond in practice to the components of between-group wage changes in each year of the underlying data set. This is quite a departure from the usual applications of discriminant function analysis, in which the elements of the eigenvectors have no intuitive interpretation. Here, they do.

The fact that the elements of the various discriminant functions may be interpreted as economic time series raises a tantalizing conjecture. Do these elements correspond, in fact, to *known* data from the historical record? The perhaps surprising fact – we were astonished when we first realized it – is that, in many cases, they do. Thus, in Chapter 3, we show how much of the between-group variation in industrial (and agricultural) wages in the United States in the interwar period can be tied to the movement of nominal gross national product (GNP), while distinct but lesser sources of between-group variation can be associated with strike activity and with movements of the dollar exchange rate. In this way, one can arrive in some cases at a quite precise accounting of the sources of variation in wages that underlie changes in inequality measured from the same data.

The precise identification of a weighting function (or eigenvector, or canonical root) with a particular historical time series remains a difficult empirical task. It can be assisted by the trick of computing a *canonical score* on each of the weighting functions for the elements in the original observation set – in this case, for each industry or industrial group. The canonical score is simply the vector product of the weighting function and the rates of wage change for the entity being scored. That is, it is the sum of the products of the relevant vector element for each year and the rate of wage change for that year.

By simply listing scores for each industry or group, one can sometimes find a clue to the force underlying a particular canonical root. For example, were one to find ammunition, steel, aircraft, chemicals, and electronics ranking high on one root, while hats, apparel, and home building ranked low (as Galbraith, 1998a, did for U.S. manufacturing from 1958 to 1992), one might be forgiven for suspecting that military spending might be the differentiating force. Once one has the clue, the next step is a search for relevant variables in the historical record. Sometimes, as Chapter 3 illustrates, these are easily found, and it does not take much effort to persuade reasonable people that an association between the root and the force probably exists.

In other cases – as we explore in Chapter 5 – identifying an association may be much more difficult, perhaps partly because the researchers themselves may be on the unfamiliar terrain of the industrial structure of some distant country. In these cases, one may have to be content with a plot of the major scores against each other; such a plot simply shows by how much the major sources of wage variation can be reduced to a handful of discrete, separable, independent (but unidentified) forces. Or one may adopt the device of plotting canonical scores against a "pseudoscore" computed in the same way but with a candidate force – the change of a variable from the historical record – substituted for the weighting function coefficients. In this case, a tight-fitting linear association between canonical scores and pseudoscores can be taken as a sign of a relationship. Chapter 5 illustrates the application of this technique in a few cases.

Discriminant function analysis, applied to the output of a cluster analysis conducted on time series data, has provided us with many insights into the macrodynamics of changing industrial structures. It is no easy business – the matrices often do not invert! But, we believe, it is worth the time and energy we have invested in it so far. And we further believe that, given the normal tendency of societies to organize themselves into groups, these techniques together form a powerful combination quite well suited to research in social science.

2.5 Conclusion

We have built this book around the idea that statistical techniques should be chosen in view of available data. The mass of industrial data sets available to economists have remained an underutilized resource, in part, because they are not usefully adapted to statistical techniques designed to operate mainly on sample surveys. Our techniques are chosen precisely with the characteristics of grouped, hierarchical, evolutionary industrial data sets in mind. The Theil statistic has provided us with a way to mine these data sets for evidence of the change in inequality through time. Cluster analysis has enabled us to make some sense of the underlying patterns of wage change. And discriminant function analysis has enabled us to deconstruct, after a fashion, the sources of between-groups variation in order to begin to gain some insight into the macroeconomic, political, and external events that have played the largest roles in driving changes in the distribution of industrial incomes.

We hope that readers will find the effort involved in pursuing these techniques through the studies that follow to be worthwhile. We also hope that, in a few cases, readers will be prompted to try these techniques for themselves. The measurement of inequality and the explanation of industrial change are ongoing projects. They should not end with this book.

PART II

INEQUALITY, UNEMPLOYMENT, AND INDUSTRIAL CHANGE

CHAPTER 3

The American Wage Structure: 1920–1947

Thomas Ferguson and James K. Galbraith

This chapter uses industrial wage data to examine changes in the interindustry structure of wages between 1920 and 1947. We first sort among the available data on wage changes by industry and occupation to identify blocs that exhibit common patterns of wage change over time. We then analyze the sources of wage variation across groups and through time. We identify four such forces that together explain 97 percent of the variance in wage change across groups, and we identify variables in the historical record that appear to correspond to these forces. In a reversal of the usual notions of micro-to-macro causality, we argue that a small number of macroeconomic variables thus account for a large proportion of distributional changes.

3.1   Introduction

Impressed by the sweeping implications of the mind–body problem, the German philosopher Arthur Schopenhauer referred to that famous conundrum as the *Weltknoten*, the "World Knot." Economic history is more prosaic. Yet the economic experience of the United States between World War I and the end of World War II did generate one problem with nearly as sweeping repercussions in its field: the behavior of wages.

This period spans the slump following World War I, the Roaring Twenties, the Great Depression, the New Deal, and World War II – times of turmoil encompassing every form of economic, technological, political, and social change. Studies of wage determination during this time can therefore illuminate many competing hypotheses, perhaps more effectively than studies of the allegedly more tranquil postwar period.[1] Such

---

[1] The persistence of the middle to late forties wage structure and the role of pattern bargains are widely acknowledged; see, e.g., Goldin and Margo, 1991, p. 1, who cite Thurow, 1975, p. 111. See also Eckstein and Wilson, 1962, and Maher, 1961a. In an interesting reversal, we have come to question whether this very widely held view is, in fact, correct. Chapter 4 provides new evidence suggesting a different story.

33

inquiries also have intriguing implications for other fields, including history, political science, and even international relations.

Yet *systematic* assessments of the relevant empirical evidence are rare; previous studies tend to be monographic.[2] The earliest studies can be traced back to the thirties, when data collected by the federal government (and studies by Paul Douglas) became widely available. This wave crested between the end of World War II and the late fifties. A second, very recent wave has followed the decay of the postwar American wage system. In line with the focus of much recent research on inequality, it emphasizes workforce characteristics, technological change, and the acquisition of skills.[3]

The major studies of the first wave agreed that interindustry wage differentials narrowed substantially during World War II, as did skill differentials. But these studies differed sharply in other respects, particularly in their assessment of the stability of wage structures in both the long and the short run. These early studies were also marked by inconsistent conclusions about the pattern of relative wage changes at important junctures, such as during parts of the Depression and the 1920–1921 downturn.[4] Differences in measurement and method accounted in part for these inconsistencies.[5]

The early studies also made little effort to investigate whether political events such as the New Deal or economic developments such as changes in international trade or the devaluation of the dollar in 1933

---

[2] A good, if sometimes curiously selective, overview of recent work in English on interwar wage adjustment and the controversies over relief is Eichengreen, 1992. See especially pp. 216–218. See also Eichengreen and Hatton, 1988, and Borchardt, 1991, Chapters 9–11. Wallis, 1989, is another interesting analysis of the relief and wages controversy in the United States.

[3] Our dating of the earlier wave of wage structure studies follows Dunlop, 1988, p. 58; the second wave of wage studies now includes a huge number of papers. See, e.g., the references in Goldin and Margo, 1991. On the notion of *wage structure*, see the classic reference by Ross, 1957.

[4] Compare Cullen, 1956; Backman and Gainsbrugh, 1948; Slichter, 1950; Reder, 1962 (especially p. 269); Bell, 1951; Lebergott, 1947; Keat, 1960; Maher, 1961a; and Dunlop, 1988. While not an interindustry study, Ober, 1948, also contains much of interest.

[5] Some of these differences, as the investigators quickly realized, were artifacts of data or method; rank orderings of industries usually looked more stable than alignments founded on ratio or interval measures such as absolute differences in cents per hour. The common technique (which we, too, employ in our study) of tracing levels of wages in a consistent set of industries over a generation or more may mislead by leaving out of account new industries that arose during the period or older ones that collapsed. Still, the first wave of wage structure studies topped out without resolving how much of a difference such differences ultimately made. See especially Cullen, 1956, which is quite complete.

affected the evolution of the wage structure; unionization is the only politico-economic event to receive extensive discussion. And most investigators in this early Keynesian era appeared to share the conviction that changes in the interindustry wage structure over several decades occurred in a neoclassical long run and were not consequences of wage policy, market power, or changes in aggregate demand.[6]

The modern studies frankly avow that the "Great Compression" of the 1940s in American wages was strongly rooted in the full-employment policies of World War II. Progress, to be sure, has been made.[7] Still, many threads from the wage-historical World Knot continue to dangle. What were the roles of politics, trade, technology, unions, and the year-to-year fluctuations of the business cycle? How much can be attributed to the rising educational levels of the workforce? What happened to inequality in this period and why? With these questions in mind, a fresh look at wage behavior between 1920 and 1947 should be rewarding, particularly if it draws on data that other studies have not fully exploited and on techniques that illuminate these data in fresh and interesting ways. It also provides a useful introduction to the analysis of wage structures and inequality more generally – the larger task of this book.

3.2   The Present Study

Our approach requires regular and complete time series, and for this volume we have brought together annual data from a variety of sources on (nominal) average hourly earnings for workers in eighty-three different industries or industry branches, including two cases broken down by region, from 1920 to 1947. We reach beyond manufacturing, where most of our data come from surveys conducted by the National Industrial Conference Board.[8] Eventually, we succeeded in locating data for railroads, electric utilities, coal mining, gas utilities, construction (where

---

[6] See Haddy and Tolles, 1957; by comparison, Haddy and Currell, 1958, is more conventional. Reder, 1962, pp. 276ff., brings out particularly clearly the neoclassical frame of reference in which most of these discussions moved. Discussions of market power did predominate in regard to one subject, labor unions, on which a vast literature arose. See, e.g., Lewis, 1963.

[7] See Goldin and Margo, 1991; Goldin and Katz, 1995; in regard to the role of education, the former is quite reserved, though suggestive.

[8] Our data come from published sources, and most of them have been used in earlier papers, though we believe we are the first to use all of them in a single analysis. While many previous studies rely on detailed data from either the Census Bureau or the Bureau of Labor Statistics, before the mid-1930s these sources reported data for many industries only at fairly long intervals, sometimes only once or twice a decade. They are not suitable for our purposes and techniques.

we have separate series for skilled and unskilled labor), public roads disaggregated by region, and agriculture (also broken down by region); these are described in detail in Appendix 1. The series for railroads are divided into thirty-one occupational subcategories; these are described further in Appendix 2.[9]

Given that most workers in most of these industries were assuredly males and predominantly white, it is also difficult to unravel influences of race or gender. But thanks to the diligence of the Conference Board in those years, a subset for manufacturing covering the period 1921–1937 reports wages separately in each industry by gender and skill levels; data for skill levels are also available for a few other sectors. By combining these bits of information, we are able to hazard some generalizations about how the New Deal and the rising demand for labor during World War II may have altered the ways in which gender and skill figured in labor markets.[10]

We analyze our data in several stages. Inspired by Dunlop's classic discussion of wage contours and more recent work in business history,[11] we first attempt to sort among the eighty-three categories for blocs that exhibit common patterns of wage changes. The basic idea of industry-specific labor rents is that under some conditions employees, in addition to owners, can succeed in capturing part of the gains from an imperfectly competitive market structure. If capital markets clear but labor markets

[9] This data set provides a solid base for testing important hypotheses about the wage structure. But one also has to acknowledge its limitations. First, some parts of the economy, notably the retail trades, are shortchanged. Second, these data are aggregated; all the series that cover the period as a whole refer to all workers within each industry except for two sectors, roads and farming, where we have breakdowns by region. Inevitably, therefore, one runs risks of slighting important differences within industries, between firms, across cities, within companies, and in some cases between skilled and unskilled labor.

[10] Useful cautions appear in Dunlop, 1988; in Slichter, 1950, especially its sobering note 1; and in Douglas, 1930; for geography, see especially Earle, 1993. For a review of data broken down by gender, see Goldin, 1990; in regard to race, see Sundstrom, 1993; for both race and gender, see also Amott and Matthaei, 1991. During most of our period, fringe and supplemental benefits were quite unimportant. They began to appear in some contracts in the late thirties and became more important as a way to evade wage controls during World War II. See the discussion and data presented in Lewis, 1963, pp. 234ff. For this chapter, it is impossible to believe that neglecting them – which all analysts known to us perforce have to do, because available statistics are meager – could possibly make much difference, because our cutoff is 1947. Economists writing about this period have usually been clear on this point, despite a vast literature by historians on the "welfare capitalism" of the twenties. The pathetically limited character of this movement is obvious in, for example, Lewis's data.

[11] Dunlop, 1957. Among recent works on business history, see especially Jacoby, 1985; Chandler, 1962; Lazonick, 1991; and Katz and Summers, 1989.

do not, we should expect that rates of profit equalize across industries but that rates of pay – even skill-adjusted rates of pay – do not. The next step is to argue that differences in patterns of wage *change* across industries through time reflect differences in the economic performance (and therefore in the gross rents) of the industries themselves. It follows that if two industrial subgroups have similar patterns of wage change through a sufficiently extended period, marching up in some years and down in others but always substantially in step, then it is likely that they are being influenced by the whole range of external forces in similar ways. We may then infer that they are, in an economically meaningful sense, closely related to each other.

To summarize this argument: First, anything that alters the relative performance of an industry – whether technological advance, a changing structure of materials prices, or a changing pattern of competition – will eventually show up to some degree in the average wage that the industry can pay. Second, when a pattern of such changes is essentially identical in two separate industrial subclassifications over a long period of time and a wide range of historical experience, it becomes increasingly unlikely that this similarity is accidental. Instead, similar effects result from structural characteristics that produce like reactions to common causes. And that being so, patterns of similar effects can be used for industrial classification.

Precisely how many groups one distinguishes depends in the end on one's sensitivity to small differences in performance. As we will see momentarily, our analysis yields a set of tables and a striking tree diagram indicating that the eighty-three industries and branches can be divided quite cleanly into eight distinct groups. This indicates that there are eight usefully distinct patterns of wage change in the data; lesser variations may be treated as occurring within groups.

We then investigate how these variations might be affected by differences in skill and gender within the workforce. Our analysis, which is based on the smaller sample of industries and the shorter time period for which relevant data are available, leads to a surprising conclusion. Differences in the rates of wage change between skilled or semiskilled and unskilled workers mattered little; such differences within industries were almost always smaller than differences in wage change between industries. On the other hand, our evidence on gender suggests that in this period women's work constituted something of an industry in its own right. Because it was, in effect, a special form of common labor practiced across conventional industry lines, it was affected dramatically by improvements in the position of the lowest-paid workers during the New Deal and World War II.

The next stage is an exploratory data analysis. By plotting the average annual rates of wage change of the various industries and industry segments in our clusters, we can illustrate how each group reacted to landmark events. We also compare how wages in each group performed through time with respect to the others. This stage, though necessarily informal, provides a feel for the data that will prove useful in interpreting the more formal analysis to follow.

Following this, we present a systematic decomposition of the sources of wage variation across groups and through time. We compute the canonical roots of a discriminant function, designed so as best to separate the wage change performance of each group of industries over the period. This yields a set of eigenvectors consisting of weights or impulses, each of which represents a lineally independent force acting on the wage structure. The fact that our cluster analysis relies on wage-change observations in percentage form produces eigenvectors in time-series format; thus, each eigenvector is itself an artificially constructed economic time series. We identify four such forces that together explain 97 percent of the variance in wage change across groups. Of these, the first two account for 75 percent of all cross-cluster variations and the first one alone accounts for over half.

To summarize, by this point we will have established, first, that a very high proportion of total wage variation in this period was interindustrial; second, that interindustrial variations were dominated by the relative movements of eight large clusters; and third, that most cross-cluster variations can be reduced to just two canonical time series, with four accounting for virtually all of them.

This raises a beguiling possibility. It may be that simple explanations account for most of the relative wage changes during the tumultuous twenty-seven years under study. In a reversal of the usual notions of micro-to-macro causality, it may be that a small number of *macroeconomic* variates account for a large proportion of *distributional* changes. The fact that our eigenvectors have a time-series representation suggests that they may also have a historical interpretation, a meaning. Can these forces be identified as substantially similar to, as in effect reflections of, known and perhaps even familiar events?

The traditional method of assigning meaning to a weighting function in discriminant or factor analysis involves computing a *canonical score* (or factor score) for each object and inferring meaning from the distribution of scores across objects. This is a purely post hoc procedure; and absent some form of hypothesis test, the resulting inference cannot be regarded as final. Our procedure permits such a test, albeit a crude one, for the fact that our eigenvectors are time series allows us to compare the root to the time path of other historical economic time series. We find the visual evidence in several cases compelling, and on occasion simple correlation or bivariate regression coefficients are, in fact, significant. On the other hand, the fact that we are often dealing with multiple, closely collinear explananda for our explanandum – for instance, exchange rate ratios for several different countries for a root apparently associated with the terms of trade – means that multivariate regression coefficients are unstable in certain cases.

In the final section, we return to the underlying data. The groupwise decomposability of Theil's T measure of inequality permits us to compute an estimate of the evolution of inequality in the wage structure over time. This estimate is independent of our clustering procedures and of our discriminant analysis; and unlike those procedures, it produces a measure of changing relative wage dispersion that is weighted by the relative size of the working population in each of the underlying classes of economic activity; in particular, it gives the heavy weight to agriculture that the large size of the farm population in those days demanded.[12] This measure is well suited to regression analysis. Using it, we test a simple macroeconomic explanation of inequality in the wage structure. The results are spectacular.

3.3   Cluster Analysis

Figure 3.1 presents the cluster analysis. The figure should be read as though it depicted the American economy as a sort of multidivisional corporation à la Chandler (1962). By beginning at the top and tracing down through each major fork in the chart, increasingly detailed groupings of industries become visible.

How much clustering one wants to work with finally depends on the researcher. Few interesting questions in economic history are likely to be answered by reference to the two giant clusters revealed in the upper parts of the figure – essentially railroads, coal, and utilities on one side and everything else on the other. Nor would it serve to keep clustering until the differences between industries became so fine that one reached

---

[12] We used the census figures for 1940 from U.S. Department of Commerce, 1975, to measure relative employment in twenty-six industrial groups, and we compressed our eighty-three wage series into these twenty-six categories by taking simple averages of wage rates from the Conference Board and other data sets. In the case of farm wages, we estimated a pseudohourly wage rate from monthly earnings data. These procedures are necessarily rough. However, small errors in estimating individual groupwise wage rates, due to lack of appropriate within-group employment weights, are unlikely to have a significant effect on the large movements of the resulting Theil statistic.

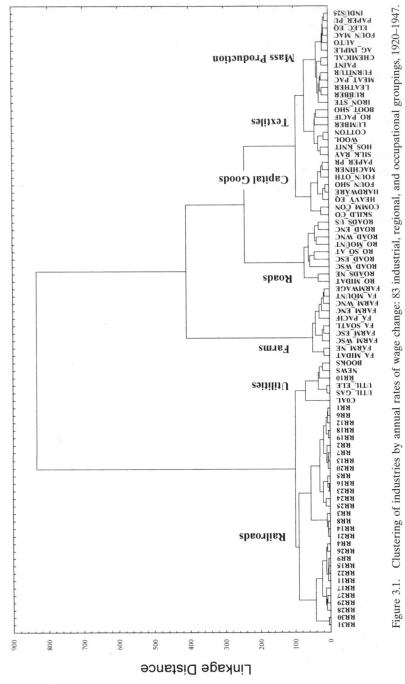

Figure 3.1. Clustering of industries by annual rates of wage change: 83 industrial, regional, and occupational groupings, 1920–1947.

a Euclidean distance of zero at the bottom of the graph, when one would be back to eighty-three different groups including thirty-one occupational subdivisions of the railroads. Instead we work with the eight rather large clusters identified in stylized form by the names on the figure: "Railroads," "Utilities," "Farms," "Roads," "Capital Goods," "Textiles," and "Mass Production" – the first representing two clusters.

These clusters appear sensible on both casual and close examination. Virtually the entire large cluster indicated by the top left fork in Figure 3.1 refers to the railroad industry. Two of the big lower-level clusters nested within the broader railroad grouping represent branches of that industry exclusively. They separate, broadly, the through-freight and passenger workers from the local line and office workers of this by then heavily regulated industry. The third branch (denominated "Utilities") includes the coal industry, the gas and electric utilities, and two industries with exceptionally strong unions, books and newspapers. This last branch also includes one entity from the railroad group, "Yard Firemen and Helpers," that seems anomalous but probably isn't. Firemen and their helpers handled fuels – in this period, mostly coal.

The right-hand prong of the great top fork breaks down into two large clusters. The first, flaring to the left, consists entirely of one sector broken down by region: agriculture. The second, leading down to the right, divides into several nested subclusters. Off by itself on the left is a cluster containing all the regional branches of public road building, with a single instructive exception. On the right, we find all the rest of manufacturing industry.

This final right fork contains three subclusters, stylized in Figure 3.1 as "Capital Goods," "Textiles," and "Mass Production." This part of Figure 3.1, with its restricted range of variation, is essentially what papers that analyze data only for manufacturing have examined. Within these subclusters, there are well-defined patterns. The leftmost subcluster – our "Capital Goods" – roughly defines what in the USSR at that time was symbolized by the name "Stakhanov": foundries, heavy equipment, machines and machine tools, hardware and small parts, paper products, and both skilled and unskilled construction.[13]

The remaining two subclusters contain the rest of American manufacturing for which we have data. The first – "Textiles" – consists of several sub-subclusters with readily intelligible internal linkages: cotton and wool, linked to another subcluster of silk and rayon and hosiery

---

[13] True, the eponymous hero was in fact a coal miner. But he worked in an economy whose degree of vertical integration would have been the envy of Carnegie or Frick. And it was the heavy industrial complex, not the coal mine, that captured imaginations.

knitting, plus lumber and boots and shoes. All were labor-intensive but essentially non–mass production industries that were sensitive not only to labor costs but also to the prices of commodities and raw materials.

Two industries that also processed commodities but were celebrated examples of mass production – rubber and meat packing – cluster with a bloc of other industries: paint, chemicals, leather, furniture, and iron and steel. Like the sectors in "Textiles" and most of the industries in our "Capital Goods" group, these industries were recurrently tempted by economic nationalism in the interwar period, either because they faced strong international competition in export markets or because they depended directly on tariff protection in the home market. In our cluster analysis, however, they link up with another subcluster of mass production industries: autos, foundry machinery, agricultural implements, electrical machinery, and paper and pulp. This latter group includes some of the most internationally successful American firms in this period. The lesson we draw from the proximity of the nationalistic sectors to the international success stories is one that contemporaries also drew: A dominant effect of protectionism is to protect.[14]

By the end of our period, it is well known that wage settlements in steel, autos, and a handful of other large unionized industries were setting the pattern for many other industries. But how and when did this system get underway? Some authorities trace its beginnings to the years just prior to World War II, partly because heavy unionization in autos, rubber, and steel came only in the late 1930s. But this is not the only possibility. Because the underlying technologies, market structures, and demand relationships long antedated the Congress of Industrial Organizations (CIO), it could also have been that the postwar wage system actually evolved from preunion patterns and merely represented a more formal version of something that was already evolving in the years after World War I.[15]

Here our results tend to support the mainstream view. Consider how steel, rubber, and autos fare in our classification. By comparison with the gulf that divides these industries from the rest of the economy, the distance separating them from each other does not amount to much. So,

---

[14] For the political economy of various sectors in the interwar period, see Ferguson, 1995a; the key point is that many protectionist firms did some exporting into particular regions even as they argued strenuously for tariffs in their home market. During most of the period, the decisive political cleavage lay between firms that were truly successful multinationals or exporters and those that weren't; their comparative statuses fluctuated with the world economy.

[15] Compare the various economic criteria discussed in, e.g., Mehra, 1976, Ross, 1957, or Eckstein and Wilson, 1962.

while linkages between these three pattern setters run back to the 1920s, linkages from them to the rest of the economy evidently do not. While the postwar system of national patterns assuredly emerged out of processes and events that we discuss here, it represented genuine development, not simply an extrapolation of previously existing trends.[16]

A tighter if less momentous set of linkages emerges in the relationship of wages in public road construction to those in agriculture. During the interwar period, analysts and advocates for the rural poor complained repeatedly that rural elites were manipulating wage levels on public relief projects to ensure a suitably compliant, truly low-wage workforce for the farms. Subsequent work by economic historians suggests that, at least in the South, those complaints were justified.[17] Our clustering reflects the fact that, throughout the twenties, wage changes on public road projects closely resembled those in agriculture. In the thirties, however, wages in road building – a quintessential New Deal activity – moved toward the manufacturing pattern. As a consequence, in a cluster analysis for the entire period, wage patterns in public roads resemble a halfway house between the two worlds of agriculture and industrial production.

The one outlier among the regional subsectors for public roads is the Pacific region. This shows up in an entirely different (right-hand) prong of the fork in Figure 3.1, where most of American manufacturing industry can be found. At first glance, this separation of roads in the far Northwest from agriculture and the rest of public roads appears anomalous. But with a closer look, the puzzle disappears; the public roads wages in the Pacific region track wages not in farming but in the locally dominant lumber industry. This exception thus conforms nicely to a larger rule.[18]

[16] Just how highly developed the pattern became is suggested in Maher, 1961a and 1961b. On the contribution of unions, see also Soffer, 1959, and Mehra, 1976. A consistent application of the latter's viewpoint would lead to important modifications of the "labor rents" view.

[17] For complaints during the Depression, see, e.g., Wyckoff, 1946. For the correctness of the complaints in the South, see Alston and Ferrie, 1985.

[18] It is reasonable to ask how sensitive these and other results presented in this chapter are to slight variations in our methods. In particular, would our results differ if we were not restricted to annual data? Our attention was drawn to the first possibility by John Dunlop, who asked us how our methods would register industries that were in fact patterning their wage settlements after each other, but only after a lapse of some time (as, for example, when the lagging industry's contract expired early in the following year). Fortunately, Conference Board data for most of the manufacturing industries in our data set are available on a monthly basis between 1920 and 1937. When we analyzed all the industries for which complete monthly data exist, only two industries switched positions vis-à-vis the annual data. One should also note that while possibilities like these occasioned much discussion in the postwar literature over pattern bargaining, no actual

The clusters portrayed in Figure 3.1 reflect patterns of wage variation across the workforce as a whole. But one naturally asks how the results would appear if one examined the fate of particular social and demographic groups, such as female workers, skilled male workers, or individual ethnic and racial groups. Would our focus on interindustrial variation still appear justified, or would some other classification principle come instead to predominate?

We have been unable to find data that allow us to compare how racial groups fared within the industries in our data set. But we do have data on the annual average hourly earnings of male skilled and unskilled workers between 1921 and 1937 in the manufacturing industries as well as in printing and news; these data come from Conference Board surveys that requested each establishment to distinguish between purely unskilled workers – those whose jobs required no training at all – and all others. Similar data also exist for skilled and unskilled construction workers under the safe assumption that female workers in that sector were few.[19]

Figure 3.2 shows the result: The skilled and unskilled portions within each industrial category virtually all appear close together. In most cases, they are side by side.[20] This is a simple showing of an important fact. In the period we are concerned with, changes between industries were – almost always – more important in explaining patterns of wage change than was the evolution of the skilled–unskilled differential within industries. Further discussion follows, but the basic result is that once interindustrial variations are controlled for, variations in the skill differential are minor, with exceptions mainly in printing and construction, which may indeed reflect a high proportion of craft workers in those trades.

argument over which industries were actually in a hypothesized pattern ever seems to have turned on this question. Compare the discussions in Ross, 1957; Maher, 1961a and 1961b; Mehra, 1976; and Eckstein and Wilson, 1962.

[19] Obviously, a classification that lumps semiskilled with highly skilled workers is not ideal. But over a wide range of industries, this latter distinction, if it is important, might be expected to show up in different patterns for industries requiring large proportions of highly skilled craft workers (such as printing) as against those where the "skilled" group was dominated by semiskilled factory hands. Classifications across industries, in other words, should contain information relevant to an analysis of changing wage differentials across skill levels. Of course, the predominant direction of causality would remain an open question in that case.

[20] The data for the skilled and unskilled men, as well as the data for men and women in manufacturing, come from the Conference Board; see Appendix 2, which also indicates the source of the construction data.

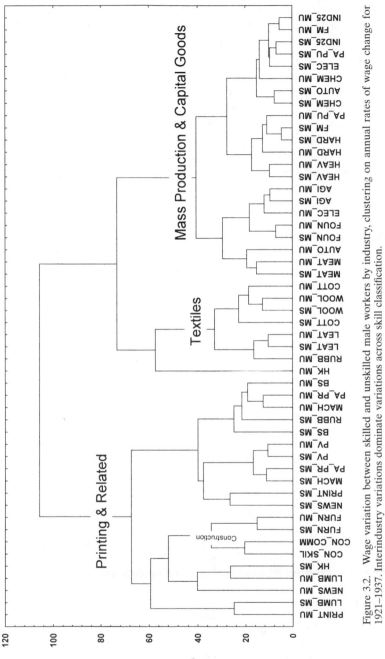

Figure 3.2. Wage variation between skilled and unskilled male workers by industry, clustering on annual rates of wage change for 1921–1937. Interindustry variations dominate variations across skill classification.

45

For the same time span, data are also available for the annual average hourly earnings of men and women in our manufacturing industries.[21] As Figure 3.3 indicates, gender is a different story. Sex proves to be a more important marker of intraindustry wage change than skill. On the right-hand side of the figure (which, again, refers exclusively to manufacturing industries between 1921 and 1937), we find groups of industries in which the wages of males tracked each other closely – autos, foundries and machinery, or chemicals. On the left are several clusters in which industry played the dominant role in determining wage changes for both genders; printing is a representative case. In the center-right are those industries whose female workers had closely co-moving wages.

In interpreting these clusters, it is useful to note that the proportion of women working in different industries varied hugely. In hosiery and knitting, for instance, women comprised a large percentage of the workforce. Other industries, such as foundries, employed very few. And in many industries, such as automobiles, the work done by women differed markedly from that performed by men, so one is in effect looking at an intraindustry occupational classification into which female workers were steered.[22]

Looking at the evidence for individual industries, we notice that many show a reduction in the *gender gap* – the ratio of women's to men's average hourly earnings – in the early New Deal years. We will have more to say about this process later, when we consider how various New Deal policies, including unionization, minimum wages, and dollar devaluation, affected industries in which women worked in large numbers. For now, our conclusion is simply that the low pay ratios are evidence that women's work in this period was essentially a special form of common labor. Precisely because of this, female workers benefited from the developments that improved the relative position of the lowest-paid workers during the New Deal and World War II.

3.4   Exploratory Data Analysis

Figures 3.4, 3.5, 3.6, and 3.7 explore some of our findings. They are in effect a graphical commentary on the debates mentioned earlier over how wages changed within and between industries.

[21] Note that the restricted sample of industries and different periods of coverage ensure that the resulting clusters differ from those in Figure 3.1.

[22] Besides the sources listed in Appendix 2, see also the table in Woytinsky, 1942, p. 169, for one set of statistics illustrating the differing percentages of women in various industries during the 1930s. The segmentation of jobs by gender within industries is obvious in many case studies. See, e.g., Gabin, 1990, pp. 12ff.

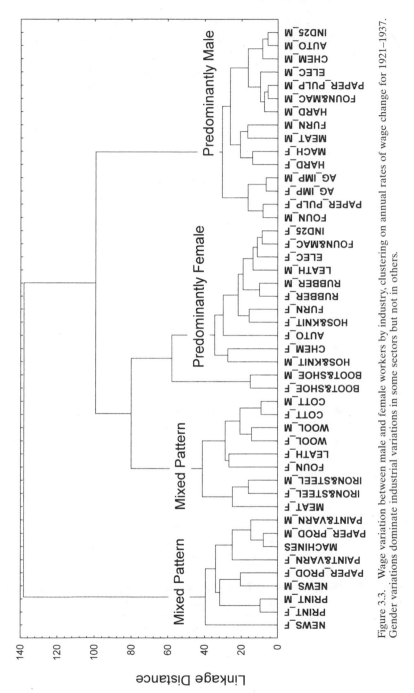

Figure 3.3. Wage variation between male and female workers by industry, clustering on annual rates of wage change for 1921–1937. Gender variations dominate industrial variations in some sectors but not in others.

47

Figure 3.4 begins by separately plotting wage changes in each of our major clusters over time, except that the two railroad groups have been consolidated. Figure 3.5 displays rates of wage change for a number of individual industries extensively discussed in the literature, but here consolidated within the seven large groups. We present them as concrete examples of the more general patterns.

Figure 3.5 shows a dramatic collapse of construction wages in the severe downturn of 1920–1921. It also testifies to another sharp fall in the wages of construction workers between 1930 and 1932, which bottomed out only as wages in other sectors, which had fallen less, were turning up after passage of the Davis-Bacon Act defending the prevailing wage in construction in 1931. The rise in farm wages in the Second World War jumps off the page and will play an important role in our story later on. So does the sharp runup in coal miners' wages in 1934.

The most suggestive fact recorded by Figures 3.4 and 3.5 together concerns the relative rise of wages in textiles and related industries at the outset of the New Deal. ("Textiles" in Figure 3.4 refers to the whole cluster as defined earlier; Figure 3.5 plots the cotton industry separately.) Along with the coal miners' union, unions in these industries are widely credited with kicking off the historic wave of strikes and union recognition struggles that began shortly after the passage of the National Recovery Act in 1933. The textile and coal unions also spearheaded the campaign that led to the famous split within the ranks of the AFL and the formation of the CIO.[23]

What explains the sudden upsurge of militancy within this sector, which had never before and would never again witness such success in raising its wages relative to those in other industries?

What may possibly explain it, we think, is something that labor historians have neglected: the differential effects of dollar devaluation and the Roosevelt administration's decision to go off the gold standard as it inaugurated the National Recovery Administration. Textiles and garment companies at that time were pressed vigorously by foreign competitors. Not only had the British recently floated the pound and erected the Ottawa System (creating problems for many American

---

[23] The key role of unions, either in the textile industry or very closely tied to it, is apparent in all accounts of the formation of the CIO. Along with the United Mine Workers, the International Ladies Garment Workers Union and the Amalgamated Clothing Workers of America appear to have been the biggest investors in the early drive for what became the CIO. See the brief discussion of the early financing in Ziegler, 1995, p. 23, as well as the discussion in Galenson, 1960, Chapter 1. The much smaller United Textile Workers and (parts of) the Hatter, Cap and Millinery Workers also figured in this effort (Ziegler, 1995, p. 24).

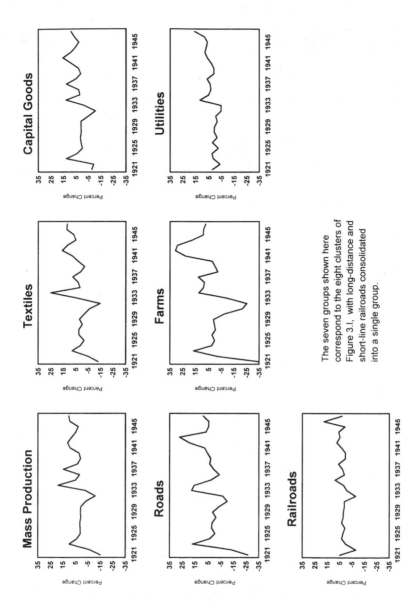

The seven groups shown here correspond to the eight clusters of Figure 3.l, with long-distance and short-line railroads consolidated into a single group.

Figure 3.4.   Percentage wage change in seven industrial groups, 1920–1947.

49

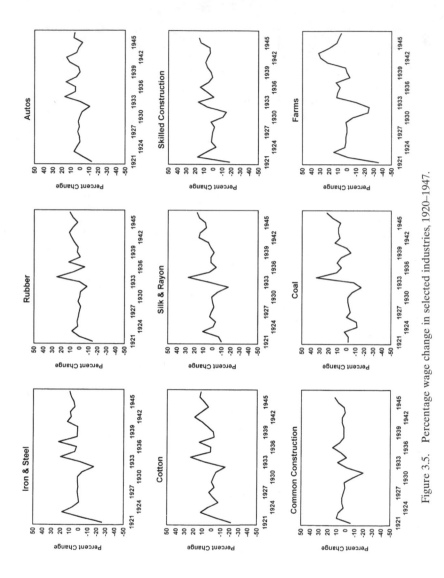

Figure 3.5. Percentage wage change in selected industries, 1920–1947.

manufacturers) but, in addition, textiles, garments, and their supplier industries (notably rayon) faced a special challenge: low-cost competition from the Orient, particularly Japan (see, e.g., Wright, 1995). Along with the demand stimulus arising from the New Deal's relief activities (at that time, very limited) and its equally slow-moving efforts to unfreeze frozen banking assets, dollar devaluation suddenly created demand and thus the possibility of profits. This was something to fight over in an industry that had stagnated since the end of the First World War.[24]

The early success of the textile unions in capturing some of those gains, in turn, helped fuel the broader drives for unionization. First, although one usually associates textiles with cities and coal mining with the countryside, in parts of the Northeast and the South these two industries importantly overlapped. In many instances, the textile industry appears to have drawn much of its workforce from the wives, children, or other extended family members of miners. The dramatic successes of their kin and neighbors could hardly have dampened spirits among male miners; John L. Lewis famously sounded the trumpet soon *after* the United States abandoned gold and textile wages had commenced their dramatic rise. Second, what was sauce for the business goose could also, in the special conditions of the devaluation(s), become sauce for the labor gander. By recycling a portion of its newly replenished treasury into the CIO's organizing efforts, organized labor, too, showed that it appreciated the logic of the investment theory of party competition.[25]

[24] For the long decline in textile manufacturing since World War I, see, e.g., Galambos, 1966, as well as the discussion of the Taylor Society and the New Deal in Ferguson, 1995a, pp. 137–138. On the Japanese export drive in textiles, see, e.g., Matsui, 1958, pp. 50–54, and Wright, 1995. Note that in many instances cheaper Japanese imports of higher-quality products (e.g., silks) were squeezing lower-grade American products, such as rayon. This sort of pressure does not always register in standard trade statistics organized by particular product lines.

There is no reason to overstate a good case: There is no question that the full force of devaluation was stayed, not least by conservative monetary policy (Eichengreen, 1992, pp. 342–347, though we would analyze the whole episode rather differently). Also, as discussed later, the prevalence of high tariffs and exchange controls in the rest of the world inevitably limited the success of U.S. exports. The prospect of cartelization – the inner meaning of the NRA – also probably held special attraction for the long-depressed textile industry. The inventory boom that accompanied the early days of the NRA (as many firms sought to restock before prices rose) and the administration's slowly moving plans for unfreezing bank assets and increased public works spending no doubt also helped fire up industrialists – and their workers – with visions of potential profits. But in a world of depreciated currencies, devaluation was helpful to many industries seeking to reclaim the home market, if not the rest of the world, particularly from Japanese competitors.

[25] For the geographical overlap between some of the militant coal mining areas and textiles, see Montgomery, 1994, pp. 344–345, and Bernstein, 1970, pp. 76–77. Montgomery

The textile workers had not, of course, discovered a foolproof way to hold on to the gains from devaluation in the long run. As Figure 3.4 shows, workers in this group of industries did not do as well, in terms of annual rates of wage improvement, as those elsewhere in manufacturing through the middle and late 1930s. By 1936 – at which time monetary stabilization, represented by accords like the Tripartite Monetary Agreement among the United States, Britain, and France, was becoming acutely controversial[26] – wage gains in textiles were falling behind those of most other industry groups. It nevertheless appears that the devaluation of 1933 may have played a distinct role in the causal chain leading to the creation of the CIO, setting up a path-dependent and perhaps spatially conditioned sequence of events that would have otherwise played out differently.

As the arrows in Figure 3.6 indicate, in many industries the gender gap narrowed (it was not, of course, eliminated) early in the New Deal. While some of this narrowing doubtless reflects the impact of unionization and minimum wage laws, including those incorporated in many National Recovery Administration codes, the crucial point is that, taken together, these political and economic developments did actually confer relative gains on female workers. And the rebirth of the women's movement that marked the years of the High New Deal surely owed at least as much to this sudden broad empowering of female workers as it did to the

notes the wildcat nature of many of the early 1933 strikes and indicates that the link with textiles was strongest in the anthracite coal region. That our own data series for coal mining is for bituminous coal is irrelevant in this context: Both areas were in an uproar and were strongly affected by the UMW; data specifically for the anthracite regions showing parallel wage movements in this period can be found in U.S. Department of Commerce, 1936, p. 33. Foner, 1980, p. 286, also mentions an overlap between textiles and mining in parts of the South. These latter mines probably were bituminous; note that in this period, while Southern textile workers were not striking with anything like the frequency of their Northern counterparts, the (less comprehensive) data indicate that their wages were rising, too.

Given the critical role played by the "alliance" between the UMW and the unions in textiles (broadly construed), John L. Lewis's own attitude toward women was plausibly of real importance to the workings of devaluation. While Lewis and other UMW leaders undoubtedly shared some attitudes toward women's social roles that could charitably be termed "Victorian" (Dubofsky and Van Tine, 1977, p. 201), and while the CIO was never likely to be confused with the Women's Trade Union League (Gabin, 1990), Kenneally (1981, p. 164) observes that Lewis had long been an annual contributor to the Women's Trade Union League, "vigorously" supported the equal-pay movement in the NRA codes, and in a *New York Times* interview he committed the new CIO to equal pay for "substantially the same work." See also Foner, 1980, especially pp. 320–322. For the investment approach to party competition, see Ferguson, 1995a.

[26] See Ferguson, 1995a, p. 155, for a discussion.

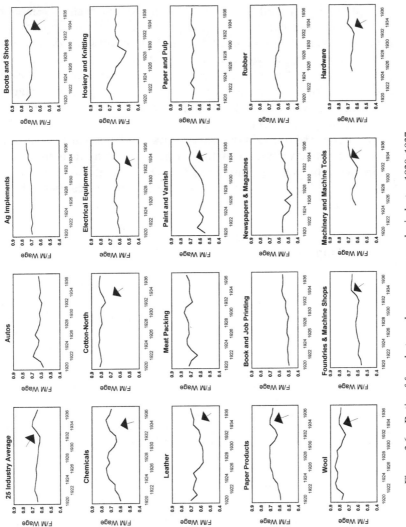

Figure 3.6. Ratio of female to male average wages by industry, 1920–1937.

53

personal influence of well-known individual women such as Eleanor Roosevelt or Frances Perkins.[27]

Because we do not have employment weights for our individual industries, we cannot compute weighted average wage levels by year for our clusters. The next best thing is to compute the evolution of the relative wage structure from a common base year, and this is possible because we know that the within-cluster departures from a common growth rate are small. Figure 3.7 plots relative wage movements, with 1920 set to 100, for all of the major groups in our cluster analysis. This figure thus summarizes the relative evolution of the entire American wage structure, beginning with the postwar slump of 1920.

As the speculative boom that followed the 1918 armistice gave way to the sharp recession in 1920, the wage structure split apart.[28] In agriculture (and public roads), where wages were lowest, wages fell the most. In coal and utilities, where wages were among the highest, they fell the least. Indeed, though federal troops were called out repeatedly to quell resistance in the coalfields, and though statistical studies of judicial behavior indicate that an unprecedented wave of injunctions crashed over unions in this period, still, in coal and utilities wages held up rather well and then soon began to rise again.[29] On the railroads (where the courts also repeatedly intervened, virtually always on management's side), wages first fell, though not by as much as in manufacturing or nearly as much as in agriculture. As the cycle turned up, railroad wages

[27] Kenneally, 1981, pp. 156ff., has a short but illuminating discussion of the NRA's equal-pay movement. He notes that some 25 percent of the codes still clearly discriminated against female workers, though the episode was widely acknowledged to have given the equal-pay movement an enormous lift. His discussion is a warning of the pitfalls of any econometric effort to neatly divide politics from economics in this period or to parcel out the influence of "government" from "unions." The only woman appointed to the NRA's Labor Advisory Board (who strongly and rather successfully championed the principle of equal pay) was on leave from the Women's Trade Union League.

[28] Contractionary monetary policy appears to have played an important role in bringing about the 1920–1921 recession; see Hicks, 1974, pp. 209ff. The U.S. case is clear-cut, particularly in regard to why the policy of tight money continued so long: "Governor Strong and Dr. Miller thought wages were still too high" (D'Arista, 1994, p. 61, summarizing material from Federal Reserve minutes and policy directives from early 1921. See also Friedman and Schwartz, 1963, p. 234).

[29] For the striking rise in injunctions, see the data in Witte, 1932; after 1920, the trend could be mistaken for a power series; for the use of troops, see the discussion and sources in Ferguson, 1995b. See also Goldstein, 1978, for statistics on meetings broken up by the authorities. Secretary of the Treasury Andrew Mellon, himself a major Pittsburgh mine owner, was quoted as saying that "You can't run a coal mine without machine guns." (What Mellon actually said was: "You could not run without them"; cf. Koskoff, 1978, p. 304.)

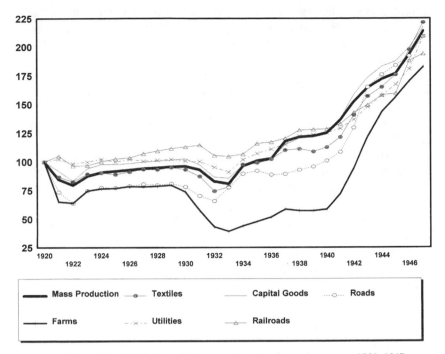

Figure 3.7.   Evolution of the wage structure by major groups, 1920–1947.

rose very slightly (amid a wave of strikes). Following the passage of the Railway Labor Act of 1926, which can be viewed as a precursor of the Wagner Act, they rose more steeply until 1932. In the thirties, manufacturing wage settlements caught up with wages on the railways, and the 1920 parities were restored from 1937 to 1940. During World War II, however, railroad wage settlements fell further and further behind (even though the absolute level of railroad wages remained quite high). This outcome might be held to reflect the long-term decline of the railroads or the eventual success of the Railway Labor Act in incorporating the unions into the bargaining process or both.

The recession of 1920–1922 hammered nominal wages in heavy manufacturing as well as in textiles and garments, though neither suffered as much as agriculture and public roads. However, as Figure 3.7 also shows, these sectors recovered after taking a second beating, like all other clusters, early in the Great Depression. Our annual data also suggest that the recession of 1938 – the first downturn in which the federal government employed a deliberately countercyclical macropolicy on a large scale, accompanied by the first broad minimum-wage laws, the Fair Labor Standards Acts of 1937 and 1938 – temporarily halted the rise in manufacturing wages but nowhere seriously reversed their course.[30]

Then, as many studies including that of Goldin and Margo (1991) have observed, with World War II the great upward pull of demand began to operate on the wage structure as a whole. The combined force of demand, military enlistment, and rising wage standards on the wages of unskilled farm workers, still 40 percent of employment in 1940, is especially dramatic. This is the Great Compression of the 1940s. By 1945, it had nearly erased the Great Decompression of the early 1930s.

Indeed, by including sectors beyond manufacturing, notably public roads and agriculture, and carrying our data back to 1920, our study sharpens the discussion of the effects of the New Deal and World War II on the wage structure. The wage structure that evolved during the war essentially represented a restoration of the wage structure that had briefly existed at the end of the Great War in 1920. World War II's Great Compression was, in truth, the Second Great Compression, the first having occurred in 1917–1919.[31]

3.5   Discriminant Analysis

In the third stage of our analysis, we apply discriminant function analysis to the eight clusters derived in the first stage. The basic idea is straightforward. Having previously found the best (minimum-variance) clustering of industries into groups, we have groups that are as strongly differentiated as any structure of aggregation based on wage behavior will yield. The differences among these groups thus contain most of the

---

[30] The pursuit of minimum-wage policies embraced far more than passage of the well-known minimum-wage laws in this period. See, e.g., Strackbein, 1939; rules on government procurement were one such policy lever.

[31] The links between economics and politics in this period are complex but very powerful. It is futile to attempt to untangle all of them. Wartime policy affected wages not only through the policies of the National Labor Relations Board – itself, of course, one of the earlier fruits of the High New Deal – but also through wartime controls that deliberately favored unionization under moderately conservative trade union leaders but also frequently sought to level up the wages of the lowest-paid workers and to prevent wage cuts. Many parts of organized labor supported this project; indeed, prominent labor leaders favored continuing wage controls after the war, along with wage policies that awarded the largest percentage raises to the lowest-paid rather than the most senior workers. This era has virtually vanished from historical memory (but see Montgomery, 1994). Employer resistance to these trends was quite fierce and spilled over into major conflicts over state as well as national labor laws. The issue of equal pay also received attention during the war, particularly from the National War Labor Board. See, e.g., National Industrial Conference Board, 1943.

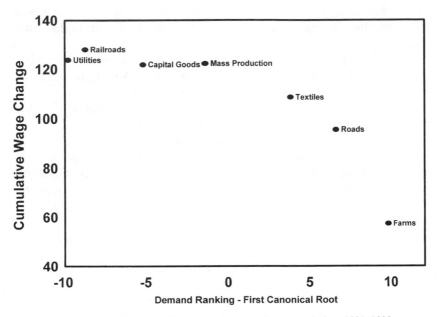

Figure 3.8.   Scores on the demand root and wage variation, 1921–1939.

economic information that may appear in the wage structure overall. To extract this information in its most compact form, we find the set of canonical roots, or eigenvectors, that best discriminates the disparate patterns of wage behavior exhibited by the clusters. These eigenvectors are ranked in importance by their associated eigenvalues, which measure the proportion of intergroup variance explained by each.

Our analysis yields four roots that together explain 97 percent of the variance in the intergroup wage structure; the first two of these alone account for 75 percent, and the first one accounts for over half. Because the roots are composed of year-specific weights, we can treat them as economic time series in their own right. Now, as explained earlier, the task is to try to determine whether these roots correspond to known variates in the historical record.

The First Root and the Movement of Aggregate Demand

Figure 3.8 presents the distribution of factor scores on the first canonical root, which we plot here against the cumulative change in nominal wages from 1920 through 1939. A remarkable association emerges. Clusters scoring below zero on this root showed relatively high and uniform cumulative wage gains through this period; clusters scoring above zero show cumulative wage gains that are progressively lower as the score declines.

A possible, albeit post hoc, explanation emerges when one considers the identity of the groups splayed across the figure. Agriculture and textiles were low-wage, competitive sectors; the former remained un-unionized throughout the period and the latter substantially so until the early to mid-1930s; these are industries that Dunlop (1957) long ago identified as heavily dependent on unskilled labor. Road wages, as previously discussed, were kept tied to those in agriculture for political reasons until the New Deal. In contrast, in mass production, in the capital goods sector, and in railroads and utilities, wages were comparatively high, workers comparatively organized, and firms monopolistic. Capital goods production naturally rises and falls with gross investment; to some extent, so does the mass production of consumers' durable goods.

We therefore hypothesize that the differences in scores across sectors may reflect differences in the ability of workers to capture the benefits of increasing aggregate demand. This is precisely a question of variations in industry-specific labor rents, as outlined in Chapter 1 of this volume, or, in the language of that time, a pass-through from Kalecki's famous degree of monopoly power.[32] In the period through 1939, weak growth of demand would work against relative wages in textiles, in road building, and on the farms.

This thought motivates a search for a proxy for the movement of aggregate demand. A reasonable proxy is easily obtained: estimates of the movement of gross national product (GNP). Figure 3.9 plots the yearly values of our first root (scaled for expository clarity) against the annual rate of change of nominal GNP.[33]

Magnitudes and timing do not accord precisely. It may be that aggregate supply factors affect GNP in some periods; lags and perhaps interdependencies in both directions are possible. But the general correspondence between these two series is striking, considering that one series is constructed from gross expenditures on goods and services, while the other is extracted from a matrix of changes in relative wage rates. The simple correlation coefficient between the two series is 0.41; we think it is an understatement.[34]

[32] See, e.g., Dunlop, 1957, Chapter 7; on Kalecki's "degree of monopoly" and subsequent controversies about this notion, see especially Sebastiani, 1994, particularly Chapter 2, and Sawyer, 1985, pp. 28–42. Mehra's discussion (1976, p. 307) is also relevant.
[33] GNP data are as recorded by Gordon, 1986.
[34] Another potential proxy for the change in aggregate demand might be the negative of the change in the unemployment rate. Not surprisingly, a plot of this series against the

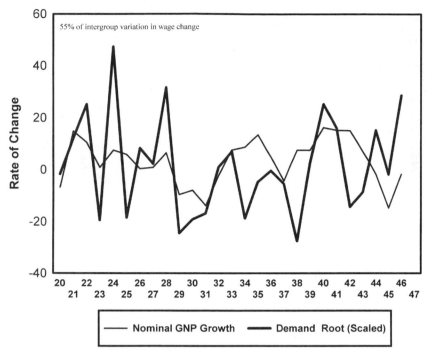

Figure 3.9.   GNP and the demand root.

The Second Root: Strikes and Strikers

The second root accounts for 20 percent of the variance in the intergroup wage structure. Following the previous procedure, Figure 3.10 plots scores along this root against cumulative wage change in the interwar years. The ranking isolates textiles and roads at the high end of the spectrum and farm workers at the low end. Mass production, railroads, and capital goods hold the middle ground, with utilities ranking below them. Notably, while the very-low-ranking farm sector showed the lowest wage gains, the highest-ranking sectors did not show the greatest gains.

Railroads, heavy manufacturing, and mass production industries were all heavily unionized by the end of this period. Although textiles were

first root also shows a good fit, with a nearly identical correlation coefficient of 0.41. The correlation of real GNP movement to this root is somewhat lower: 0.31. We should note here that for expository purposes in Figure 3.9 we have taken the negative of the calculated first root from the discriminant function; for consistency, we have also taken the negative of the calculated canonical scores. So long as consistency between coefficients and scores is preserved, this should have no effect on the analysis.

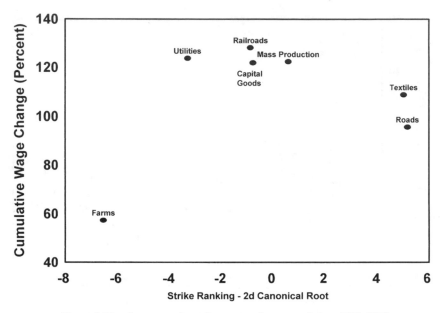

Figure 3.10.   Scores on the strike root and wage variation, 1921–1939.

not unionized in the South, the Conference Board data we use are drawn heavily from Northern mills, and these became unionized in the great drives of the early 1930s. Agriculture and public roads, in contrast, were essentially un-unionized, but the wage behavior in road building was altered dramatically during this period, as we have seen, by a political decision.[35]

It thus seems plausible that this root is capturing not the degree of labor power but the change in it, the relative degree of labor militancy across sectors. A suitable proxy for this may be the total number of days lost to strikes, particularly strikes that ended in labor victories or in compromise.[36] This information is plotted against the second root in

[35] Estimating which parts of the economy were unionized at what points in this period can be tricky, but the cases we discuss here are not controversial. See the discussion in Lewis, 1963, pp. 258ff. Troy, 1965, is also helpful.

[36] Unsuccessful strikes usually do little to enhance the power of labor. In the thirties, there is no doubt that labor's success rate skyrocketed. But statistics, in fact, exist for part of our period and confirm that the percentage of successful-won strikes began rising – at first very gently – in the late twenties. See Griffin, 1939, and the discussion in Edwards, 1981, p. 139. There is no question that the Wagner Act, originally passed in 1935 and influenced by the earlier Railway Labor Act (Ferguson, 1995a, p. 171, n. 104), eventually made a major difference in the outcomes of labor disputes in this period. But it should

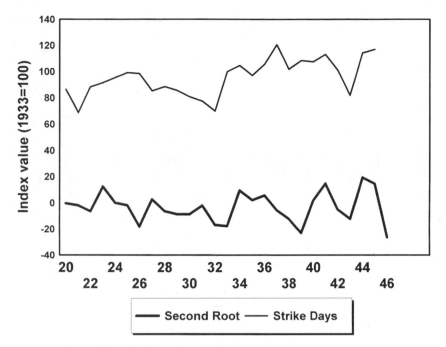

Figure 3.11.   Strikes and the strike root.

Figure 3.11. Though the match is again imperfect, the two series share a pattern: Both show the abrupt upsurge of the early 1930s and again at the end of World War Two. Once again, there is a significant positive correlation between them (rho = 0.35). Correlations to measures of total work stoppages and the number of workers involved are even higher: 0.40 and 0.46, respectively. Figure 3.12 illustrates.

It does not follow, of course, that a high ranking on this root produces the highest overall rates of wage gain. The root captures only 20 percent of the intergroup variation; its effects are therefore dominated by those of the first root. Textile wage gains overall were low, though textile workers were militant; though railroad workers were less militant over the whole period, railroad wage gains were high. Still, overall, these figures suggest quite clearly that strikes and related political decisions made a difference, particularly in separating the wage performance in unionized textiles from those on the farm.

be noted that only continued political pressure secured its effective implementation and that membership in unions truly soared during the war. See Appendix 2 for the data on successful and unsuccessful strikes.

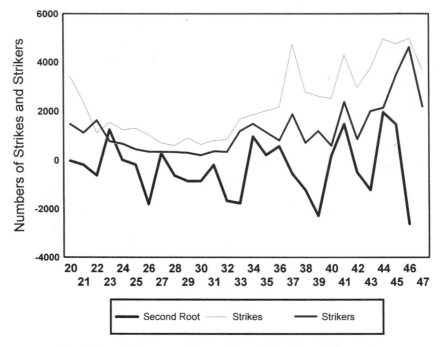

Figure 3.12.   Strikers, work stoppages, and the strike root.

The Third Root: Terms of Trade and Exchange Rates

The first two roots explain 75 percent of the total variance. But there is
a third root that accounts for another 15 percent. Again following pro-
tocol, we plot in Figure 3.13 the canonical scores on this root against
cumulative interwar wage change and notice that now mass production,
textiles, capital goods, and utilities all rank high, while farms, roads, and
railroads rank low. Can it be that this root is picking up the influence of
trade in manufactured commodities?

Figure 3.14 puts this hypothesis to a preliminary test by plotting the
third root in index number form against an index of crude food to manufactured import prices and an index of total import values. The family
resemblance is not bad; the sharp fall in imports that accompanied the
outbreak of war in Europe is telling. But in Figure 3.15 we show
something even better: the exchange rates against sterling and against
other major currencies – the former showing terms of trade against an
advanced economy and the latter approximating the terms of trade
against economies that exported commodities and low-wage manufactures to the United States.

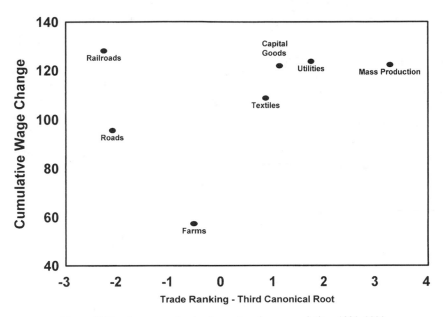

Figure 3.13.   Scores on the trade root and wage variation, 1921–1939.

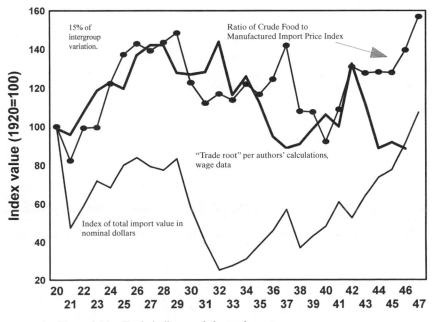

Figure 3.14.   Trade indices and the trade root.

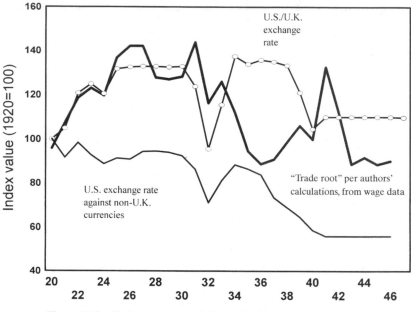

Figure 3.15.   Exchange rates and the trade root.

Looking back at the scatter plot in light of this evidence, only utilities seem curiously out of place. Leontief's famous study of the interwar economy observed that while direct exports from this sector were modest, it profited strongly from its customers' growth. By contrast, wages on roads and railroads often zigged (in the twenties, usually improving) as the international economy zagged. And while one normally thinks of American agriculture as a successful export industry, in the interwar period this bromide was just close enough to the truth to be seriously misleading. Many crops dominant in certain regions – for example, many dairy products or fresh vegetables – were not traded at all or on only a very small scale (save in the form of canned goods). Others were scarcely competitive with imports at any price and sought (and received) tariff protection. More internationally competitive crops, such as wheat, cotton, or tobacco, all too frequently faced shrinking foreign markets as governments around the world sought to protect their agricultural producers.[37]

---

[37] See Leontief, 1951, pp. 178ff. Leontief's industrial categories probably differ somewhat from ours; this is particularly the case for utilities, where he included petroleum as well as coal. But given coal's continuing enormous importance, it probably matters little. An

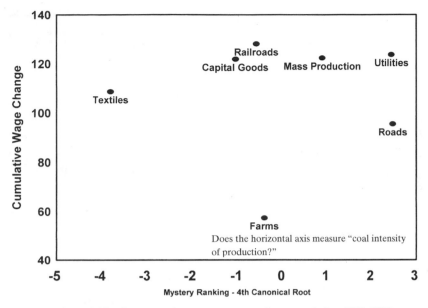

Figure 3.16.   Scores on the mystery root and wage variation, 1921–1939.

The Fourth Root: A Mystery?

At this point, just 10 percent of cross-cluster variation remains, and our analysis reveals a fourth root that explains seven percentage points of that variation. This root is not so easy to characterize. Figure 3.16 shows that utilities ranked highest on this root. Combined with the choppy downward trend after 1925 shown in Figure 3.17, this suggests to us that the root might perhaps reflect the long-term structural transition of the economy from coal to oil. But we have no historical series with which to test this thought, and for the time being we leave the question open.

But What About Education and the Increasing Supply of Skill?

Education plays no apparent role in our analysis at all. Why not? Considering the importance of this issue for policy, it is worth asking whether

excellent summary of many trends in foreign trade, with details about how particular industries fared in the United States and worldwide, is Woytinsky, 1955, especially pp. 120ff. An extremely interesting summary of trends in agriculture is Ezekiel, 1932, which notes that many countries protected their agricultural populations to preserve peasant proprietors as bulwarks against communism.

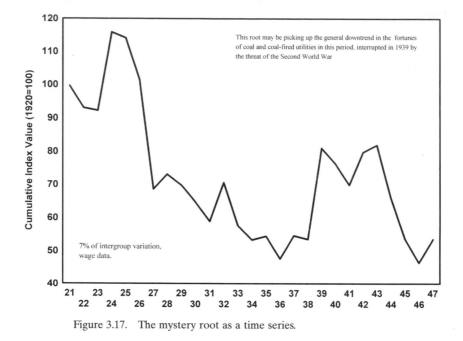

Figure 3.17.   The mystery root as a time series.

there is something in our methods that might mask the influence of an educational effect on the labor supply.[38] Or is it possible, as one referee has suggested to us, that entirely separate determinants can drive the year-to-year movement of relative wages on the one hand and the long-term trend of differentials on the other?

The first possibility can be excluded. The trend in total school enrollments is well documented; its plot shows a gently rising trend, except during the Depression and World War II. The rise in the number of workers who had completed high school, perhaps the most relevant construct for a measure of labor supply, is even steadier, falling only during World War II. Thus, changes in the educational status were happening continuously over the period; education was not like immigration, which slowed abruptly at the outset of our period.

---

[38] Goldin and Margo, 1991, and Goldin and Katz, 1995, have offered arguments for believing that education and perhaps technological change played important roles in the movement toward greater equality of wages in the period from the early thirties to the end of World War II. They argue that the increasing supply of high school graduates, in particular, increased competition for skilled jobs, depressed skill differentials, and compressed the wage structure. Several empirical analyses involving certain specialized occupational groups, such as clerks in New York State and railroad machinists, appear to lend weight to this claim.

Moreover, we have direct evidence that changes in pay related to skill differentials were minor. In Figure 3.3, we show that in most industries the movement of the skill-to-unskilled differential for the period 1920–1937 is less than the wage variation between these industries and even their near neighbors. As Figure 3.18 confirms, most of the important wage variation was interindustrial, not across skill levels. The printing trades were conceivably an exception – but if so, they were a minor one in the larger scheme of industrial wages.

Finally, we reject the argument that long-term trends can somehow supersede the patterns detected in our analysis. This argument amounts to a claim that the endpoints of an arbitrarily chosen time period can be explained without reference to the events occurring in between. We don't think so. The interindustry wage movements we identify occurred; we think they occurred because of particular movements of aggregate demand, labor action, and exchange rates. Had these movements been different, so, too, would have been the major variations in relative wages. To show an effect of education, one must therefore show either that one of our identifications is incorrect or that changing skill levels controlled one of our three identified proximate causes.

One final point: During World War II, the enormous increase in wages of the truly unskilled workers who toiled in agriculture and on the public roads owed nothing to any Roads Scholarships program. The spectacular rise in their wages was surely the effect of demand, spurred by record public deficits, and the absorption of some ten million men into uniformed government employment. And the result was an almost perfect inversion of Protestant ideology and conventional thinking about education and labor markets, for the prime beneficiaries certainly included millions of workers who were functionally illiterate and possessed of the lowest educational credentials of all.

3.6   Explaining the Evolution of Inequality as a Whole

To conclude our analysis, we return to our original data set. With some compression, so as to match our wage data to 1940 data on employment, and with some approximations (mainly filling in a few years of missing wage data here and there by interpolation), we can compute a single annual index of inequality in the wage structure.

To be precise, we have calculated the between-groups component of Theil's T statistic, a well-known measure of inequality, for the eighty-three industries in our sample, by averaging them into twenty-six major groups and using 1940 employment weights from the *Historical Statistics of the United States*. Figure 3.19 displays the result; Chapters 2 and 15 provide details of the method. As an absolute measure of wage

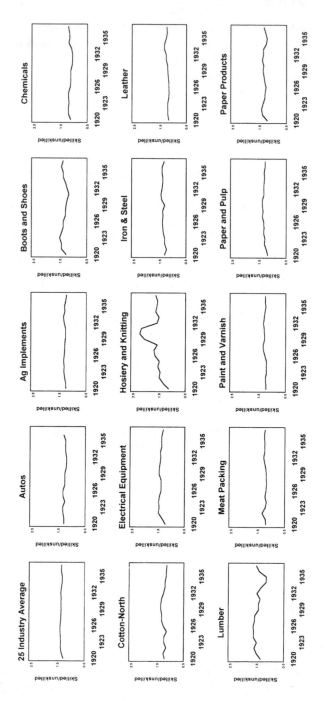

68

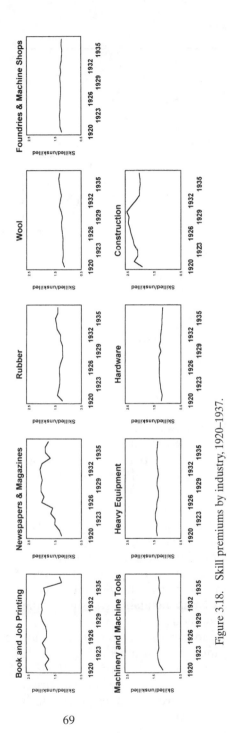

Figure 3.18.   Skill premiums by industry, 1920–1937.

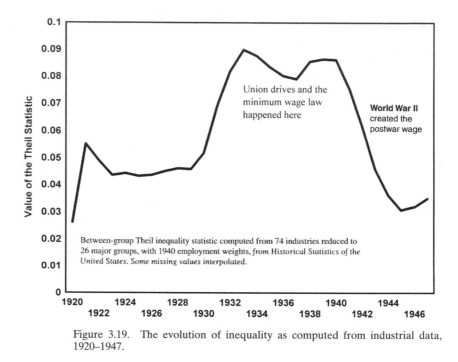

Figure 3.19. The evolution of inequality as computed from industrial data, 1920–1947.

inequality, our measure means little. But as a measure of *changes* in inequality, it turns out to be very interesting indeed.

Our estimate rises in 1920–1921, falls to a plateau in the 1920s, rises sharply in the Great Depression, and only comes down again, in a dramatic rush, during World War II.

Figure 3.20 adjusts our inequality measure by a factor of 200 for visual comparison and reveals clearly what does track inequality in the wage structure: the unemployment rate. In a bivariate regression (not shown), unemployment accounts for 83 percent of the variation in the Theil statistic. It is worth noting that we are looking here at the dispersion of wages among the *employed*. The falling incomes of the unemployed have no direct effect on the computation of this inequality statistic (as they would affect a Gini coefficient based on household incomes).

What then is the contribution of the forces associated with the canonical roots to the movement of wage inequality as a whole? There is no reason a priori for clear associations to exist for two reasons. First, the between-group Theil statistic is employment-weighted, while our clusters are not; it could be that major variations across clusters, picked up by

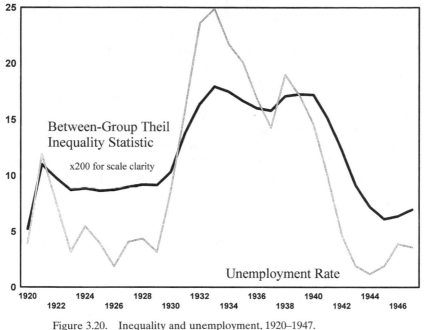

Figure 3.20.   Inequality and unemployment, 1920–1947.

the discriminant functions, affected only small groups of workers and therefore carried little impact on the Theil statistic. Second, even where some force significantly affects cross-cluster differentials, it may or may not affect the overall dispersion of wages, depending on whether initial differences in average wage levels between the clusters are large or small.

A reasonable first test of the influence of our canonical forces on inequality is simply to add the variable most strongly correlated with each canonical root to the Theil regression. For the first root, we have two potential proxies of equal power and no strong a priori reason to prefer one over the other; they are change in GNP (real and nominal changes are hard to distinguish in this noninflationary period) and change in unemployment. We use total workers involved in strikes as our proxy for the second root. As far as the third root is concerned, we use the foreign exchange index for the United Kingdom on one side and an average of such rates for seven countries – Argentina, Brazil, Canada, France, Italy, Japan, and Mexico – on the other. We would expect the signs a priori to be positive for GNP growth, negative for unemployment, and negative again for the strike variable. It appears from our earlier analysis that high growth rates benefited relatively high-wage workers – because the surge of investment would raise the incomes of construction, capital goods, and durable-goods producers – while strikes benefited relatively less well paid workers. For the sign of the exchange rate variable, we offer the following speculation: A depreciation with respect to sterling should mainly help high-wage workers who competed with the British in machinery markets, both foreign and domestic, while a depreciation with respect to other countries should mainly benefit low-wage workers, who competed with their imports in home consumer markets. Thus, the sign on the U.K. exchange rate would be positive and that on exchange rates with other countries would be negative.

Unemployment raises inequality and does most of the work in this equation. The growth of GNP has the expected effect: Initially, increases in aggregate demand increase inequality; it is only with sustained high employment that inequality declines. Both results underscore the primacy of aggregate demand effects on the wage structure.

The coefficients on both the labor and exchange rate variables are also significant, with the expected signs. Their economic significance is, of course, a good deal less – something we already know from our disaggregation of between-group changes. Overall, the regression explains 94 percent of the variation in the Theil statistic. Durbin–Watson statistics do not indicate serial correlation in these residuals. Appendix 3 displays the results in detail.

3.7   Conclusion

At the end of World War I, the structure of wages in the American economy resembled what it would look like almost a generation later. But after the brief postwar boom, this relatively egalitarian wage alignment disintegrated under the hammer blow of the recession of 1920–1922, when unemployment soared. A recovery in the early 1920s led to a plateau for the rest of that decade until the Great Crash of 1929.

The Depression of 1929–1932 drove inequality up as the low-wage farm sector, still 40 percent of all employment, collapsed. The dollar depreciation against sterling in 1933 exacerbated this effect. Overall in the 1930s, exchange rate movements tended to increase inequality in two ways: The dollar fell and remained low against the British pound but rose against low-wage currencies, thus working to increase inequality on both fronts. Only the full-employment policies and direct controls of World War II, accompanied by a strong push for greater wage equality within the trade union movement, returned the wage structure by 1946 to something that resembled that of 1920.

Indeed, so powerful was the wartime rise in the lowest wages that the whole labor market began to change in ways not well captured by our study. As the price of unskilled labor rocketed up, employers began accepting and in many instances recruiting new sources of unskilled labor. Depending on the nature of the work process, the location of production, and other variables, they began to hire larger numbers of women, Negroes, Mexicans, and Puerto Ricans (as these groups were then called). In effect, sustained full employment restructured the market for unskilled labor. And many of its biggest beneficiaries were groups that had been largely excluded from both manufacturing employment and education before the war.[39]

Theorists who see this process as importantly driven by education and changing skill levels are, we believe, in danger of putting the cart before the horse. The GI Bills came at the very end of the period we are concerned with, and the National Defense Education Acts and the Great Society's education programs lay far in the future. For all the success of the public schools, access to education between 1921 and 1947 remained very far from equal. Indeed, though the question would require another chapter, it seems likely that the vast increase in education levels that followed the war owed much to the prior leveling of the wage structure and the new political structures engendered by the New Deal. And we suspect that those business groups that accepted the GI Bills but worked hard to prevent the Employment Act of 1946 from becoming what its original sponsors intended – a Full Employment Act – well understood that the World Knot could be unraveled.[40] They had already grasped what our study has told us. They knew that no public policies work so reliably to reduce inequality as the deliberate, simultaneous effort to combine full employment with collective-bargaining rights and rising wage standards.

[39] Haddy and Tolles, 1957, make the interesting point that substantial numbers of employers appear to have restructured their work schemes in order to tap into these untraditional reserves of labor.
[40] On the politics of the 1946 Employment Act, see Collins, 1981, and Burch, 1973.

Appendix 1

Description of Data

The principal source of hourly wage data for manufacturing industry in this study is M. Ada Beney, National Industrial Conference Board Studies No. 229, *Wages, Hours and Employment in the United States, 1914–1936* (New York: National Industrial Conference Board, 1936). Most of these data series were continued through December 1937 in the Conference Board publication *Wages, Hours, and Employment in the United States, July 1936–December 1937*, which was issued as a Supplement to the Conference Board Service Letter of June 1938. Data for later years are drawn from issues of the Conference Board's *Economic Almanac.*

Construction wages are drawn from the 1942 and 1949 supplements to the *Survey of Current Business* (U.S. Department of Commerce). These series cover union and nonunion work sites.

Wages in the printing trades are from *Union Wages and Hours: Printing Industry – July 1, 1967 and Trend 1907–67*, Bulletin No. 1592 (Washington, DC: U.S. Department of Labor, May 1968), and Part I of *Historical Statistics of the United States.*

Gas and electric distribution wages are in the Conference Board, *Economic Almanac for 1948*, p. 188.

Wages on public road-building projects are from U.S. Department of Commerce, *The Statistical Abstract of the United States, 1951*, p. 202, and the *Survey of Current Business, 1936 Supplement*, p. 42.

Railroad wages are from Harry E. Jones, *Railroad Wages and Labor Relations, 1900–1952: A Historical Survey and Summary of Results* (New York: Bureau of Information of the Eastern Railways, 1953). The data came originally from the Interstate Commerce Commission.

Hourly-equivalent wages for farm workers are estimated by the authors from annual data on *monthly* farm wage rates in U.S. Department of Labor, *Handbook of Labor Statistics, 1950 Edition*. The method is to convert 1920 farm wages to an approximate hourly equivalent by dividing by average hours in manufacturing and then to use the observed rates of change in monthly wages to generate the path of the corresponding pseudohourly series. Because farm hours exceed manufacturing hours by an unknown amount, this overstates the average hourly farm wage and understates the initial degree of inequality between agricultural and other wages when estimated on an hourly basis. But the patterns of change in wages or inequality should not be affected.

Employment data by industry for 1940 are drawn from the *Statistical Abstract of the United States, 1947*, Table No. 210, p. 191.

Data on strikes and unionization are from the Census Bureau, *The Statistical History of the United States from Colonial Times to the Present* (Stamford, CT: Fairfield Publishers, 1965) and from William Goldner, *Strikes* (Berkeley: Institute of Industrial Relations, University of California, 1951).

Data on trade and commodity prices are from R. E. Lapps, *Price and Quantity Trends in the Foreign Trade of the United States* (Princeton, NJ: National Bureau of Economic Research, 1963), Tables A-3 and A-6.

Macroeconomic data are from Robert J. Gordon, ed., *The American Business Cycle: Continuity and Change* (Chicago: University of Chicago Press, 1986).

Exchange rate data are from Board of Governors of the Federal Reserve System, *Banking and Monetary Statistics, 1914–41* (Washington, DC, 1943) and *Banking and Monetary Statistics, 1941–1970* (Washington, DC, 1976).

Appendix 2

List of Industry Variables Used and Variable Codes

Name	Figure 3.1 Code	Figure 3.2 Codes
25-industry average	Indus25	Ind25_MU,Ind25_MS
Agricultural implement	Ag_Imple	Agi_MU, Agi_MS
Automobile	Auto	Auto_MU,Auto_MS
Boot and shoe	Boot_Sho	BS_MU,BS_MS
Chemical	Chemical	Chem_MU,Chem_MS
Cotton–North	Cotton	Cott_MU,Cott_MS
Electrical manufacturing	Elect	Elec_MU,Elec_MS
Foundries and machine shops	Foun_Mac	FM_MU,FM_MS
Foundries	Foun_Sho	Foun_MU,Foun_MS
Machines and machine tools	Machiner	Mach_MU,Mach_MS
Heavy equipment	Heavy_Eq	Heav_MU,Heav_MS
Hardware and small parts	Hardware	Hard_MU,Hard_MS
Other products	Oth_Foun	Not used
Furniture	Furnitur	Furn_MU,Furn_MS
Hosiery and knit goods	Hos_Knit	HK_MU,HK_MS
Iron and steel	Iron_Ste	Not used
Leather tanning and finishing	Leather	Leat_ MU,Leat_MS
Lumber and millwork	Lumber	Lumb_MU,Lumb_MS
Meat packing	Meat_Pac	Meat_MU,Meat_MS
Paint and varnish	Paint	PV_MU,PV_MS
Paper and pulp	Paper_Pu	Pa_Pu_MU,Pa_Pu_MS
Paper products	Paper_Pr	Pa_Pr_MU,Pa_Pr_MS
Printing – book and job	Books	Print_MU,Print_MS
Printing – news and magazines	News	News_MU,News_MS
Rubber	Rubber	Rubb_MU,Rubb_MS
Silk (and rayon)	Silk	Not used
Wool	Wool	Wool_MU,Wool_MS
Farm wages	FarmWage	Not used
Mid-Atlantic	Fa_Midat	Not used
Northeast	Farm_NE	Not used
East North Central	Farm_ENC	Not used
West North Central	Farm_WNC	Not used
West South Central	Farm_WSC	Not used
East South Central	Farm_ESC	Not used
South Atlantic	Farm_SA	Not used
Mountain	Fa_Mount	Not used
Pacific	Fa_Pac	Not used
Public roads	Roads_US	Not used
Mid-Atlantic	Ro_Midat	Not used
Northeast	Roads_NE	Not used
East North Central	Road_ENC	Not used
West North Central	Road_WNC	Not used
West South Central	Road_WSC	Not used
East South Central	Road_ESC	Not used

Appendix 2

(cont.)

Name	Figure 3.1 code	Figure 3.2 codes
South Atlantic	Ro_So_At	Not used
Mountain	Ro_Mount	Not used
Pacific	Ro_Pacif	Not used
Coal	Coal	Not used
Gas utilities	Util_Gas	Not used
Electric utilities	Util_Elec	Not used
Railroads	RR (1 to 31)	Not used
Common construction	Comm_Con	Con_Comm
Skilled construction	Skild_Co	Con_Skil

Key to reading the Railroad Categories in Figure 3.1

Following are the thirty-one subcategories of wages by industrial subsector and occupation for the railroad industry, listed in order of their appearance from left to right in Figure 3.1.

21 Road Freight Brakemen and Flagmen (Through Freight)
14 Road Freight Conductors (Through Freight)
 8 Road Freight Firemen and Helpers (Through Freight)
 3 Road Freight Engineers and Motormen (Through Freight)
25 All Other
24 Switch Tenders
23 Yard Brakemen and Yard Helpers
16 Yard Conductors and Yard Foremen
 5 Yard Engineers and Motormen
20 Total Road Freight Brakemen and Flagmen
13 Total Road Freight Conductors
 7 Total Road Freight Firemen and Helpers
 2 Total Road Freight Engineers and Motormen
19 Road Passenger Brakemen and Flagmen
18 Road Passenger Baggage Men
12 Road Passenger Conductors
 6 Road Passenger Firemen and Helpers
 1 Road Passenger Engineers and Motormen
31 Maintenance of Way Group
30 Stationary Engine and Boiler Room and Shop Laborers Group
28 Shop Crafts Group
29 Clerical and Station Employees Group
27 Floating Equipment (Marine) Group
17 Assistant Road Passenger Conductors and Ticket Collectors
11 Outside and Inside Hostlers and Helpers
22 Road Freight Brakemen and Flagmen (Local and Way)
15 Road Freight Conductors (Local and Way)
 9 Road Freight Firemen and Helpers (Local and Way)
26 Train Dispatchers Group
 4 Road Freight Engineers and Motormen (Local and Way)
10 Yard Firemen and Helpers

Appendix 3

Determinants of Changing Inequality in the Wage Structure, 1920–1947

Dependent Variable: THEIL (T statistics in parentheses) $N = 26$	
Independent Variables	
UNEMP	**0.84**
	(17.27)
DRGNP	**0.17**
	(3.60)
STRIKERS	**−0.23**
	(3.82)
FOREXUK	**0.19**
	(3.82)
FOREXOTHER	**−0.37**
	(5.66)
CONSTANT	**0.034**
	(3.11)
Adjusted R^2	0.94
D-W	1.92
Coefficients significant at 0.01 level shown in bold face.	

Variables used:
THEIL: between-group Theil statistic computed for twenty-six industrial groups using 1940 employment weights; authors' calculations.
UNEMP: unemployment rate, from Gordon (1986).
DRGNP: percentage rate of change of real GNP, also from Gordon (1986).
STRIKERS: number of workers involved in strikes, in thousands.
FOREXUK: exchange rate of the British pound, in cents per pound, presented as an index number with 1920 = 100.
FOREXOTHER: average of the exchange value of the dollar against the currencies of Argentina, Brazil, Canada, France, Italy, Japan, and Mexico, presented as an index number with 1920 = 100.
CONSTANT: coefficient of intercept.
Coefficients reported are Durbin Betas.
D-W: Durbin-Watson statistic.

CHAPTER 4

Inequality in American Manufacturing Wages, 1920–1998: A Revised Estimate

James K. Galbraith and Vidal Garza Cantú

Using a monthly data set for wages and employment of production workers in eighteen sectors for which continuous data are available back to January 1947, we compute new measures of earnings and wage inequality in U.S. manufacturing. We confirm that there is a close connection between the dispersion of hourly wage rates and unemployment. But we also show that, contrary to general belief and some of our own previous assumptions, in the 1950s manufacturing wage rate inequality rose sharply, reaching the extreme levels of the 1930s. An implication is that inequality in manufacturing hourly wage rates in the late 1970s and 1980s, previously thought to be lower than during the Great Depression, was in fact much higher. The new series also shows that wage rate inequality began declining again in 1994 and has now fallen to just below the peaks of the interwar period. The data are current to the end of 1998.

4.1   Introduction

The previous chapter showed how unemployment and inequality were closely related during the interwar and World War II years. Here we extend that analysis to the late 1990s. New, highly detailed data, as well as calculations by Garza-Cantú, permit us to offer continuous *monthly* series for inequality in U.S. manufacturing wage rates, beginning in January 1947 and up to date as of December 1998. This series tracks Galbraith's measures for the 1958–1992 period closely.[1] It strongly supports

---

[1] In *Created Unequal*, Galbraith has presented estimates of the evolution of inequality in hourly wage rates in American manufacturing for two periods, 1920–1947 and 1958–1992. The earlier series is based on historical data assembled from many sources by Thomas Ferguson and Galbraith (this volume), while the later one is computed from the U.S. Department of Commerce's Annual Survey of Manufactures. They are linked together by an interpolation based on the observed correlation between T′ and a Gini coefficient based on household income data during the years when both are available, 1958–1992, applied to the years 1947–1958, for which the latter was available but not the former.

the argument that there is a close association between the dispersion of hourly pay rates and unemployment – in effect, that wage rate inequality is a macroeconomic phenomenon. The new measures also show a decline in wage rate inequality beginning in 1994, just as the unemployment rate began to decline from recession levels.

The new series also shows a sharp rise in wage rate inequality between 1947 and 1958 – the years for which a Theil measure was not available in the earlier study. The assumption that wage rate inequality in manufacturing tracked the much broader and stable measure of household income inequality in this period was thus incorrect. It appears instead that wage rate inequality returned to levels characteristic of the Great Depression by the late 1950s. It declined in the 1960s, particularly toward the end of the decade, but to levels that remained substantially higher than those prevailing in the 1920s or at the end of World War II. In the 1970s and 1980s, manufacturing wage rate inequality rose to levels far higher than those existing during the Great Depression of the 1930s. The decline during the second half of the 1990s has only now brought this measure of inequality back below the peak levels of the Great Depression.

4.2   A Monthly Measure of Wage Rate Inequality in U.S. Manufacturing, 1947–1998

The new measure is calculated across eighteen highly aggregated manufacturing sectors. Figure 4.1 presents this measure alongside the monthly rate of unemployment. Table 4.1 lists the sectors covered.

This is perhaps a crude measure, but when presented as an annual series, it closely tracks Galbraith's measure of the same phenomenon, which is based on three-digit Standard Industrial Code (SIC) categories. Figure 4.2 provides a picture of both series.

As noted previously, the new series declines sharply beginning in 1994. While there is general agreement that some improvement in wage inequality has occurred in recent years, actual measures are few and far between. Our measure is consistent with other findings, though it would probably date the beginning of improvement earlier than most other studies.

Wage rate inequality also rises sharply in this series in the decade immediately following World War II. This is surprising, as the 1950s are widely regarded as a time of stability in the wage structure. Our evidence

---

This interpolation is superseded by the results reported here; however, the general accuracy of the separate Theil measures is strongly reconfirmed.

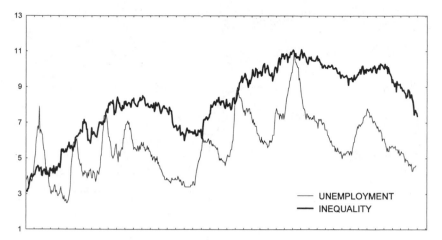

Figure 4.1. Unemployment and inequality in manufacturing wages, January 1947–December 1998 (monthly data).

Table 4.1. *Eighteen Manufacturing Sectors for Which Continuous Wage and Employment Data Are Available, 1947–1998*

Lumber and wood products
Furniture and fixtures
Stone, clay, and glass products
Primary metal industries
Fabricated metal products
Industrial machinery and equipment
Transportation equipment
Miscellaneous manufacturing industries
Food and kindred products
Tobacco products
Textile mill products
Apparel and other textile products
Paper and allied products
Printing and publishing
Chemicals and allied products
Petroleum and coal products
Rubber and miscellaneous plastics products
Leather and leather products

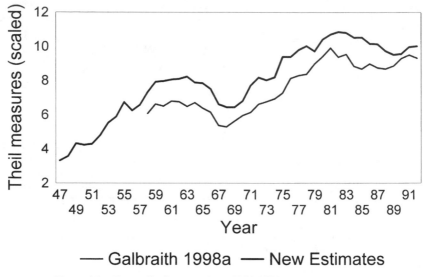

Figure 4.2.   Inequality in wage rates, 1947–1998.

strongly contradicts this image and suggests that the observed stability of the household income distribution in this period must be due to factors outside the manufacturing wage structure: to the growth of services, retail, government employment, and the Social Security system, for example. On the other hand, the finding that wage rate inequality did rise in the 1950s resolves an anomaly of the earlier assumption, for in this period there were two recessions with sharply rising unemployment, and we now see that there did exist, in fact, a relationship between these spikes in the unemployment rate and rising wage rate inequality.

4.3   Computing an Unbroken Inequality Series Back to 1920

This new series also has strong implications for efforts to extend the measurement of inequality in wage structures back to the interwar period. Put simply, if wage rate inequality rose sharply in the 1950s, it must have been lower in the 1940s and in earlier years.

Figure 4.3 presents a measure of inequality that is unbroken from 1920 to 1998. The problem in constructing such series is that the data are from different sources and are collected at different levels of disaggregation; the level values of between-group components of the Theil statistic are not directly comparable when group structures differ. But because the movements through time of such series are likely to be highly similar,

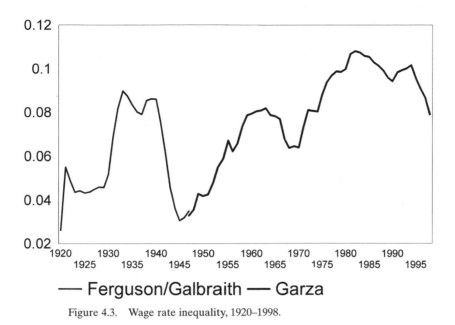

── Ferguson/Galbraith ── Garza

Figure 4.3.   Wage rate inequality, 1920–1998.

series computed from different sources can be linked. We do this simply by adjusting the levels of the new postwar series so that they correspond to those of the Ferguson-Galbraith series for the earlier period in the one year of overlap, 1947. Thus, the new series assumes that proportionate changes in the inequality measure for the earlier period are comparable to equivalent proportionate changes in the measure for the later period.

If this assumption is correct, then previous understandings of the long evolution of manufacturing wage rate inequality must be revised. While the earlier linked series offered by Galbraith in *Created Unequal* shows inequality at all-time highs in the 1930s, the new series shows that Great Depression levels were regained within a decade of the end of World War II. The Kennedy–Johnson years showed improvements, but even at their best, in 1967–1969, wage rate inequality remained higher than in the late 1940s. And from that high base, inequality soared in the 1970s and 1980s, reaching levels far higher than those existing during the Depression. The recovery after 1994 brings inequality down again, but only to just below that of the worst years of the 1930s.

How good is the proportionality-of-change assumption on which these observations rest? The question can be tested directly in two ways. The first is to examine industrial categories that are substantially the same in

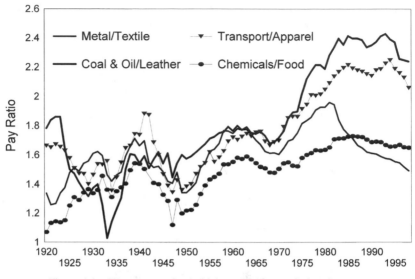

Figure 4.4.   Wage rate ratios in high- and low-wage industries.

the earlier and later data sets. Figure 4.4 presents the ratio of average hourly wages in four high-wage industries compared to those in four lower-wage industries for which one can construct time series that are continuous across the entire time frame. The results broadly confirm the assumption: Direct measures of interindustrial pay gaps also return to the 1930s levels in the 1950s and then rise beyond those levels in the 1970s and 1980s.

The second way to confirm the continuity of the time series is to extend the Theil measure of inequality back in time, albeit for higher levels of aggregation. Garza-Cantú has calculated a twelve-sector measure of T' that extends back to January 1939, again on a monthly basis. This measure, annualized, is presented alongside the composite Ferguson-Galbraith-Garza measure shown in Figure 4.5. Once again, the correspondence is very close for all years of overlap, which indicates that the across-industries Theil method is quite robust with respect to differing classification schemes and levels of aggregation in the data set from which it is constructed.

4.4   Inequality and Unemployment

Figure 4.6 presents the relationship of inequality to unemployment in the new monthly series as a quantile-quantile scatterplot. This form is

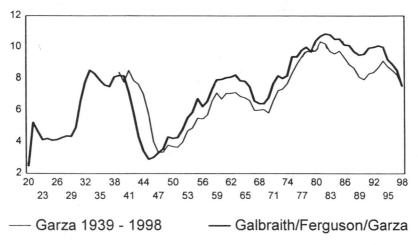

— Garza 1939 - 1998   — Galbraith/Ferguson/Garza

Figure 4.5.   Inequality in wage rates, 1920–1998.

particularly telling: Inequality maintains a linear relationship with unemployment, indicating that the two series are drawn from the same distribution, but only over a middle range of values of the unemployment rate. At very high rates of unemployment, say 10 percent and above, there is little additional effect on the wage structure. And at low rates of unemployment, improvement speeds up. From the figure, that critical value appears to be about 4 percent, or just below present-day unemployment rates at the time of writing. It should be stressed, however, that this is no more than a historical regularity.[2]

Figure 4.7 presents a similar plot on annual data for inequality and unemployment over the entire time frame under study, that is, back to 1920. The data show a similar pattern: sharp differences in the response of inequality to high and low unemployment and rough linearity in the inequality–unemployment relationship between unemployment rates of 4 and 10 percent.

4.5   Conclusions

New monthly measures of inequality in the structure of manufacturing wages back to 1947 and even to 1939 permit us to refine and extend past measures of wage rate inequality back to 1920. They also permit us to calculate the evolution of wage rate inequality to very recent dates. We believe that these new measures support a Keynesian and

---

[2] Galbraith has at various times referred to this threshold variable as the "ethical rate of unemployment."

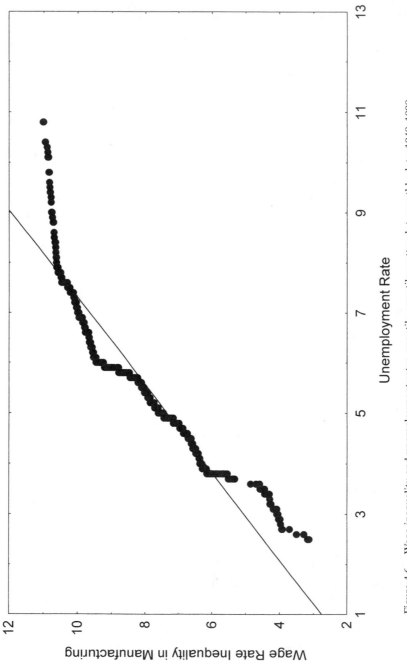

Figure 4.6. Wage inequality and unemployment rates, quantile-quantile scatterplot, monthly data, 1948–1998.

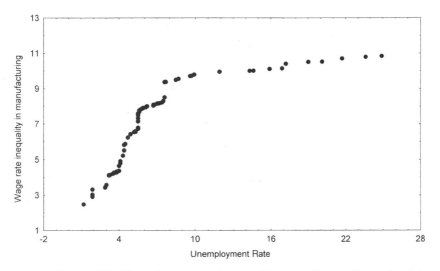

Figure 4.7. Unemployment and inequality, quantile-quantile scatterplot, annual data, 1920–1998.

macrotheoretic view of changing wage distributions, according to which the unemployment rate stands out as a principal determinant of the wage rate distribution.

Additional work remains to be done to develop the relationship between wage rate inequality in manufacturing and that in the rest of the economy, and particularly to account for the stability of household income inequality in the United States in the 1950s while manufacturing wage rate inequality was rising rapidly. What we have seen so far supports the commonsense notion of the time: The growth of government and the welfare state, not equality of private wage rates, produced a stable income distribution during those years.

88	Galbraith and Garza Cantú

Appendix

Earnings Inequality in the United States Economy, 1939–1999:
A Comparison of Alternative Measures
(Calculations by Peter P. S. Bradford)

These charts present calculations of the between-groups component of
the Theil statistic (T') for the U.S. economy, using data from different
sources and at different levels of aggregation and disaggregation. The
charts thus provide a visual check on the consistency of alternative measures of the evolution of earnings inequality in the United States. The
first chart presents measures of earnings inequality in the U.S. manufacturing sector, comparable to most measures of inequality presented in
this chapter. Five inequality series are shown. Of these, three are drawn
directly from the Bureau of Labor Statistics (BLS) employment and
earnings data set; they represent monthly calculations of T' at the two-,
three-, and four-digit levels of the SIC system. As one might expect, these
series are highly correlated with each other through time. The difference
between them is chiefly that the level estimate of the statistic rises as
the underlying data set is sliced into finer components. Discontinuities
in the series, on the other hand, are produced by periodic revisions in the
number of SIC categories included at each level of aggregation in each
survey month. These revisions have only minor effects on the manufacturing estimates, but they more seriously affect estimates of earnings
inequality in the larger economy, presented subsequently.

The remaining two series show annual estimates of T' as computed
from the Organization of Economic Cooperation and Development's
(OECD's) Structural Analysis (STAN) data set (thirty-nine industrial
categories) and from the industrial statistics data set published annually
by United Nations International Development Organization (UNIDO)
(twenty-nine industrial categories). These data sets are intended for
international comparisons, and while measures of inequality derived
from them are useful for that purpose, they are at best crude approximations of the measures available from the BLS.

The second chart presents measures of earnings inequality for the U.S.
economy across the full range of employment and earnings data, including data for mining, services, and the financial and public sectors. Again,
monthly measures are presented at the two-, three-, and four-digit levels
of disaggregation.

These data are not as complete or continuous as those for manufacturing, and they exhibit considerable changes with revisions in the classification schemes. Nevertheless, they follow a distinctly recognizable

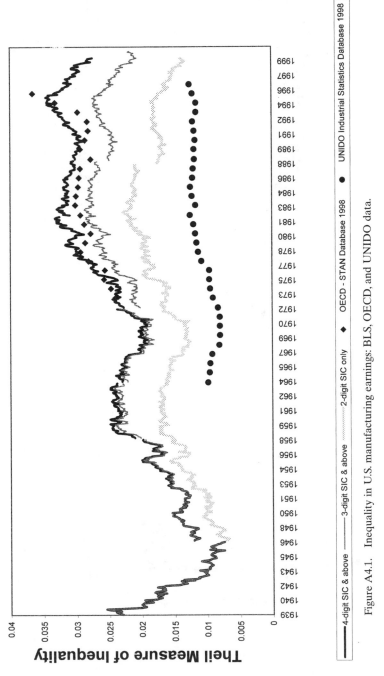

Figure A4.1.   Inequality in U.S. manufacturing earnings: BLS, OECD, and UNIDO data.

89

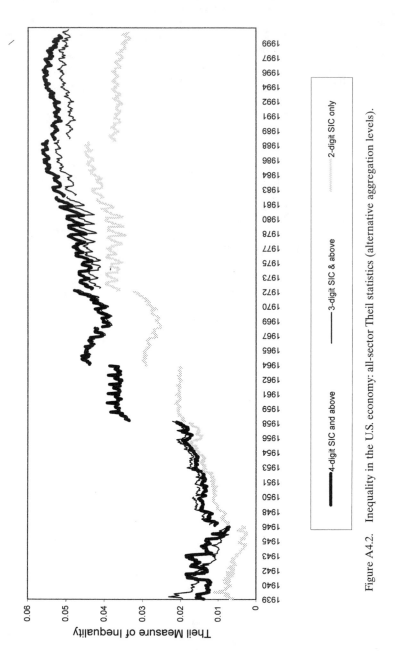

Figure A4.2. Inequality in the U.S. economy: all-sector Theil statistics (alternative aggregation levels).

pattern, consistent in general terms with the measures of earnings inequality in manufacturing alone. There are sharp declines in inequality in World War II, rises thereafter, declines in the 1960s, and a strong rise through the 1970s and early 1980s, followed by some reduction of inequality in recent years. Note also the annual flux in these estimates, which appears to be strongest in the 1970s and may be related to the within-year pattern of annual cost-of-living adjustments in certain sectors.

CHAPTER 5

Interindustry Wage Structures: New Evidence from the OECD

Amy D. Calistri and James K. Galbraith

This chapter presents an analysis of the evolution of industrial wages in a selection of Organization of Economic Cooperation and Development (OECD) countries, using data drawn from the structural analysis database and a sequence of techniques that apply cluster and discriminant analysis to time series of wage change by industry. The principal finding is that a small number of well-defined groups of industries usually exist whose cross-group differences account for almost all interindustry wage variation. While the specific structure of groups varies according to patterns of natural resources, comparative advantage, and trade union organization within each country, the between-group variation across time usually reflects the movement of macroeconomic variables, some of them internal and other external, such as inflation and exchange rates.

> The chaos which *seems* to prevail in the labor market conceals a pattern of order which can be explained and which sheds light on the influences that determine the inter-industry wage structure of the community.
>
> Slichter (1950:81)

5.1 Introduction

Since the time of Slichter's (1950) groundbreaking work, the literature on wage structures has often used the concept of *rent sharing* to explain differences in pay between similar workers in different industries.[1] In a recent article, Blanchflower, Oswald, and Sanfey (1996) reaffirm Slichter and Lester's (1952) analysis, which shows that the distribution of profits to workers accounts for almost a quarter of interindustry wage differ-

---

[1] Studies of interindustry wage differentials by Dickens and Katz, 1987; Krueger and Summers, 1987, 1988; Katz and Summers, 1989; and Carruth and Oswald, 1989, have all used the idea.

entials. And yet, although (as Blanchflower et al. delicately put it) rent sharing is inconsistent with conventional competitive models, the literature continues to rely largely on the competitive framework to interpret changes in the distribution of pay.

This chapter develops and extends an alternative approach, based on the insight that changes in degrees of market power must lie behind changes in the distribution of rents, and that macroeconomic and specifically Keynesian forces – changes in consumption, investment, commodity prices, and exchange rates – often lie behind the rise or decline, over time, of a group of industries and their place in the wage structure. Galbraith has summarized the theory behind this argument.[2] This chapter extends its empirical application to a selection of countries outside the United States. We show that while details of institutional structure differ from case to case, the idea that just a few macroforces drive the wage structure has wide application. In fact, we have yet to encounter an exception.

The order within is often simple. The long lists of industrial categories characteristic of standard industrial classification schemes are usually redundant when it comes to explaining patterns of wage change. Instead, the differential movement between three or four large, well-chosen *groups* of industries can usually capture most of the evolution of the wage structure. Equally, one can usually reduce the between-group changes to an even smaller number of component forces; taken together, these forces explain a very high proportion of between-group variations. Finally, it is often possible to make an intelligent judgment as to the economic nature of those forces. In other words, by reducing a complex, redundant, multivariate, and inchoate block of historical data to its essential informational content, one may frequently arrive in the end at a reasonable assessment of the major sources of change in the distribution of industrial pay.[3]

Cluster analysis applied in this way groups variables that behave similarly. Discriminant analysis develops lineally independent weighting functions that expose the principal between-group differences. It also evaluates the relative importance of each such function (eigenvector) and permits the calculation of scores that show the relative influence of each function on each industry. In this chapter, we identify groups of industries, as defined by similar patterns of wage behavior, for Germany,

[2] In *Created Unequal* and Chapter 1 of the present volume.
[3] Ferguson and Galbraith provide an example of such an analysis in Chapter 3 of this volume. Galbraith and Lu (see Chapter 16) present details on the combination of cluster and discriminant analysis applied to blocks of time series as a research tool in social science.

Japan, and Italy. We then develop the functional scores that differentiate the groups within each country. Finally, we compare these to economic time series drawn from the historical record to arrive at inferences about the forces that influence the evolution of wage differentials.

Clear group structures can be identified in each of the countries we examined. Industries group into recognizable clusters according to natural resources, technological process, comparative advantage, and sectors linked by bargaining or as the common targets of industrial policy. While different countries display individual structures, these groupings and between-group characteristics are evident in all the OECD countries that we have examined so far. The key sources of between-group variation, on the other hand, appear to be exogenous macroeconomic forces such as commodity prices, interest rates, inflation, or changes in gross domestic product (GDP), to which the groups are differentially sensitive.

5.2   Data and Method

We apply cluster and discriminant analyses to time series of changes in average annual earnings by industrial category. We investigate three developed countries that differ from each other in many ways – Germany, Italy, and Japan – and we provide summary information in an appendix on three others – Canada, New Zealand, and Norway – chosen for no particular reason other than to provide an eclectic selection. Some of these countries are large, others small, some diversified, others specialized. They are spread across the globe, and they have widely differing patterns of trade. Our data are drawn from the OECD's Structural Analysis (STAN) database using a nonoverlapping subset of that database's forty-nine International Standard Industrial Classification (ISIC) Revision 2 industries.[4]

Our method follows the Galbraith-Lu procedure. First, we compute a matrix of percentage changes in nominal average earnings by industrial category. We then apply cluster analysis to the resulting *paths* of wage change, a procedure that for most countries permits us to reduce twenty or thirty industrial categories to between four and six groups; these groups experience small to negligible within-group wage variation over time. Discriminant function analysis then permits reduction of the pattern of between-group variations to a small number of linearly independent canonical forces, or eigenvectors, of a standardized matrix of

---

[4] Missing observations, which are not numerous, are filled in using cross-industry averages for the relevant year.

between-group variations.[5] These eigenvectors may be used to compute canonical scores for each industry in the original data set, and the pattern of scores can be examined in several ways to arrive at an interpretation of each root.[6]

Our preferred device is simply to report scatterplots of two kinds. First, we plot canonical scores of the first two roots, ranked by their explanatory power, against each other; this procedure illustrates the effectiveness of the cluster and discriminant procedure in constructing change as a comparatively simple between-group phenomenon. The distribution of industries along the scale of scores often also provides clues to the nature of the economic forces that are differentiating wage performance along that dimension. These forces may have to do with technology, patterns of unionization, patterns of trade, or other factors.

Second, for each root we seek to identify, we plot the calculated canonical scores against what might be termed a *pseudoscore* derived from candidate variables in the historical record. The pseudoscore is computed in a way analogous to that of the original canonical score.[7] Where the fit between scores and pseudoscores is good, one may reasonably infer a relationship – not necessarily causal but plausibly indicative – between the root and the historical variable from which the pseudoscore is computed. We are able to provide reasonable identification of three roots in this manner, one each for Germany, Italy, and Japan.

5.3   Results

The application of the method just described is uniformly successful in two key respects. First, for each country we examine, nearly all of the interindustry pay variations can be isolated into the between-group differentials for a small number of groups. The Wilks's lambda statistic – the ratio of the determinant of the within-group variance-covariance matrix to the determinant of the total variance-covariance matrix – is

---

[5] The canonical score for each industry on a particular root is simply the vector product of the eigenvector associated with that root and the time vector of wage changes for that industry.

[6] In addition, the eigenvectors themselves take the form of a time series, which can in some cases be compared directly to historical time series to obtain a visual or statistical matching of time patterns. However, to execute this step effectively – as in Ferguson and Galbraith's chapter on the United States in 1920–1947 – usually requires more detailed historical evidence on each country under study than we were able to muster in this study.

[7] The pseudoscore is the vector product of percentage wage changes for each industry against the time vector of changes in the candidate explanatory variable, which may be the path of consumption spending, exchange rate, commodity price, or some other variate drawn from the historical record.

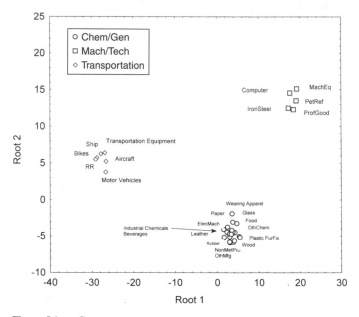

Figure 5.1a.   Germany: scatterplot of canonical scores.

below 0.005 in every case. Second, we find that the first two eigenvectors of the discriminant matrix account for more than 75 percent of the between-group variation in all cases. This suggests that knowledge of just two external influences on the wage structure is usually sufficient for an understanding of the most important sources of interindustry wage change. These results are summarized in Appendix 1.

Scatterplots of the scores on the first and second roots for Germany, Italy, and Japan are found in Figures 5.1a through 5.3a. These provide a kind of profile of industrial structure and wage bargaining in each country examined. The very tight clusters found in Japan, for example, indicate the close conformity of wage settlements by group membership in that country. Industrial specialists may recognize these groups as wage bargaining units, national monopolies or protected sectors, import-sensitive industries, advanced technology and export industries, and so on.

The relative wage performance of each group is depicted in Figures 5.1b through 5.3b. In each case, the figures show average earnings for the cluster in relation to the average for manufacturing as a whole. Thus, the figures provide a capsule history of interindustry wage changes. Movements toward the average (as in Italy in the 1970s) indicate a general compression of the wage structure, whereas movements away from the

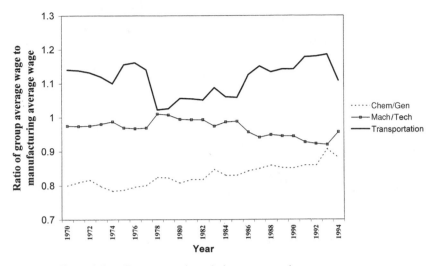

Figure 5.1b.   Germany: major relative wage trends.

average (as again in Italy in the 1980s) not only indicate expanding inequality but also point to the industrial groupings that are most responsible for it (in the Italian case, advanced technologies and oil). These movements thus help to characterize the forces underlying measures of inequality computed using the Theil statistic – which, for instance, show wage compression followed by decompression in Italy at this time.[8]

The remaining figures, 5.1c through 5.3c, show our preferred identifications of selected roots. This project remains the most challenging aspect of the present research, yet we remain convinced that the other identifications are out there, waiting to be made. Discriminant plots for Canada, New Zealand, and Norway are provided in Appendix 2.

Germany

The German industrial wage structure resolves itself into three distinct groups (Figure 5.1a). One group represents all the transportation industries, irrespective of mode: aerospace, rail, shipping, and automotive, even motorcycles (Transportation). The second is the machinery/technology (Mach/Tech) sector, including computers, machinery, professional goods, iron and steel, and oil. The third comprises the balance of Germany's industries, including chemicals (Chem/Gen). Of these three groups, Germany's Transportation sector has traditionally had the highest wages,

---

[8] These measures are presented in Figure 8.1 in Chapter 8.

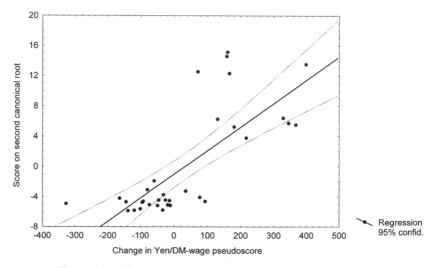

Figure 5.1c.   Germany: scatterplot of second root score and yen/DM pseudoscore. Correlation: $r = 0.75$.

and this remains the case to the end of our data. The Mach/Tech sector has also paid an above-average wage, but its position has been eroding, and it is almost convergent with the general manufacturing sector as of 1992 (Figure 5.1b).

What to make of this? Figure 5.1a provides certain clues. We see that the Mach/Tech sector ranks highest on both roots, while the transportation groups ranks lowest on the first root and the Chem/Gen sector ranks lowest on the second. We do not have a statistical interpretation for the first and dominant root, which accounts for 80 percent of between-group variation and may be related to the investment cycle in Germany. But as for the second root, which accounts for 19 percent of the between-group variation, we notice that both the Mach/Tech and Transportation sectors are advanced exporters. Meanwhile, the comparatively low-tech and low-scoring members of the Chem/Gen group tend not to be. This suggests a trade-related source of wage differentiation. One may further notice that the Mach/Tech group contains a number of industries that have come under particularly intense competition in world markets from Japan.

We choose the change in the yen–Deutsche mark exchange rate as our candidate explanation. We find a 0.75 correlation between scores on the second canonical root and the pseudoscore on this variable. This is illustrated by the scatterplot in Figure 5.1c. As the yen depreciates relative to the deutschemark, industrial wages come under pressure to a degree determined by the extent to which the industry competes with Japanese exports. This is most true of the Mach/Tech sector, which includes the manufacture of computers, machine equipment, iron and steel, and optical products such as cameras and microscopes. It is also true, to a much smaller degree, of the transportation sector. It is not true at all in the food, textile, leather, and chemicals sectors, where Japanese and German industries do not go head to head for world markets.

Italy

Cluster analysis on patterns of industrial earnings change for Italy reveals five distinct groups, which we denote as Oil, Transport/Sin, Fashion, communications and computers (Comm/Comp, including computers and radio-TV) and, as in Germany, a Chem/Gen sector covering the rest of manufacturing.[9]

The oil sector is the wage leader, with wages almost twice the average at the start of our observations. But oil sector wages decline relative to the average throughout the 1970s and early 1980s, recovering in part in the late 1980s and early 1990s. The Transport/Sin sector also records above-average earnings that converge gradually toward the average over this period. The Comm/Comp group is represented by state-controlled and/or protected industries that are average wage performers until the mid-1980s, at which time relative earnings in these sectors rise sharply. The Chem/Gen sector, in contrast, sees only modest improvement in its relative wage position at a few moments during the period under study. Italy's Fashion sector, though renowned, is not well paid by national standards, as Figure 5.3b shows.

The first two canonical roots of the Italian wage structure account for 46 and 31 percent of the total between-group variations, respectively. Once again, the first root appears to separate industries along some criterion of capital intensity in the production process, with process industries such as beverages and nonferrous metals scoring high, while handcrafts such as footwear and pottery score low. But we have been unable (so far) to identify a time-series variable in the Italian accounts that effectively replicates the time-series pattern of the first eigenvector.

---

[9] For reasons we do not attempt to fathom, the Sin sector (beverages and tobacco) are grouped with the otherwise homogeneous transport industries in Italy. Meanwhile, wage changes in motor vehicle production in Italy are grouped with nontransport sectors such as chemicals and food.

The second root, which strongly distinguishes the oil sector from the rest of manufacturing in Italy, provides a more clear-cut clue. Relating this root to the change in the refiner's acquisition price of oil (in lire) yields a significant −0.46 correlation. But this relationship is almost completely driven by the oil sector and virtually disappears if the sector is eliminated from the analysis. Thus, oil prices alone cannot account for the considerable discriminating power of this root.

What about inflation? During the period under study, oil prices and inflation were closely related. And indeed, if we substitute the rate of inflation in Italy for the oil price, we find a differentiator closely associated with the pattern of second-root scores. The correlation between our inflation-wage pseudoscores and scores on the second canonical root is −0.70; if the calculation is run without the oil sector, the correlation is a still significant −0.59.[10]

How does inflation affect wage differentials? We think the mechanism must essentially be one of a squeeze on supply prices. Italy is a medium-sized open economy, and although high average rates of lira inflation were endemic in the pre-Euro period, *changes* in the Italian inflation rate were driven substantially by external events – such as changes in oil prices. For domestic industry, an increase in external supply prices means a squeeze on profits, which translated into a squeeze on rents and hence on relative wages. Industries that saw the erosion of margins due to government price controls would also suffer losses in their wages share at this time, and the Italian system of wage indexation, the famous Scala Mobile, did not fully offset this effect.[11]

Japan

The wage patterns of Japanese industry cluster into four very distinct and highly homogeneous sectors (Figure 5.3a). One group, Major Export, is composed of key manufacturing and export industries, including motor vehicles, iron and steel, and computers. A second group,

---

[10] Because inflation also affects the exchange rate, we test to see if this, and not inflation per se, might have been the more important force. (For instance, the primary driver could be the inflated cost of intermediate imports as a result of a devalued lira.) Although we find a significant relationship between the lira exchange rate and second-root scores, -0.6 and -0.4 with and without the oil sector, respectively, the relationship to supply-price inflation appears to be stronger.

[11] Erikson and Ichino, 1994, point out that during the 1970s, indexation programs and labor policies were wage compressing. Both indexation and labor policies saw a shift against egalitarianism during the period 1983–1986. Our industry group wages are convergent throughout the 1970s and start diverging in the mid-1980s and are therefore consistent with these findings.

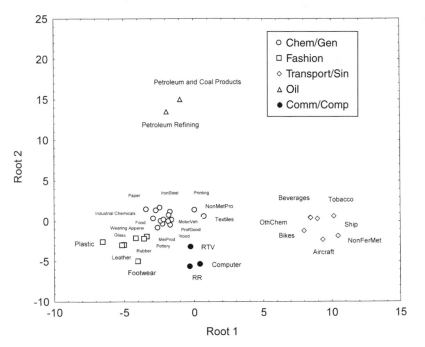

Figure 5.2a.   Italy: scatterplot of canonical scores.

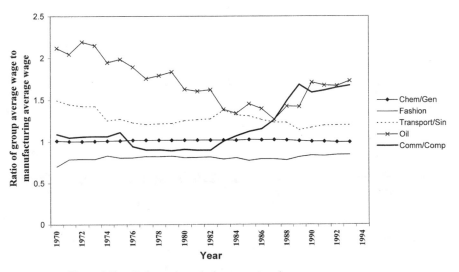

Figure 5.2b.   Italy: major relative wage trends.

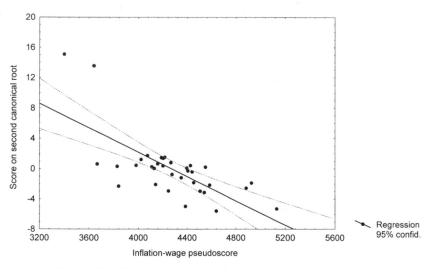

Figure 5.2c.   Italy: scatterplot of second root score and inflation pseudoscore.
Correlation: $r = 0.70$.

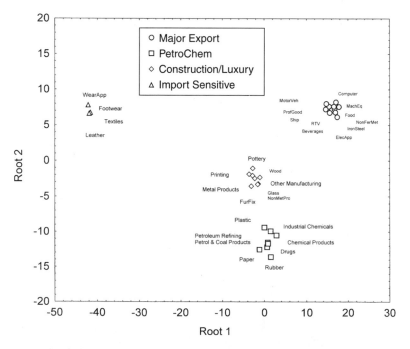

Figure 5.3a.   Japan: scatterplot of canonical scores.

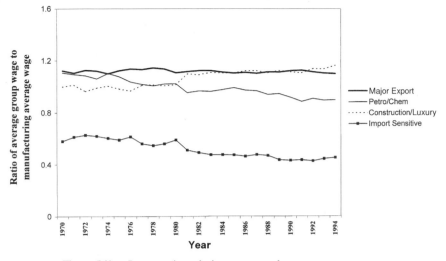

Figure 5.3b.   Japan: major relative wage trends.

Import Sensitive, contains the labor-intensive, import-sensitive industries: textiles, apparel, footwear, and leather. A third group contains all
of the oil and chemical industries (PetroChem). The last group, Con-
struction/Luxury, is a mixture of construction industries and such spe-
cialty, craft, and luxury items as china, jewelry, and musical instruments.

Japan's Major Exports sector paid consistently high earnings throughout our period of observation (Figure 5.3b). In the early 1980s, however,
this sector was equaled, and later slightly overtaken, by the sector in
which construction work predominates – perhaps a wage consequence
of the Japanese property boom? Chemicals and petrochemicals emerge
comparatively as losers: they start at the high end of the wage scale but
lose relative ground throughout the 1970s, 1980s, and 1990s; average
earnings in the chemical industries in Japan are now below those for
manufacturing as a whole. Meanwhile, the traditional labor-intensive
sectors remain, as always, at the low end of the wage scale. Indeed,
relative wages in this sector declined during this period.

The first two roots of a discriminant function for Japan account for 80
and 15 percent of the between-group wage variations, which in turn
account for the overwhelming share of total cross-industry variations.
Though the first root strongly separates the export leaders from the
import followers, we did not find a close association between any trade
or exchange rate variable and this root. Inflation, lagged one year, is
strongly correlated with this root (0.63), suggesting a difference in the
effectiveness of wage indexation across industries as a strong factor.

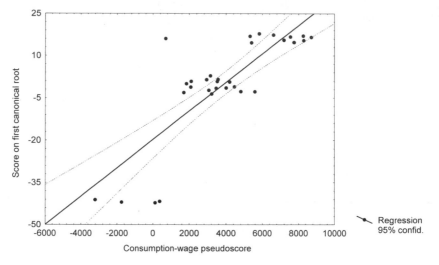

Figure 5.3c.   Japan: scatterplot of first root score and consumption pseudoscore.
Correlation: $r = 0.81$.

However, this variable successfully distinguishes only the lowest-wage
sector from the other three; the correlation disappears when the most
labor-intensive industries are removed from the analysis.

Clearly, Japan's import-sensitive traditional industries lost wage
ground most severely in the inflationary periods. The reason seems plain:
These sectors enjoy the least market power in the Japanese economy.
This simple insight leads us to look away from trade-related explanations
of the first root and to consider instead a variable related mainly to the
internal strength of Japanese domestic demand. Change in consumption
spending per capita is such a variable, and it does the job: The correlation of pseudoscores on this variable with scores on our first canonical
root is a highly significant 0.81, falling only to 0.67 when the import-
sensitive sector is excluded. Figure 5.3c illustrates. We believe this provides evidence for the simple Keynesian idea that the strength of consumer demand, interacting with the degree of monopoly power across
different sectors of industry, is the critical factor underlying changes in
the Japanese wage and earnings structure.

5.4   Conclusions

This chapter illustrates a technique for exploring the macrodeterminants
of changing patterns of income distribution, particularly with respect to

the distribution of wages and salaries in industrial sectors. We have shown, we believe, that in an eclectic subset of developed countries, there exist comparatively simple patterns of between-group variation, which account for a very large share of the total change in interindustry relative wages through time. Arriving at a firm judgment as to the nature of the forces behind industrial change is a more difficult task, and one whose completion will await the energies of additional researchers armed with more detailed national data sets and more knowledge of individual national economies than we possess. But, we believe, these methods will prove useful to researchers who would like to go beyond the conventional microanalyses of wage change and attempt to arrive at explanations that can be supported by close reference to the historical record.

Appendix I

Summary Properties of the First and Second Canonical Roots: Wage Change Between Industrial Groups in Six OECD Countries

CANADA
Discriminant analysis: Wilks's lambda = 0.000098, approx. $F(72,15) = 4.598063$, $p < 0.0007$

Root	Eigenvalue	Prop.*	p Level
1	116.5530	0.8747	0.000000
2	9.1086	0.06837	0.003659

GERMANY
Discriminant analysis: Wilks's lambda = 0.0000864, approx. $F(48,14) = 31.07956$, $p < 0.0000$

Root	Eigenvalue	Prop.	p Level
1	216.5649	0.8059	0.000000
2	52.1727	0.1941	0.000000

ITALY
Discriminant analysis: Wilks's lambda = 0.0000500, approx. $F(92,30) = 3.679267$, $p < 0.00007$

Root	Eigenvalue	Prop.	p Level
1	27.16082	0.46137	0.000000
2	18.47832	0.31388	0.000018

JAPAN
Discriminant analysis: Wilks's lambda = 0.0000018, approx. $F(72,12) = 14.70896$, $p < 0.00000$

Root	Eigenvalue	Prop.	p Level
1	367.5749	0.8018	0.000000
2	70.8889	0.15461	0.000000

NEW ZEALAND
Discriminant analysis: Wilks's lambda = 0.0000042, approx. $F(69,9) = 8.859464$, $p < 0.00037$

Root	Eigenvalue	Prop.	p Level
1	1530.977	0.984	0.000000
2	17.814	0.01128	0.003664

NORWAY
Discriminant analysis: Wilks's lambda = 0.0048912, approx. $F(69,9) = 4.432875$, $p < 0.00105$

Root	Eigenvalue	Prop.	p Level
1	31.97910	0.86015	0.000006
2	5.19940	0.13985	0.045626

* Denotes proportion of between-group variations explained by the root.

Appendix II

Canada: Discriminant Plots

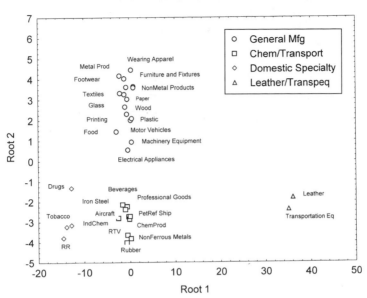

Figure 5.A1. Canada: scatterplot of canonical scores.

New Zealand: Discriminant Plots

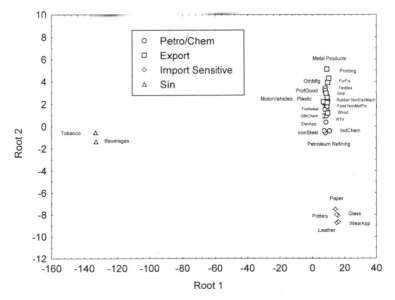

Figure 5.A2. New Zealand: scatterplot of canonical scores.

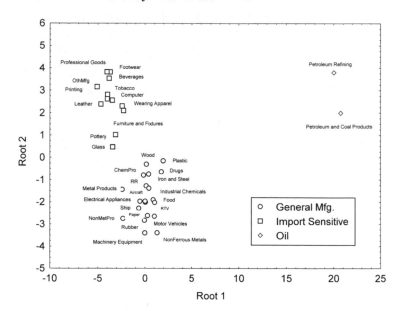

Figure 5.A3.   Norway: scatterplot of canonical scores.

CHAPTER 6

Inequality and Unemployment in Europe: The American Cure

Pedro Conceição, Pedro Ferreira, and James K. Galbraith

There is a common view that unemployment in Europe is attributable to rigid wage structures, high minimum wages, and generous social welfare systems. In fact, countries that possess the low inequality such systems produce tend to experience less unemployment than those that do not. We show that inequality and unemployment are related positively across the European continent, within countries, between countries, and through time. Large intercountry inequalities across Europe also appear to aggravate the continental unemployment problem, and we find evidence that when these inequalities are taken into account, overall earnings inequality is higher in Europe than in the United States. We therefore suggest that the key to reducing unemployment in Europe lies in measures that reduce, not increase, inequalities in the structure of pay – and that do so at the continental level. This is a long-standing and often overlooked characteristic of social welfare policy in the United States.

6.1 Introduction

What is the relationship between inequality and unemployment? This question is perhaps the most important issue in the political economy of Europe, and it has relevance for other regions with developing transnational ties, including the United States and the North American region.

One widely held view is that high unemployment rates in Europe are due to that continent's generous social welfare systems and "rigid" wage structures, or, in other words, to the equality that is the characteristic goal of social democracy. Though this view has lately come under attack,[1] it

---

[1] In an important paper, Nickell, 1997, examined particular features of European labor markets and reached conclusions broadly similar to ours: Institutions that promote equality are not generally associated with higher rates of unemployment across European countries. Glyn and Salverda, 1999, also challenge the conventional view that greater wage disparities are associated with better employment prospects for less skilled workers.

remains the received wisdom for most economists, for the new policymakers of the so-called Third Way, and, of course, for the business press.
In this view, low unemployment in the United States is credited to that
country's "flexible labor markets," willingness to tolerate increasing wage
inequality, and high absolute levels of inequality in wages.

This view is strikingly inconsistent with the facts. For example, it
implies that, *within* Europe, countries with more inequality should have
less unemployment. It also appears to imply that countries with high
wage levels should perhaps have more unemployment, and certainly not
less, than countries with lower wages. But the opposite is true in both
cases. Unemployment has always been higher where inequality was
greater in Europe. And now, as Europe has integrated, a corresponding
transnational pattern has emerged. It was never the case that the richer
countries had more unemployment as a rule. Twenty-five years ago,
unemployment across countries in Europe was, in fact, largely uncorre-
lated with per capita national income; labor markets perhaps cleared, or
did not, on a national basis. But in the late 1970s, a strong and systematic *negative* relationship emerged that has been sustained ever since.[2]
Today, national unemployment rates are systematically *lower* in the
richer and more equal countries of Europe, where wages are high and
social welfare systems are strong. Meanwhile, it is the lower-income
countries with the weakest social welfare systems and the most inequality, such as Spain, where unemployment is highest in Europe.

The conventional view also implies that inequality in the United
States, where unemployment is presently quite low, must be higher than
in "Europe." But while this *is* generally true for comparisons between
the United States and individual European countries, such comparisons
ignore differences in income levels among the countries of Europe. When
these differences are accounted for – and Europe is today an integrated
continental economy – it is not obvious that the United States is in fact
less equal. Our methods, which employ measures of inequality that can
be "grouped up" to the European level, permit the calculation of a dispersion index that is directly comparable between the United States and
Europe; this index shows a higher value for Europe.

Further, the conventional view implies that in the United States unemployment should have fallen when inequality rose, in the 1980s, and vice

---

[2] As of 1992, the correlation between income level and unemployment rates across fourteen countries had risen to an impressive −0.75. As for correlations between measures of
internal inequality and unemployment rates, they peaked in the mid-1980s, declining
somewhat later on as high unemployment hit the Nordic countries, especially Sweden
and Finland.

versa in the 1990s. But wage rate inequality, in manufacturing at least, rose and fell *in step with* changes in unemployment in the United States, year to year and even month to month, over virtually the entire twentieth century.[3] To the extent that we can measure the *evolution* of inequality in Europe as a whole, the same appears to have been true for Europe in recent years.

We suggest two simple reasons why inequality and unemployment may generally show the positive association that we observe, while the associations between unemployment and income and between inequality and average income are both negative.[4] One is that unemployment causes inequality. The other is that inequality may cause unemployment. Regions with low average incomes are marked by large numbers of relatively impoverished people in low-productivity occupations and thus by high inequality across occupations, industries, and sectors. Many such people seek any available exit from their status, even if they recognize that the chances of finding a substantially better job are low. In other words, so long as appealing alternatives to low-income employment exist, even (indeed, especially) when they are not widely accessible, the unemployed line up.

This does not happen to the same extent in high-income countries. It is true that the lures of truly high-wage jobs are even greater in such countries. Unemployment insurance and other safety nets are stronger in rich countries than in poor ones. Conventional thinking focuses on such measures of social welfare generosity as benefit replacement rates and predicts higher unemployment in more generous countries. And yet, contrary to the views of the antilabor right, such open invitations to unemployment are not, in fact, accepted to the same degree. Why not?

One possible explanation might be that the richer countries of Europe lack low-*productivity*, dead-end, uninteresting jobs from which people might be seeking to escape. But this is not the case. High-wage countries are characterized by a diverse cross section of industries and services, including many that are low in productivity and that must compete with

---

[3] This line of causation is explored in detail in Galbraith's *Created Unequal*, 1998a. Galbraith's wage rate inequality estimates for the United States are revised in Galbraith and Garza Cantú (Chapter 4 of this volume).

[4] The "wage curve" analysis of Blanchflower and Oswald, 1994, provides striking evidence that within any *given* economy, regions with high average incomes have lower unemployment than regions with low average incomes. This suggests that barriers to mobility are not merely national; however, national and language barriers surely add powerfully to those based on family ties, housing supply, and so on.

low-wage imports and with immigrants. The high-wage countries are, in fact, typically *more* diverse in their employment structures than the low-wage countries; somehow they manage to have high wages alongside many low-productivity jobs. How do they do it?

The answer is scandalously simple: *High-income countries subsidize and support the pay of low-productivity people.* They do not rely on markets. They provide high minimum wages, buyers for farm produce, jobs in vast public bureaucracies, free health care, and higher education. As a result, low-productivity people stay put in their low-productivity jobs. They do not migrate in large numbers toward the high-productivity sectors in the pursuit of higher pay. The pay in such jobs is not so much higher, all aspects of living accounted for, to make the trouble of earning it worthwhile. And this is the secret, it appears, of fuller employment in richer countries.

This suggests that the real and relevant rigidities of today's Europe are entirely different from those proposed by the conventional view. *Indeed, they have nothing to do with the supposed inflexibility of relative wages in any particular country.* To the contrary, increasing relative wage differentials would only cause even more low-productivity people to abandon their present employment in favor of job hunting and welfare.

The relevant rigidities lie instead in rigid thinking on the part of Europe's central authorities in two respects. First, the latter are unable or unwilling to foster the development of *macroeconomic* policies that can effectively build Europe's peripheral economies through *national* programs of full employment – and that indeed once did so in the heyday of national Keynesianism from 1945 to 1970. Second, they have been unwilling to make the vast income transfers, across national lines, that would be required to make rural or service sector or even civil service life in Spain as attractive as it is in Sweden.

Indeed, present European policy is designed to work in just the opposite direction. Through monetary union and the Maastricht treaty, Europe has moved to restrict the autonomy of both monetary and fiscal policies and to impede the achievement of full employment on a national scale. Meanwhile, barriers to migration and resettlement obstruct the citizens of the European periphery from taking full advantage of the more generous social welfare systems to their north. This concentrates unemployment in Spain, Italy, and Greece and reduces the pressure on Northern Europe to pursue full employment policies. And, of course, European fiscal policy places relentless pressure on individual countries to cut back on their welfare states.

In sum, there are good reasons why *lower* incomes and *more* inequality should mean *more* unemployment – and why, therefore, present

European policy is a formula for continued failures to reduce unemployment. There is undoubtedly a long-term structural aspect to the European unemployment problem. It does not consist, as characteristically in the United States, of short-term involuntary displacement – a phenomenon that places unemployment in the causal driver's seat. In European conditions, rather, *interregional inequalities cause unemployment*. The latter is, indeed, in part a voluntary response to a deeply unfavorable set of choices facing low-income people in the low-income countries. Better welfare and the grimy suburb than life in the village or on the farm. But structural conditions are policy driven; *these* inequalities are created.

As for the United States, it is true that the 1970s and early 1980s were a time of sharply rising wage inequalities by national-historical standards. But one must recall that as late as 1970 the United States was viewed, and had been for a century, as the preeminent country of the middle class.[5] While lacking European *socialist* traditions, the United States also lacked European *fascist* traditions. And it did experience a vast expansion of the role of government during the New Deal and Great Society eras, as well as a sharp reduction in wage and earnings inequalities during World War II. Again, contrary to much received belief and in contrast to Europe, American policies have remained open to the joint reduction of inequality and unemployment. Measures of earnings dispersion for manufacturing show a steady decline after 1994, alongside the reduction of unemployment to rates just above 4 percent.

We suggest that the true American advantage is not inequality, which by our measures is lower than that across the whole of Europe, but America's national policy means for income redistribution and the pursuit of full employment, and perhaps the pressure for full employment brought to bear by a mobile population on the richer regions. Indeed, one can argue that compared with Europe the United States may be the true social democracy these days, a social democracy founded on liberal access to credit, on a national Social Security system, and, since 1994, on a rapidly expanding earned income tax credit that has bolstered the real earnings of lower-income Americans and may therefore have played a critical role in lowering unemployment. Americans take low-wage jobs because the gaps are not in fact that high and because the after-tax gaps are even lower – particularly when one considers that Americans pay a federal progressive income tax, not the regressive European value-added tax.

[5] As Karl Marx had written, in a letter of congratulation to Abraham Lincoln on his second inauguration in 1865: "From the commencement of the titanic American strife, the working men of Europe felt instinctively that the star-spangled banner carried the destiny of their class" (!).

114   Conceição, Ferreira, and Galbraith

Europe therefore faces three choices. The first is impossible, the second is unacceptable, and the third is therefore necessary. Europe could, in principle but not in practice, restore *national* means for the pursuit of full employment in the form of independent monetary, fiscal, and trade policies alongside capital controls. It will not do this, of course. Or Europe could break down its national and regional enclaves, establishing a unified labor market from the Baltic to the Algarve, so that the poor populations relocate to the rich countries, like Mississippi's blacks to Chicago. It could do this, but we do not think it would be well received.

And if not this, then Europe *must* establish, on a continental and international scale, the kinds of social welfare transfer and employment subsidy mechanisms that have heretofore existed only within the smallest, richest, and most resolutely socialist nations of the Continent – and that are also routine in the United States. We shall discuss later exactly of what these consist.

The remainder of this chapter presents the evidence on which we rest our claim for a systematic positive association between inequality and unemployment. In Section 6.2, we present Theil's measure of inequality in manufacturing earnings within the countries of Europe from 1970 to 1992, computed from the Structural Analysis (STAN) database of the Organization for Economic Cooperation and Development (OECD). These measures have significant advantages, of coverage and of accuracy, over the conventional measures of income inequality maintained by the World Bank. In addition, they are inexpensive and easy to compute. Using them, we show that the cross-country correlation between industrial earnings inequality and unemployment is consistently positive in every year from 1970 to 1992. So, even more strongly, is the correlation between unemployment and the ratio of average manufacturing wages to per capita gross domestic product (GDP) – a measure that captures, very crudely, the relationship between manufacturing and services incomes. As that ratio rose in every country, so did unemployment.

In Section 6.3, we present measures of countrywide average income levels – per capita GDP – compared to rates of unemployment in Europe. The rise in unemployment in Europe in the 1980s and 1990s was tightly linked to differences in average income across countries: less in richer countries, more in poorer ones. Rising unemployment did not create the differences in per capita income levels apart. Rather, we believe the best explanation of this geographic pattern is that preexisting differences in income levels determined the distribution of rising unemployment.

In Section 6.4, we examine the structures of industrial employment in Europe and their relation to income and inequality. We show that the high-income, low-inequality countries of Europe are not generally those that specialize in particular industries – for instance, the advanced sectors. Rather, high-income countries tend to have more-diverse industrial structures than low-income countries, and those high-income countries that specialize, for instance in oil and natural gas, tend to have low manufacturing shares in total employment. Low inequality in high-income countries is therefore not generally a question of specialization in a narrow class of high-productivity goods, but rather of egalitarian pay structures across high- and low-productivity sectors, both of which rich countries possess in abundance.

In Section 6.5, we offer measures of industrial earnings inequality across the whole of Europe compared to the United States, taking account of differences between industries and between countries. Finally, Section 6.6, presents conclusions and policy recommendations.

6.2   Inequality and Unemployment in European Countries

Appendix 1 presents measures of inequality in the industrial earnings structures for fourteen countries of Europe, computed from the Structural Analysis database of the OECD, using the between-group component of Theil's T statistic (T' hereafter). Galbraith (1998c) has provided time-series analysis of this data set, showing inter alia that when one controls for changes in employment structure within each country, changes in wage dispersion vary positively with changes in unemployment over time. Rising (declining) *wage* inequality and rising (declining) *unemployment* tend to go hand in hand within most European countries – as Galbraith and Garza-Cantú demonstrate is also the case for the United States.

But what about the cross-sectional and comparative properties of these data? We have been reluctant to advance cross-country comparisons of the levels of a T' statistic for two reasons. First, the (much larger) within-category component of inequality is unknown. Second, while one may reasonably suppose that T' estimated on industrial earnings covaries through time with the larger income distribution, there is no strong reason a priori to suspect that *differences* in levels of T' observed within manufacturing across European countries are particularly correlated with differences in inequality outside of manufacturing or between manufacturing and the nonmanufacturing sector. Thus, it is possible in principle that differences in an inequality measure in manufacturing, while

Table 6.1. *European Countries Ranked in Ascending Order of Income Inequality by the World Bank*

1970	1992
United Kingdom	Spain
Sweden	Finland
Belgium	Belgium
Netherlands	Netherlands
Finland	Italy
Germany	Germany
Denmark	United Kingdom
Greece	Sweden
Spain	Denmark
Norway	Norway
Portugal	France
Italy	Greece
France	Portugal

Source: Deininger and Squire (1996a). Data are for the nearest available year.

surely interesting in their own right, may not be representative of the whole income distribution.

Still, everything must be considered in light of alternatives. The World Bank has provided a data set that purports to measure inequalities in household income across countries, using the Gini coefficient, providing broad measures that are comparable among countries. A ranking of these data for Europe, using the nearest available dates where the exact year was not covered in the World Bank data set, is given as Table 6.1 for 1970 and 1992. According to these data, in 1970 the United Kingdom was the lowest-inequality country in Europe, followed by Sweden, Belgium, and the Netherlands; the highest-inequality countries at this time were, in ascending order, Spain, Norway, Portugal, Italy, and France. In 1992, according to the same data set, the ranking had changed drastically. Now Spain was the lowest-inequality country (!), followed by Finland, Belgium, The Netherlands, and then Italy, which is now purportedly less unequal than either Germany or the United Kingdom. The United Kingdom, in turn, is said to be less unequal than Sweden, Denmark, and Norway, and the highest-inequality country in Europe is now supposedly Portugal.

Table 6.2. *European Countries Ranked in Ascending Order of Industrial Earnings Inequality According to the Theil Statistic*

1970	1992
Norway	Norway
Finland	Denmark
Denmark	Finland
Germany	Netherlands
Netherlands	Sweden
United Kingdom	United Kingdom
Belgium	Germany
Sweden	Belgium
Greece	Austria
France	Greece
Austria	Portugal
Italy	France
	Spain
	Italy

Source: OECD STAN and authors' calculations. Data are for the year reported.

Table 6.2 provides a contrasting ranking of T′ computed over industrial earnings data.[6] The low-inequality countries in 1970 are Norway, Finland, Denmark, Germany, the Netherlands, and the United Kingdom. In 1992, the low-ranking countries are Norway, Denmark, Finland, the Netherlands, Sweden, the United Kingdom, and Germany; the high-inequality countries are Greece, France, Austria, and Italy in 1970 (data for Spain and Portugal not being available) and Greece, Portugal, France, Spain, and Italy in 1992. These rankings are much more consistent over time than the Gini rankings published by the World Bank, and we believe that they are also much more sensible.[7]

---

[6] Among the convenient properties of the Theil statistic is invariance to scale. So, measures of T′ need not be adjusted for inflation, whose effects cancel in the calculation, or for differences in exchange rate valuations across countries. So long as the industrial categories are the same, which is true of the STAN data set by construction, T′ turns out to be comparable across countries. We remain wary of overinterpreting level comparisons of T′ for larger data sets, such as the UNIDO numbers presented in later chapters, because differences in employment structure become very large when one leaves the industrialized world for the developing world.

[7] One may also compare our ranking to that of the LIS, which, taking the available years closest to 1992, is Finland, Sweden, Belgium, Norway, Denmark, Germany, the Nether-

The issue is important, for one can easily correlate inequality and unemployment across countries for each year from 1970 to 1992. Using the World Bank data set, one arrives at the result that inequality and unemployment were positively correlated in 1970, but the correlation declines throughout the period and turns negative in 1976, falling thereafter to reach –0.66 in 1992. Pleasing though that result might be to a partisan of the "wage rigidity" hypothesis, it depends mainly on soaring unemployment in Spain, which the World Bank ranks preposterously as the most egalitarian country in Europe, and in undeniably egalitarian Finland, which suffered a severe recession following a property bubble and the collapse of its Soviet markets after 1991.

When one correlates unemployment and industrial earnings inequality across European countries using the Theil statistic, the correlation coefficients are always *positive*. Over all years, the average of correlation coefficients is 0.37, with a standard deviation of 0.20. The correlation does decline in 1992 as Finnish unemployment soars, but due to exceptional conditions not driven by events inside the OECD. Figure 6.1 presents a time-series graphic of the cross-country correlation coefficient between inequality and unemployment in Europe.[8]

Next, we examine a rough measure of inequality between manufacturing sectors and the rest of the economy. This is the ratio of average manufacturing wages to GDP per capita. This measure is well correlated to the within-manufacturing Theil statistic.[9] Countries with high inequality in their manufacturing sectors also tend to be more unequal between manufacturing and everything else. The correlation coefficient across the fourteen countries is positive in every year and averages 0.60 across all years from 1973 to 1992.

Across countries, the ratio of average manufacturing wages to per capita GDP is positively correlated with unemployment in every year

lands, France, Spain, Italy, and the United Kingdom. The LIS rankings are closer to ours than they are to the World Bank rankings, even though ours are based on industrial earnings, while both the LIS and World Bank purport to measure inequality in household income. The World Bank's data set is the odd one out in this triangle, and our inequality measures have two additional advantages: more countries covered and regular annual observations.

[8] We have annual observations for both inequality and unemployment from 1970 through 1992 in eleven European countries: Austria, Belgium, Denmark, Finland, France, Germany, Italy, Netherlands, Spain, Sweden, and the United Kingdom.

[9] This is perhaps not surprising in light of the good correspondence between the Theil measures and the LIS Gini coefficients. But more generally, it illustrates the unitary character of income distributions. When inequality is growing between low- and high-wage sectors within manufacturing, the same will generally be true of inequality between manufacturing on average and low-wage agriculture or services on average.

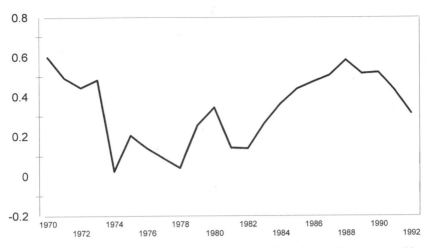

Figure 6.1. Correlation of inequality in manufacturing earnings, measured by the Theil statistic, to rates of unemployment in fourteen European countries, 1970–1992. Observations for Portugal begin in 1974 and for Spain in 1978. Data for France are adjusted to correct for missing industries in years before 1978, and data for Belgium are adjusted to correct for an undetermined error in the years 1970–1972.

except the last (again, mainly due to the depression in Finland). Figure 6.2 illustrates this situation. Within countries through time, the movement of this ratio is a good predictor of the movement of the unemployment rate: The through-time correlation coefficients are positive for twelve of the fourteen countries (the exceptions being Italy and Spain) and are above 0.7 in the cases of Austria, Belgium, Finland, Greece, the Netherlands, and the United Kingdom.

The evidence is, in short, consistent once proper measurements are taken. Indeed, it is overwhelming. Unemployment and wage or earnings inequality are related *positively*. Countries that are more unequal tend to suffer higher rates of unemployment. Though this fact defies the conventional view, it is in line with our conception of the process of structural unemployment as driven largely by the pay gap between low- and high-productivity employment or, in other words, by inequality itself.

The time-series and cross-sectional relationships between inequality and unemployment are evidence that the notion of a trade-off between the two social goals is incorrect. Within any given country, higher inequality and higher unemployment go hand in hand. Our suggested reason is that inequality reduces the subjective opportunity cost of leaving a low-productivity job. But because the occupants of low-productivity

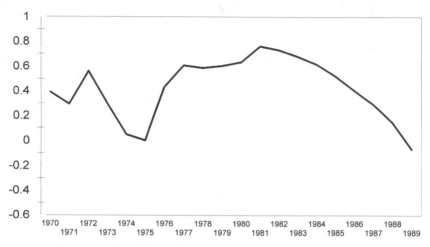

Figure 6.2. Correlation of the ratio between average manufacturing wage rates and per capita GDP to unemployment rates in fourteen European countries, 1973–1992. Observations for Portugal begin in 1974 and for Spain in 1978. Data for France are adjusted to correct for missing industries in years before 1978, and data for Belgium are adjusted to correct for an undetermined error in the years 1970–1972.

employments are numerous, while the number of high-productivity, high-wage jobs is necessarily few, especially in poor countries, many seeking such jobs will not find them. Thus, unemployment bred of inequality can persist. So long as wages rest on productivity differentials, exactly contrary to the standard intuition, labor markets do not clear.

6.3   Unemployment and Income Differentials across Countries

Europe is not a country; it is a multicountry region. It is a region in the midst of a profound process of economic integration, with expanding intraregional trade, a single internal market, common fiscal policies, and now a common money. What it lacks, compared to the United States, is only a common set of social policies[10] and a single financial or credit market – precisely the devices that work to reduce inequality at the continental scale.

In the early 1970s and for many years before that, measured unemployment in Europe was everywhere quite low. It was, at that time, only slightly correlated with income levels across countries. In the

---

[10] We thank Waltraud Schelkle for focusing our attention on this point and acknowledge her important contribution to our thinking on this subject.

high-income countries, full employment, social democracy, and the welfare state prevailed. The low-income countries were substantially peasant societies, often with comparatively recent fascist governments, as in Spain, Portugal, Greece under the colonels, and Italy from a generation before. In these countries, much of the rural population had not become intranationally mobile. There were few industrial jobs and few cushions for those who might seek but not obtain them. Except for emigrants and exiles, people stayed on the farm.

Since the early 1970s, Europe has experienced democratization in the poor countries and yet rising unemployment as well. In Spain, the extreme case, unemployment rose from 3 to 19 percent in the decade from 1974 to 1984 and has stayed near that level for many years. In 1993, Italy, Belgium, France, the United Kingdom, Denmark, and Finland all had unemployment rates above 10 percent. Only socialist Austria (the country with the sharpest decline in manufacturing earnings inequality in Europe over the previous twenty-two years by our measures) was near full employment. Still, some countries were doing better than others: Unemployment in Norway was just 6 percent, in the Netherlands 6.2 percent, in Sweden 8.2 percent, and in Germany 8.8 percent.

When one correlates European income levels and unemployment rates across countries and over time, a key fact emerges: Unemployment in Europe has risen almost strictly in inverse relation to per capita GDP. Today, high-income countries in Europe systematically have less unemployment than low-income countries. Figure 6.3 illustrates these correlations.

What is going on? Where per capita GDP is high, either of two possible situations may prevail. It may be that most people are employed in moderately high-productivity employments and are paid according to their productivities, and so, by their individual and collective productivities, they raise the average national income. Alternatively, a fairly small number of very highly productive income earners, including profit earners, may provide truly massive subsidies to the living standards of low-productivity workers. In this way, high average incomes are achieved in an equal society by raising the average pay of low-productivity workers far beyond their average productivities.

In the first case, low unemployment would be no mystery to anyone. The free markets of textbook theory would indeed allocate resources and remuneration in just this way; firms would arise to demand the services of such high-productivity employees. Still, one might wonder how the rich citizens of a country that specialized in, say, oil refining would satisfy their tastes for Thai cooking and acupuncture without allowing immigrants to provide these services or their own citizens to learn them.

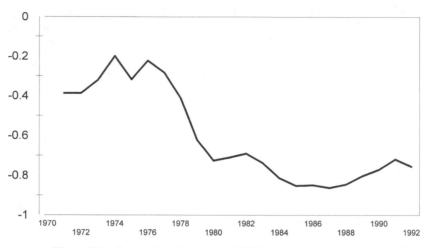

Figure 6.3.   Correlation of per capita GDP and unemployment rates in four-teen European countries, 1970–1992.

There is the difficulty, too, that if all the high-productivity jobs were in one country, all the low-productivity jobs would have to be in another. In that case, because low-productivity jobs are necessarily more numerous, it would be difficult to understand why the low-productivity, low-income country would suffer higher rates of unemployment.

The second case is at variance with the conventional view of many economists. It argues that countries with high-productivity industries effectively redistribute income to low-productivity workers, maintaining egalitarian social structures and fuller employment in spite of radical differences between pay and productivity levels. In this case, the opportunity cost of low-productivity employment falls, and people stay where they are, growing artichokes in Brittany, crofting in Norway, or raising pigs in the high passes of the Swiss Alps.[11]

Can we demonstrate that the second case is, in fact, the pertinent one for Europe?

[11] It is worth noting that due to efficient provision of public services on a capitation basis, very high living standards can be achieved at fairly low cost, without sacrificing the textbook efficiency consideration that marginal productivity should be associated with *marginal* pay. Typically, analyses that treat wages as the only source of income ignore this fact. This leads to the common prediction that pushing up low-productivity wages will lead to unemployment (because firms will not hire workers for more than the value of their output), when in fact pushing up the incomes of low-productivity people is the key to maintaining effective demand and thus full employment.

6.4   Income Levels and the Structure of Employment

Why are rich countries rich? Are they rich because they have a dispro-
portionate share of high-productivity jobs, because they squeeze out the
low-productivity activities and either rely on imports of these goods and
services or do without them? Or, on the contrary, are they rich because
high productivity in some sectors (and perhaps also profit income from
abroad) permits them to provide high living standards to *both* high-
productivity and low-productivity workers, as well as direct employment,
in many cases, to the latter?

These questions are obviously critical to the design of national
employment and competitiveness strategies. And while there are many
ways of answering them, we will concentrate on just two that can be
managed from our data sets. The first is to ask, do high-income countries
have high or low shares of manufacturing in total employment? Manufacturing productivity is higher, as a rule, than productivity elsewhere.
And manufacturing wages tend to be high, relative at least to services
and agriculture wages, in most countries. Countries with high manufacturing shares in total employment might therefore be thought of as high-
productivity countries with correspondingly high incomes; indeed, the
strategy of industrialization was always predicated on the idea that a
strong manufacturing base was the lynchpin of a strategy to raise
national incomes.

But this is not in fact the case for today's Europe. It is no longer true,
as a rule, that higher-income countries have more manufacturing in their
employment mix. Figure 6.4 illustrates the evolution of the cross-country
correlation between the share of manufacturing in total employment in
employment and per capita GDP. Until the early 1970s, this relationship
was, in fact, positive and quite robust. But in 1975, the relationship began
to deteriorate, and by 1981 there was no longer any significant relationship between shares of manufacturing in employment and per capita
GDP in Europe. In the late 1980s, the correlation turned *negative*, and it
may have become significantly so in the last year of the data at hand.
Where once the divide between high- and low-wage occupations was
between manufacturing and agriculture, with poorer countries predominantly rural, today nonmanufacturing occupations – including public
sector employment, of course – are just as prevalent in rich countries as
in poor ones.

It remains possible, of course, that the high-income countries have a
particularly rich share of the highest-productivity *manufacturing* sectors.
Do such countries get rich by squeezing out textiles and food processing, and by concentrating on computers and aircraft, alongside, perhaps,

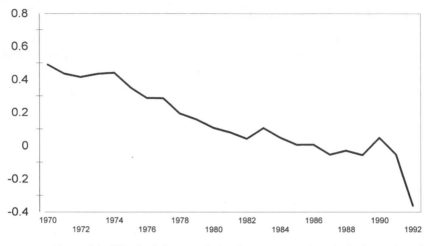

Figure 6.4.   The declining correlation between manufacturing's share of total employment and per capita GDP in fourteen European countries, 1970–1992.

a particularly rich share of high-productivity occupations in the service sectors (such as banking, engineering, architecture, and law)? This is a somewhat more difficult question, because many patterns of industrial specialization are possible in a multicountry regional economy. The theory of comparative advantage certainly predicts such specialization: here a chemical country, there aerospace, computers, and machine tools somewhere else.

Sorting out these patterns to arrive at a single index of specialization and a ranking of productivities is not straightforward. But consider the following institutional fact: The International Standard Industrial Classifications (ISIC) are designed by the OECD to accommodate the industrial structures of the large, advanced countries. It is they, after all, that dominate the most advanced sectors, such as aerospace and pharmaceuticals. Thus, the ISIC codes, simply because they try to be informative when applied to such countries, are designed to separate their economies into sectors of approximately comparable size. To do otherwise – to design a classification scheme based on the economy of Portugal, say – might lead to separate major categories for wine and port, for shoes and handbags, for cut glass and blown glass, with perhaps just one catchall category of "Other Manufacturing" for aircraft, computers, automobiles, and so on. To apply such a categorization to Germany, say, would not be useful.

Table 6.3. *Herfindahl Measures of Industrial Diversification for Fourteen European Countries, Selected Years*

	Austria	Belgium	Denmark	Finland	France	Germany	Greece
1970	0.097	0.126	0.099	0.107	0.073	0.072	0.135
1981	0.092	0.126	0.098	0.097	0.072	0.071	0.146
1992	0.088	0.125	0.097	0.093	0.070	0.072	0.141

	Italy	Netherlands	Norway	Portugal	Spain	Sweden	UK
1970	0.101	0.094	0.088	0.170	0.094	0.077	0.072
1981	0.103	0.090	0.086	0.151	0.091	0.075	0.071
1992	0.103	0.089	0.095	0.160	0.087	0.081	0.070

Given this convention in the design of industrial statistics, a measure of specialization across conventional categories can usefully tell us whether a country's economy is diversified or specialized relative to that of the large industrial states. A Herfindahl index of employment shares by ISIC category, for instance, can provide a simple such measure of industrial specialization.[12] Such indices are reported for European countries in Table 6.3. The most industrially diversified countries in Europe in 1992 and throughout our period were indeed the larger advanced countries: the United States, Germany, and France. And, as an understanding of the taxonomic conventions would lend one to expect, there is a strong negative correlation between specialization and per capita GDP: nearly −0.8 for every year we observe, as Figure 6.5 illustrates.

There are a few moderately specialized rich countries. Norway is an example. Denmark is the most specialized rich country in Europe. Sweden, though diversified, is less so in 1992 than in 1970. And as these examples indicate, to be specialized is not necessarily inegalitarian. Northern Europe contains several small, specialized, low-inequality countries. In these countries, large transfers flow from a narrow range of highly productive manufacturing, as well as extractive industries and niche agriculture, to the rest of society. All of these countries have, among other things, notably large public sectors and generous welfare programs.

---

[12] The Herfindahl index, a well-known index of concentration, is simply the sum of squared shares. Higher values indicate greater specialization. The measures are comparable across countries simply because the design of the STAN standardizes employment categories across countries.

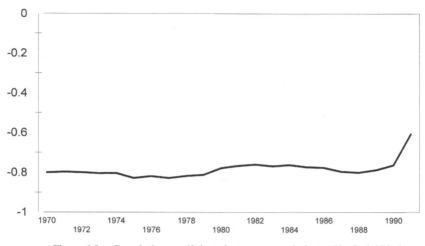

Figure 6.5.   Correlation coefficients between cross-industry Herfindahl indexes and per capita GDP for twelve European countries, 1970–1992.

But being highly specialized rarely goes with being rich. In contrast with the exceptional Scandinavian cases, industrial specialization usually means a high share of textiles, food processing, and the like in manufacturing employment; this is true in all cases of very high specialization in Europe. And such specialization is strongly associated with lower per capita income. Moreover, *where high specialization and high inequality go together, unemployment is epidemic.* In these cases, the manufacturing sectors are not diverse enough, or rich enough, or willing, or technically able to support the low-productivity sectors through taxes, transfers, and subsidies. Greece and Italy are among the examples in Europe.

The exceptional case of Portugal, finally, highlights the rule. Portugal has the most specialized manufacturing economy in Europe. Most of it is low-wage: food processing, textiles, leather, and glass. As a result, Portugal has one of Europe's lowest per capita incomes. But Portugal is also a low-inequality country, as between manufacturing and everything else. In 1992, the gap between wages in manufacturing on average and per capita GDP in Portugal was one of the lowest in Europe, having fallen sharply since the revolution in 1974. The consequence is comparatively low unemployment – or, one should say, low *internal* unemployment. People in Portugal see little advantage in competing for the available Portuguese manufacturing jobs. Should they wish higher incomes, as many do, they leave the country. Paris is the second largest Portuguese city after Lisbon.

In sum, rich European countries that have diversified manufacturing and comparative equality between manufacturing and the rest of the economy tend to have lower unemployment. Specialized lower-income countries with weaker transfer mechanisms have done much worse (the cases of Italy and Greece), until one comes down to Portugal, where emigration emerges as a major outlet for frustrated aspirations that elsewhere appear as unemployment.

6.5　Europe and the United States

We now turn to a consideration of inequality in Europe as a whole compared to that in the United States. It is true, of course, that by commonly accepted measures of household income the United States has higher inequality than any individual country in Europe. Taking the nearest available year, the Luxembourg Income Studies (LIS) report Gini coefficients for the United States in 1992 of 35.5, compared to 34.3 for the United Kingdom and 31.8 for Italy; the LIS series goes to a low of 22 for Finland. But no one, so far as we know, has attempted to compute a Gini coefficient over the population of Europe as a whole. Intra-European-country inequality numbers ignore very large intercountry differences in income levels. Average income in Spain, adjusted for purchasing power parities, is only about 60 percent of that in Germany. Average income in Texas, at roughly comparable economic and geographical extremes, is fully 85 percent of that in New York. Of course, regional income differentials are already fully accounted for in national measures of inequality for the United States.[13]

The Theil statistic, on the other hand, can be decomposed by groups, and it can be aggregated by groups – including national groups. Using standard purchasing power parity exchange-rate conversions, we have computed a pan-European, cross-industries, between-groups component of the Theil statistic for European manufacturing earnings – a first-ever measure of (one dimension of) inequality for Europe as a whole, taking account of inequality across countries and between manufacturing sectors within each country. This measure is presented in Figure 6.6. The figure shows that this measure of pan-European industrial earnings inequality increased through the middle 1980s, alongside dramatically increasing unemployment at that time. In the stagnant 1990s, inequality in Europe remained unchanged.

---

[13] Comparable differentials between the richest and poorest nations of Europe, say Germany and Portugal, are also much greater than these between, say, New York and West Virginia.

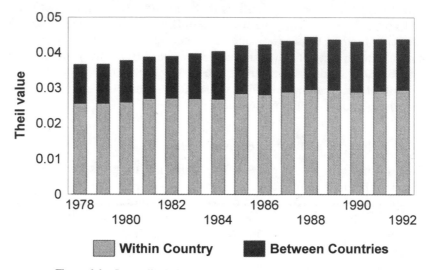

Figure 6.6.   Inequality in industrial earnings for Europe as a whole, with disaggregation into within- and between-country components.

Most of the rise in inequality in Europe in the 1980s did not occur within individual countries – a fact that may have contributed to the impression that inequality was not rising in Europe. But it was: The poor countries were slipping back relative to the wealthy ones. Monetary union will, of course, block further deterioration of this kind. But it also slows an easy route to the *reduction* of inequality in Europe, which once could be caused by real currency appreciations in the poorer countries. Henceforward, convergence of earnings across Europe will have to depend on actual convergence of Euro-denominated wages; nominal wages will have to converge in nominal terms. This may prove to be a contentious process once people realize what they are in for.

Finally, we can extend our measures of inequality to offer a preliminary comparison of *levels* of pay inequalities across Europe as a whole as compared to those in the United States. Recall that, as Table 6.2 illustrated, a T' computed across consistently classified industrial groups provides inequality rankings for Europe that are strikingly consistent with common knowledge and with the sophisticated measurements of the LIS. The comparable measure of T' for the United States is also high by the standards of almost any European country (Italy and Spain are not far off), and this, too, is consistent with the LIS findings. Why not make a comparison between levels of inequality for Europe as a whole and that found in the United States?

Table 6.4 provides estimates for such a comparison. As always, the data are drawn from the STAN, which does provide consistent industrial classifications.[14] As the table shows, cross-industry earnings inequality in the United States is approximately the same as the aggregated, employment-weighted, within-countries component of a similar measure of inequality for the European members of the OECD – a measure computed by supposing, in effect, that all the European countries had the same *average* manufacturing earnings. But this ignores the actual *between-countries* component of European differences, which are about half again as large. When the between-countries component is added in to assess manufacturing earnings inequality overall, European inequality of manufacturing earnings, adjusted for differences in purchasing power between European currencies, emerges as substantially higher than in the United States.

We offer these estimates with some reservations. It is possible, and many certainly believe, that the within-industries component of American earnings inequality, which we do not observe, must be larger than similar differentials in Europe. This might be true. There is, particularly, the case of the new technologies – high-inequality industries in which the United States specializes. But relative to total employment, these sectors remain small. In any event, a hidden within-industries component of U.S. earnings inequality would have to be 50 percent larger than its European counterpart to offset the international component of European inequalities.

It remains true, of course, that inequality within the United States remains high by its own longer historical standards, especially when broader measures of income including profit income and capital gains are taken into account. It is also probably true that capital wealth is more unequally distributed in the United States due to a low level of state ownership in the industrial sectors. And it is very likely true that unemployment measures in the United States continue to understate the full amount of underemployment in the United States.

Nevertheless, it is certainly true that unemployment in the United States is far below that in Europe. And when one considers the concept of income that is most relevant to job seeking, namely, wages and earnings, combined with governmental transfer payments, then inequality in

---

[14] They are, however, quite crude by the standards of estimates made with U.S. SIC data, and we particularly do not vouch for the time pattern. This particular series shows (outside the range of the table) rising inequality in the 1970s and in the early 1990s, so the upward movement overall is stronger in the United States than in Europe. But it does not capture increases in inequality in the United States in the 1980s that do show in other measures. See the appendix to Chapter 4 for details.

Table 6.4. *Inequality in Industrial Earnings in Europe Compared to the United States*

| | Theil Europe | | | |
	Within Countries	Between Countries	Total Europe	Theil U.S.
1978	0.026	0.011	0.037	0.029
1979	0.026	0.011	0.037	0.028
1980	0.026	0.012	0.038	0.029
1981	0.027	0.012	0.039	0.029
1982	0.027	0.012	0.039	0.030
1983	0.027	0.013	0.040	0.030
1984	0.027	0.014	0.040	0.030
1985	0.028	0.014	0.042	0.030
1986	0.028	0.014	0.042	0.029
1987	0.029	0.014	0.043	0.028
1988	0.030	0.015	0.044	0.029
1989	0.029	0.014	0.044	0.029
1990	0.029	0.014	0.043	0.028
1991	0.029	0.015	0.044	0.028
1992	0.029	0.014	0.044	0.030

the United States is probably also lower than in Europe, taken as a whole, and probably has been so for fifty years.

6.6   Questions of Policy

Inequality in wage structures and unemployment are related: When one goes up, so does the other. And where one is higher, so usually is the other. These facts are consistent with causality that might run in either direction. But in the European case, where cross-national inequalities of very long standing have only within the past several decades become inescapable features of every European's economic life, we believe that the dominant line of causation runs from inequality *to* unemployment. This is true both within and between countries and through time. Unemployment is the expression of frustration with low-wage work when significantly better alternatives are in plain view. Unemployment causes inequality: In the periodic slumps and recoveries of the United States, this appears to be the principal chain of cause and effect. But in the United States, inequality also *falls* when full employment returns, and policies aimed at reducing unemployment appear to have good effects on wage and earnings inequality as well.

In Europe, it would appear, such policies are largely prevented. When failures of effective demand and external shocks destroyed the national full-employment equilibrium of the early 1970s, existing inequalities within manufacturing, between manufacturing and services, and across countries determined the distribution of rising unemployment across Europe. And today, as regional integration has undermined national policy means for the pursuit of full employment, particularly by locking into a common currency that freezes transnational income differentials at high levels, Europe stands little chance of reducing cross-country pay differentials.

This position is radically at odds with the supply-and-demand doctrine that permeates European discussion of the wage rigidity problem. There *is* a rigidity problem in Europe, but it is not the one commonly cited. Rather, the problem in Europe appears to be transnational as well as intranational rigidities that prevent the American process of equalization from taking effect. Europe is not too equal: it is not nearly equal enough. Now, of course, the irreversible integration of European currencies into the Euro has blocked the easy channel of real exchange rate revaluation for Spain, Italy, Portugal, and other low-income European countries.

This view is consistent with the important Blanchflower-Oswald work on the wage curve and also with Card and Krueger's vital work on the minimum wage. Indeed, our work suggests a straightforward under-pinning for the latter's finding that raising the minimum wage increases employment. Such increases reduce inequality and so increase the opportunity cost of leaving low-productivity employments. Thus, turnover falls, total employment rises, and fewer people report themselves as unemployed.

The larger policy implications are not for the faint-hearted. We observe that countries that maintain very strong internal transfer mechanisms are more likely to enjoy lower unemployment than countries that reduce their welfare states in the pursuit of "efficiency." Not everyone can have a high-productivity job. Indeed, to the contrary, the entire point of having high-productivity jobs is, or ought to be, to be able to afford large numbers of low-productivity workers, either in teaching or caring professions or cleaning the streets or simply tending the landscape. This is the trick that the richer European countries have, in relative terms, continued to manage.

To eradicate unemployment in Europe will therefore require power-ful action in one of three possible directions.

In principle, Europeans *could* restore to individual national govern-ments the tools necessary to reduce inequality and unemployment at the national level – in other words, to set up the welfare states that the poorer countries in Europe still lack. But to do this, of course, one must either transfer revenues directly from rich to poor governments on a gigantic scale or else undo the project of European Union and allow national governments to compete once again in the creation of national high-productivity industries. Either seems beyond imagining at the present time.

As a second possibility, Europeans *could* encourage all nationalities to adopt the Portuguese solution and let the people come to the welfare states. To some extent, this *will* happen, over time, if nothing better is done. And it is not such a bad thing, for it will necessarily bring pressure on the rich countries to reflate.[15] Yet, the difficulties and limitations of this approach need not be dwelled upon. It will at best happen very slowly and against entrenched opposition of the xenophobic right wing that remains highly active in many European countries.

The remaining possibility is a full-employment policy at the *continental* level, involving transfers not to governments but mainly to individuals and at a common continental standard.

We know this is possible. We can see it in action today in the United States. And so we must ask, of what does full-employment policy in the United States of America actually consist?

First of all, the United States has pursued a pro-equality, low-interest-rate policy since 1995, not just on its own but in conjunction with a banking structure and a credit policy strongly favorable to the private accumulation of debts. American households fuel full employment in the United States by borrowing. So do state and local governments, school and hospital districts, and private companies, and the Federal Reserve has accommodated them all by keeping interest rates stable and refusing to be spooked by the fear of inflation. Europeans are much more reticent about private and local government debt, but if they are unwilling to allow national governments to assume the burden of directly creating new employments, then they will have to change private attitudes instead.

Second, the United States has a continental Social Security system. It is not as generous as those in Northern Europe, but we suspect that it compares favorably with retirement funding in Europe as a whole. Social Security has, since 1972, been the primary agent for the reduction of poverty among the American elderly to values below those of the general population, and it accounts for a very large share of the total

---

[15] Why are there liberals on Wall Street and none in the banks of Frankfurt? Part of the reason, surely, is that rich New York attracts America's poor people, while wealthy Frankfurt repels the poor of Europe. Thus, in Europe the progressive politicians are from the poor regions, while in the United States they come almost invariably from the wealthier states.

income of over half of America's elderly. And the comparison should favor the United States even more when one adds to the mix a health care system – admittedly an inefficient one with large gaps in coverage – whose costs remain thankfully out of control. Health care employment and services provided have risen very rapidly in recent years in the United States, and the deficiencies of the American system cannot gainsay the vast amounts of care actually provided. Further, the United States has an enormous state-supported system of higher education that uses far more resources and holds far more young people off the labor market than is the case in Europe. Any casual visitor to European and then to North American universities knows the importance of this fact. In no place on earth is low productivity so richly and happily rewarded as on the American university campus.

Third, the United States, unlike Europe and despite the theatrics of the 1996 "welfare reform," has been expanding the incomes of low-wage workers in recent years. The welfare cuts transferred resources back to the states, which did cut access to many programs. But in a general climate of full employment, no great crisis of rising poverty in fact occurred; the crisis of welfare reform will emerge only when the economy goes sour.[16] The 1996 rise in the *federal* minimum wage, to $5.15 per hour, no doubt further increased the opportunity cost of leaving low-productivity jobs and so reduced turnover and the unemployment rate. But so, too, and perhaps more significantly, did a vast expansion in the earned income tax credit (EITC) that began in 1994, just as unemployment rates started to drop. The EITC has grown by more than $30 billion since then without raising political objections; possibly this single policy has done more than any other, a low-interest rate monetary policy possibly excepted, to reduce unemployment in the United States.

Here then is a full-employment program for Europe: First, lower interest rates, credibly and permanently, and greatly promote the private, business, and local government uses of credit. Second, expand middle-class *public consumption* goods, particularly health care, urban services, and education.[17] Third, begin to extend the rich-country systems of European social insurance, particularly retirement pay, to the poorer

---

[16] News reports also suggest that the most drastic fiscal provisions of the welfare bill, which involved cutting Supplemental Security Income and food stamps for landed immigrants, many of whom are elderly and disabled, were simply not implemented in the interim before Congress restored most of the those benefits.

[17] Particular attention should be paid to the creation of major new universities of the first water, in the beautiful lower-income regions of the European periphery, and to the full funding of students to attend them. There is no true European university at the present time, let alone a European university *system*, but what better project can one imagine for the future development of European unity?

countries of Europe, raising demand and equality by helping the elderly first and foremost. Fourth, gradually raise poor-country minimum wage the European Union could and meanwhile subsidize the achievement of continental minimum earnings in lower-income Europe through a centrally disbursed program akin to the EITC.

A truly *European* welfare state with a continental retirement program, "topping up" of low wages, and a Euro-valued minimum wage. A *continental* welfare state modeled on the *comparatively successful* social democracy of the United States. That's the ticket.

Appendix: Theil Statistics Measured across STAN Industrial Sectors for European Countries

	1970	1971	1972	1973	1974	1975	1976	1977	1978	1979	1980	1981	1982	1983	1984	1985	1986	1987	1988
Austria	26.7	23.9	22.4	21.9	24.1	24.3	24.1	23.5	23.1	23.3	23.2	25.4	24.5	20.6	22.4	21.5	21.5	22.4	19.6
Belgium	10.5	10.7	11.0	11.0	11.2	11.4	11.3	11.8	11.7	12.4	12.6	12.6	12.5	12.9	13.3	13.9	13.5	14.0	13.9
Denmark	8.4	8.6	8.5	7.3	7.3	8.7	7.3	6.4	6.5	5.9	5.6	5.7	6.2	5.6	5.4	4.9	5.1	5.3	5.6
Finland	8.0	6.5	7.1	7.3	6.7	6.5	6.3	5.9	5.9	6.8	6.0	5.8	5.3	5.5	6.2	6.2	6.5	6.0	5.2
France	17.1	16.6	15.0	15.9	16.7	14.6	16.5	16.5	16.7	17.9	18.3	20.1	19.8	18.8	18.0	19.6	19.0	19.1	19.2
Germany	9.5	9.2	8.9	9.1	9.9	10.1	10.2	10.4	9.9	10.4	10.5	10.3	10.5	11.0	11.7	11.2	10.7	11.4	10.9
Greece	12.7	12.3	12.1	12.0	13.7	13.6	12.4	12.7	14.3	15.9	16.5	17.3	18.7	13.9	14.7	13.5	11.4	11.8	12.4
Italy	27.8	22.7	21.4	21.0	20.0	21.2	20.4	17.4	17.5	16.8	17.2	17.6	17.7	17.9	17.2	18.7	19.3	19.7	22.2
Netherlands	10.3	10.3	9.8	9.9	10.3	9.5	8.3	8.0	8.0	8.0	7.8	7.9	7.7	8.7	9.0	8.3	7.7	7.6	8.2
Norway	4.4	4.3	3.9	4.0	4.0	4.1	3.9	3.7	3.5	3.6	3.7	3.8	3.6	3.8	4.1	4.4	4.1	4.1	4.3
Portugal					31.3	30.9	18.9	20.8	20.0	15.9	15.4	15.2	16.7	17.8	16.9	17.9	20.8	18.0	17.5
Spain										22.0	22.4	21.1	21.0	20.4	20.6	21.7	22.3	21.9	22.0
Sweden	11.5	9.8	9.8	10.1	9.8	9.2	8.4	7.8	7.0	7.6	7.5	8.2	8.5	8.6	9.3	11.0	11.3	10.9	8.9
United Kingdom	10.3	9.5	9.9	10.0	9.0	10.2	8.3	8.8	9.0	8.7	9.3	9.3	9.7	9.7	9.4	9.3	9.5	9.4	9.6

Notes: French data corrected for missing industries, 1970–1976. Belgian data adjusted for error, 1970–1972. Computed from industrial wage data, STAN database. Actual values multiplied by 1,000 to improve readability.

PART III

INEQUALITY AND DEVELOPMENT

CHAPTER 7

Toward a New Kuznets Hypothesis: Theory and Evidence on Growth and Inequality

Pedro Conceição and James K. Galbraith

Simon Kuznets proposed a broad hypothesis on the process of development: that economic progress is accompanied by increasing inequality in the early stages of industrialization, which then tends to decline as industrialization deepens. Recent empirical tests of the Kuznets hypothesis have raised questions about this conjecture, yet most of these studies are based on limited and deficient data. Here we examine the dynamics of inequality across the Organization for Economic Cooperation and Development (OECD) using methods that allow the construction of long and dense time series of inequality. We find that an augmented Kuznets curve for developed countries, where inequality increases with income growth for the highest-income countries, is consistent with this data set. Thus, we offer a macroeconomic alternative to the skill-biased technological change hypothesis, which has been dominant in the literature as an explanation for increasing inequality.

> For the study of the economic growth of nations, it is imperative that we become more familiar with findings in those related social disciplines that can help us understand population growth patterns, the nature and forces in technological change, the factors that determine the characteristics and trends in political institutions. . . . Effective work in [the field of economic growth, inequality, and technology] necessarily calls for a shift from market economics to political and social economy.
>
> Kuznets (1955:28)

7.1 Introduction

Research on economic inequality is relatively recent, at least in the context of developed countries. In the past, most of the important contributions on economic inequality were made by scholars (such as Sen) attracted to the problems of the less developed countries and by authors

139

(such as Atkinson and Theil) inclined toward the ethical, mathematical, and statistical issues associated with the measurement of inequality.[1]

In contrast, the study of *modern economic growth* – economic progress since the Industrial Revolution – has focused extensively on technological change and its application to what is now the industrial world.[2] In Kuznets's own words: "we may say that certainly since the second half of the nineteenth century, the major source of economic growth in the developed countries has been science-based technology – in the electrical, internal combustion, electronic, nuclear, and biological fields, among others" (1966:10). Robert Solow developed the influential neoclassical conceptualization of modern economic growth; he states that models in which technology is the ultimate driver of growth are suited "perhaps to Brazil or Taiwan or Portugal [but] I do not imagine they could be [applicable to] Guyana or Zimbabwe or Bangladesh" (1997:71).

Consequently, until recently, technology and inequality were two rather disconnected concepts, with technology belonging to the realm of the developed world, where it is considered the main engine of growth and with inequality being fundamentally a problem of developing countries.[3]

This situation has changed considerably in recent years. During the 1990s, according to Atkinson, the subject of economic inequality was brought "in from the cold."[4] This development owes much to the increase in income inequality observed from the early 1970s in the United States and from the late 1970s in the United Kingdom.[5] The perhaps surprising fact is that technology, which had been credited for driving growth and prosperity, came equally to be blamed for this observed increase in inequality in developed countries.

---

[1] Sen, 1984, contains an eclectic collection of Sen's work. Sen, 1997, is this author's prime reference specifically on economic inequality. Theil, 1967, and Atkinson, 1970, are good examples and are the sources for two important measures of inequality.

[2] According to Landes, 1969, it is only after the Industrial Revolution that technology systematically affected economic growth. Technological change drives industrial development. Thus, having industrialization is a required condition for a country's growth to be driven by technology.

[3] An exception must be made for that most extreme form of economic inequality, poverty, a concern in every developed country.

[4] Atkinson, 1997, p. 299, provides a short but revealing summary of the number of articles published on the topic of income distribution from the late 1960s to 1995. He finds that most of them dealt with development economics or with empirical and theoretical statistical analysis. What was lacking were articles tying "income distribution centrally into analysis as to how the economy works."

[5] See, e.g., Levy and Murnane, 1992, for the United States and Jenkins, 1995, for the United Kingdom.

The emergence of a conceptual association between technology and the rise in income inequality may also come as a surprise in view of the widely held belief that over the long run there is complementarity between labor and technology. Thus, Samuelson (1964:773) writes: "with the advance of technology and the piling up of a larger stock of capital goods, it would take a veritable miracle of the devil to keep real wages of men from being ever higher with each passing decade. Who fails to see this fails to understand the fundamentals of economic history as it actually happened." The neoclassical model of growth, developed largely by Solow (1956, 1957), formalizes this idea, proposing that growth is based on two factors of production, capital and labor, and an exogenous flow of new technology, which works as the tide that lifts all the boats (raises the incomes of all). Competitive markets are assumed to exist in each factor of production and in output. In this context, the law of one price in the labor market leads to a wage rate equal to the marginal product of labor.

Even slicing up aggregate labor into various levels of education, as the human capital theorists suggested (Becker, 1993; Schultz, 1960), does not change the fundamental complementarity between labor and technology embedded in the neoclassical model of growth. Human capital (educated labor) is "entered" in the production function framework as just a different type of capital, perfectly substitutable in its varying grades with raw labor. In these models, there is no mechanism through which technology can affect differently the wages of workers with different qualifications.

Most of the recent work on the causes of growing income inequality has been performed in the context of labor economics. Figure 7.1 provides an overview of the major sets of conjectures suggested by labor economists, which can be broadly divided into two categories: explanations associated with differences in the demand for and supply of skills and explanations associated with changes in wage-setting institutions.

"Supply and demand of skills" types of explanations are grounded on the assumption that wages are the result of market clearing via the competitive pricing of the capabilities of people.[6] Different capabilities are associated with different levels of skill, education, and seniority in the workforce. High skill/education/experience is associated with a higher marginal product of labor that commands higher wages than low skill/education/experience. The evolution of the difference between the prices of skills depends on the interaction between shifts in the relative

---

[6] These are not always acknowledged as such, but they are often presented as matters of fact.

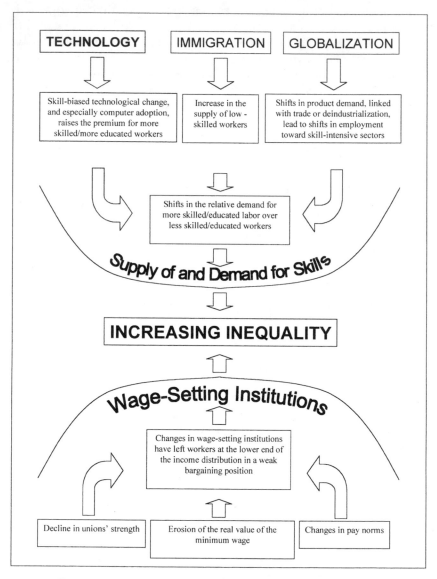

Figure 7.1.   Alternative explanations for the increase in inequality in the United States.

demand for more-skilled labor and changes in the relative supply of skilled labor.

The "wage-setting institutions" class of explanations puts much more emphasis on changes in the institutions that constrain the definition of wages, which may override competitive forces in the dynamic evolution of income associated with rising inequality. These institutional changes include the weakening of unions – which erodes the bargaining power of low-paid workers – changes in pay norms (more contingent employment and pay), and the decline in the real value of the minimum wage, which, as Freeman (1996) argues, can constitute an important redistributive tool.

A standard division in the industrialized countries, according to these two classes of explanations, places the United States, and also the United Kingdom in the 1980s, in the realm of the labor market, while wages in the remaining OECD countries are considered to be institutionally determined (Blau and Kahn, 1996). The reason, it is argued, is that the labor market in the United States, and in the United Kingdom after 1980s, is characterized by much weaker unions and less centralized collective bargaining than in the non–Anglo-Saxon countries of the OECD. However, even for the OECD countries other than the United States and the United Kingdom, the skill supply-and-demand hypothesis has been gaining momentum.[7]

As Figure 7.1 shows, there are two dimensions to the skill supply-and-demand story. The first concerns the validity of the assumption that labor market mechanisms are dominant in driving the dynamics of inequality. Then, if one does indeed accept this assumption, there remains the question of what the causes driving increased inequality in the labor market may be.

At a fundamental level, some scholars reject the validity of the labor market as a metaphor for the employment relation. For instance, many sociologists oppose the economic theory of human capital; they argue that cultural and institutional factors are more important in determining wages. Thus, Dore (1976) differentiates "education" from " schooling," which refers to "mere qualification-earning," leading to an "educational inflation" spiral. Bourdieu and Passeron (1970), Boudon (1973), Jencks (1972), and Bowles and Gintis (1976) are similarly skeptical about a direct relationship between increases in the level of education and economic performance. The differences between the economists of human

---

[7] Leuven, Oosterbeek, and Ophem, 1998, directly criticize Blau and Kahn, 1996, and argue that the skill supply-and-demand story is also applicable to a set of European OECD countries.

capital and these other authors, who come primarily from sociology, remain sharp. In fact, some of the critiques have important parallels with economic perspectives, such as Bourdieu and Passeron's theory of the social filter, whereby schools work as filters to preserve and maintain social and educational differences, and the "inheritance of inequality" perspective of Meade (1964).

For those who are ready to accept the existence of a labor market where wages reward, at least partially, productivity and skill, Katz and Murphy (1992) provide evidence that supply and demand can explain some patterns in the evolution of inequality. Most of the recent studies on inequality that focus on a single-country longitudinal analysis of the evolution of the dispersion of income follow Katz and Murphy.[8] One important benefit of these studies has been investigation of the complex microlevel patterns behind the increase in inequality, including the timing of the dynamics in the disparity of income for different demographic groups and for groups with different workforce characteristics, such as level of education and experience.[9]

However, most such studies are disappointing when it comes to dealing with the question of causes. There has been a rapid but largely ad hoc convergence toward a consensus that technology is to be blamed (Berman, Bound, and Machin, 1997). The main assumption is that technological change is (or has become) *skill-biased*, in the sense that it creates jobs that demand people with high skills. The mechanism through which technology conduces to inequality depends on the assumption that technologically driven increases in demand for highly skilled labor lead to a higher wage for highly skilled workers in comparison with nonskilled labor.

During the period of sustained growth of the 1950s and 1960s, the conventional wisdom was that there was a complementarity between technology and aggregate labor. If the skill-biased technological change hypothesis is valid, this era ended, and it gave place to an age of complementarity between technology and skill. Therefore, the questions that arise are, when did the skill-biased technological change emerge, and what were the causes behind that emergence? Despite recent sophisticated answers to these questions, such as those of Goldin and Katz (1998) and Caselli (1999), digital computers and, more generically, information

---

[8] Examples of the same methodology applied to other single-country studies include Schmitt, 1995, for the United Kingdom and Edin and Holmlund, 1995, for Sweden. Blau and Kahn, 1996, apply a similar procedure to a cross section of OECD countries for a single year.

[9] Grubb and Wilson, 1992, is another example of the same microanalysis of inequality in the United States, although it utilizes different methods.

technologies are considered the "trend-breaking technology" that is responsible for this development (Autor, Katz, and Krueger, 1997).

Yet, despite its surface plausibility, the skill-biased technological change hypothesis has faced considerable empirical and conceptual difficulties. Galbraith (1998a) provides a thorough analysis of the main criticisms. One major issue is associated with the mismatch between the timing of the diffusion of information technology and the start of the increase in inequality in the United States. Howell (1996) provides an equally critical assessment of the empirical validation of the skill-biased technological change hypothesis. Another major problem is related to the fact that computers and information technology in general do not seem to have contributed to increases in productivity. Instead, in the 1980s productivity growth was stagnant at rates much lower than the records set in the two decades that followed World War II. If there is motivation to hire highly educated people who can work with computers, aiming at increasing productivity (from which the wage premium must come), why do we not see an increase in productivity? A standard answer from students of technological change (Rosenberg, 1982, 1994; David, 1985) is that major new technologies take a long time to make their effects felt. But then the effects should not yet be seen in the labor market.

The vast scholarship on the process of technological change has largely been ignored in the literature asserting skill bias. Typically in these discussions, technology is conceptualized as an exogenous flow of innovations and as a purely public good, freely and universally available, as in the initial neoclassical models of Solow (1956, 1957). This simplified treatment comes at a time when there is growing vitality in the study of technology and its economic context. Several economists and other social scientists have fought the tendency to oversimplify the impact of technology, providing sophisticated conceptual and empirical insights into the way technology is related to economic growth.[10] Yet they have not made much headway with the inequality theorists.

Even the modeling effort of the *new growth theories*, which partially intends to introduce some of those insights into the formal neoclassical framework (Romer 1994), fails to justify fully the hypothesis of skill-biased technological change. According to Petit (1995:373), this recent work on economic growth "has been marked by a revival of Schumpeterian ideas on technological change and long term economic growth."

---

[10] Good overviews are included in Fuhrer and Little, 1996, and especially in Stoneman, 1995. However, it is important to point out the work of economic historians, such as Landes, 1969, 1998; Rosenberg, 1982, 1994; and Mokyr, 1990.

Still, despite the fact that the incorporation of the dynamics of innovation conceptualized and described by Schumpeter (1934, 1950) has been a major thrust of endogenous growth theory,[11] the relationship between technology and inequality continues to be modeled primarily through the hypothesis of skill-biased technological change delivered deus ex machina to the economic world.

Meanwhile, the dominant empirical investigations of rising inequality in developed countries continue to be single-country longitudinal studies based on labor market/human capital analysis. Most of the these studies fall back on the skill-biased technological change hypothesis without adequately measuring technology or the pace of technological change. And studies have attempted to evade the difficulties of measuring technology in general by suggesting a causal association between computer usage and wage levels. These studies have run into a host of empirical problems, such as the mismatch in the timing of the increase in inequality and the introduction of computers and the fact that the increased adoption of information technology has not noticeably contributed to increased productivity. Readers of this literature have also been alerted to the strong possibility, not sufficiently noted in the first articles on this subject, that the causality runs from inequalities in the wage structure to the use of computers rather than the reverse.

Beyond these well-known problems, most of the modern inequality literature has also ignored the tradition of studies associating inequality with macroeconomic fundamentals in the tradition of the Kuznets hypothesis. To this tradition, we now turn.

7.2   The Kuznets Hypothesis: An Inequality Macrodynamics

The origins of a theoretical relationship between income distribution and growth go back to Keynes (1936), who was concerned with the effect of income distribution on aggregate demand through the asymmetric consumption and saving behavior of individuals with different levels of income. Models by Kaldor (1956) and by Pasinetti (1962) continued the Keynesian tradition, and so in his way did Kuznets (1955).[12]

Kuznets suggested that developed countries were on a continual path toward income equalization. He hypothesized that inequality would increase in the earlier stages of industrialization but decrease continu-

---

[11] Comprehensive treatments, in textbook form, of endogenous growth theory include Barro and Sala-i-Martin, 1995, and Aghion and Howitt, 1998. The pioneering work was developed in Romer, 1990; Grossman and Helpman, 1991; and Aghion and Howitt, 1992.

[12] Galor and Zeira, 1993, make this point.

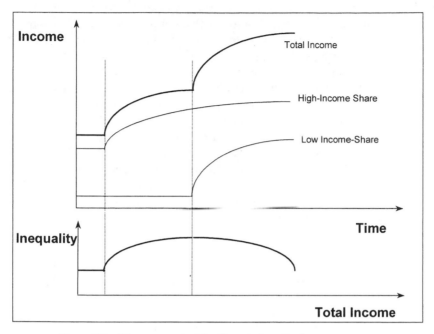

Figure 7.2.   The argument of the Kuznets hypothesis.

ously after a certain threshold of development was reached. This threshold, he argued, was reached in the later quarter of the nineteenth century in the United Kingdom and somewhat later in the United States. The important empirical work of Williamson and Lindert confirmed both Kuznets's conjecture and the timing of the turning points.[13] Most interpretations of Kuznets's hypothesis predicted that inequality would increase steadily in developing countries but decline steadily in developed nations (Tinbergen, 1975).

Essentially, the Kuznets hypothesis states that there is a causal relationship running from growth to inequality. Figure 7.2 illustrates the way Kuznets arrived at his hypothesis. Suppose that a country enjoys an initial situation where growth is the same for both the low- and high-income shares of the population. Total income also grows at the same rate, but the relative incomes of the high- and low-income groups of the population are constant. Thus, inequality does not change as income grows in this initial stage.

[13] See, e.g., their contributions to the volume edited by Brenner, Kaelbe, and Thomas, 1991.

Now assume that there is a first stage of development in which the income of the high-income share of the population starts rising more rapidly than that of the low-income group. This can correspond to a shift from a traditional, stable agricultural society to an industrialized urban economy. People shift from the traditional rural sectors to the more productive industrial sectors, thus gaining income. In this first stage of development, growth in income is accompanied by increased inequality. In the second stage of development, as total income rises and the process of industrialization deepens and broadens, the low-income group starts to catch up. And because it starts from a much lower level of income, growth is more rapid for the low- than for the high-income sector. In this second stage of development, growth leads to decreasing inequality.

The Kuznets hypothesis linking growth and inequality became the most influential income distribution theory of the early Keynesian period. But interest soon waned. After World War II, high rates of productivity growth in the developed countries led to a consistent and generalized increase in real wages (Abramovitz, 1986; Baumol, 1986), accompanied by increased state welfare and protection. Low levels of inequality, historically unprecedented, and apparent stability in the evolution of the distribution of income characterize the post–World War II period (Williamson and Lindert, 1980).[14] The study of economic inequality became limited to a few problems in the exploration and modeling of personal income distribution. Examples include the development of the life cycle savings model of Modigliani and Brumberg (1954), the class-based models of Pasinetti (1962),[15] and Stiglitz's (1969) modification of the neoclassical model of growth to account for possible inequality given different initial endowments of capital.

Kessler and Masson (1988) provide a snapshot of income distribution issues in the 1980s. The main issue addressed in this volume is a controversy between lifelong savings and intergenerational transfer models of wealth accumulation.[16] Commenting on a paper by Edward Wolff (1988), Russell (1988:281) writes, "Wolff's paper addresses one of the most

---

[14] Note our finding, in Chapter 4 of this volume, that the U.S. wage structure in manufacturing was not in fact stable during the 1950s. However, we do not contest the view that inequality of incomes, a more broadly based concept affected by rapid growth in employment outside manufacturing, as well as by the rise of Social Security and other transfer programs, remained much more stable from 1945 to 1970 than it had been before or would be later.

[15] Pasinetti attempted to link the functional distribution of income among the factors of production (labor, land, and capital) with the personal distribution of income.

[16] See the first two chapters in the volume: Modigliani, 1988, and Kotlikoff and Summers, 1988.

interesting questions about the twentieth-century evolution of western industrialized countries: what is the explanation for the marked downward trend in wealth inequality?" Ten years later, Cohen (1998:47) states that "rising inequality is the key preoccupation at the end of the twentieth century." Renewed interest in inequality has naturally led to efforts to explain recent increases in the dispersion of income documented for the United States, the United Kingdom, and other countries, and this has alerted a few researchers to the continuing relevance of Kuznets's ideas.

A recent treatment of the Kuznets hypothesis is included in the work of Galor and Tsiddon (1996), who develop a general equilibrium model in which growth and inequality are both endogenous. Here, the inverted U arises due to imperfections in the capital market, but Figure 7.2 is as useful as before to illustrate the dynamics according to this new mechanism. The high-income and low-income groups have different patterns of investment, which, in the initial stages of development, benefit mainly the high-income group. Capital market imperfection makes it difficult for the poor to borrow; the imperfection is characterized by free lending, but borrowing requires collateral, which the poor do not possess. This dynamic generates growing inequality, which can either persist or disappear, depending on parameter values. According to Galor and Tsiddon, investment-led growth eventually creates new opportunities for the poor, who have more chances to borrow, with higher returns, than do the rich. In these models, the persistence of inequality is harmful for growth because it leads to a suboptimal level of investment. This causal relationship running from inequality to growth can be considered an evolution of the Kuznets hypothesis and has received a great deal of attention in the recent literature.[17] Several empirical studies argue that there is a systematically negative relationship between inequality and growth.

The hypothesis of a negative relationship between inequality and growth has also motivated many theorists to propose models that can account for the mechanisms through which inequality hampers growth. One stream of scholarship, already discussed, has proposed endogenous models of growth and inequality with nonconvexities that generate inequality.

A second type of model argues that inequality can generate sociopolitical instability. An unequal distribution of income can generate pressures and opportunities for violence (assassinations or coups), corruption, and other destabilizing factors that hinder growth by increasing

---

[17] Important and influential references include Alesina and Rodrik, 1994; Perotti, 1992, 1994, 1996; Bénabou, 1996; Persson and Tabellini, 1994.

uncertainty, disrupting investment and production, and undermining government policies. Examples include the works by Alesina and Perotti (1994) and Bénabou (1996).

A third category of theories attempts to link political outcomes with inequality. More inequality can lead voters to elect governments with more-redistributive policies by which taxation is suboptimal, discouraging effort and investment and therefore slowing economic growth. The most representative study is that of Alesina and Rodrik (1994), but Bénabou (1996) also presents a model along these lines.

The major obstacle to testing, or modifying in a persuasive way, the Kuznets hypothesis is associated with the data available to measure inequality. In the following sections, we analyze the mostly commonly used data set on inequality, the Deininger and Squire data set – recently made available under the auspices of the World Bank – and show the inadequacies of these measures of inequality. We then propose a new data set and provide a new look at the relationship between inequality and growth.

7.3   The Established Data on Inequality Evolution

At the beginning of an important report on inequality for the OECD, Atkinson, Rainwater, and Smeeding (1995:13) state that "issues of methodology are central to this investigation. Any comparison of income inequality in two or more countries is only comprehensible by referring to the methods employed." Brandolini and Rossi (1998) caution that one needs to consider two qualifications. First, the analysis of inequality dynamics needs to be performed in the macroeconomic and institutional contexts of each country. Second, the measurement of inequality is not only extremely incomplete but also difficult to compare across countries and over time.[18]

Nevertheless, many authors have offered analyses of the patterns of inequality evolution in the OECD in broad strokes. The most commonly used aggregate measure of inequality is the Gini coefficient. This measure is a number between 0 and 1 (or 100, depending on how it is defined) that summarizes the concentration of income (0 corresponding to total equality, 1 or 100 to having all the income concentrated in a single individual). Normally, Gini coefficients are computed from household surveys.

Concerning the source of data, there are two main options. One is to use national sources, which typically provide many inequality estimates,

---

[18] Chapter 2 of the present volume provides additional discussion.

but with wide variation in coverage, methods, and accuracy. The other is to use international data sets based on comparable definitions and methods. Given the compatibility restrictions, these sources typically provide fewer data points over time for each country.

Many researchers have used the data compiled by Deininger and Squire (1996a) under the auspices of the World Bank. This data set is considered the most thorough and largest source of internationally comparable measures of inequality and has been the inspiration for many recent papers.

Recent work by Deininger and Squire (1996b) and by Li, Squire, and Zou (1996), for example, question the existence of any systematic relationship between growth and inequality. First, using a panel regression with country dummies, they find no systematic relationship between income distribution and growth, but they do find a negative correlation between land distribution and growth. They then specify another model in which a dummy is used to differentiate democratic from undemocratic countries. The aim is to test the importance of the political system in mediating the dynamics of the relationship: In principle, democracies should be more responsive to demands for redistribution and therefore less efficient. The authors find that the dummy is not statistically significant, a result that is said to undermine the thesis of a political relationship between inequality and growth.[19]

On what do conclusions of this kind rest? Table 7.1 summarizes what Deininger and Squire classify as "high-quality" Gini coefficient values for the OECD from 1969 to 1992. These values meet three conditions, all related to the process by which the data are collected. First, information on income must come from household surveys. Second, the household survey must provide comprehensive coverage of the population (and not be, for instance, restricted to urban areas or selected regions). Finally, the household survey must give a comprehensive coverage of income sources. These conditions required Deininger and Squire to discard many available Gini observations or at least not to include them in the "high-quality" subset. This procedure obliterated large numbers of inequality measures in developing countries, but we should note that even for the OECD, Table 7.1 looks rather rarefied, not to mention the absence of the following OECD member countries: Austria, Iceland, Ireland, and Switzerland. The United States and the United Kingdom are the only countries to have a continuous year-to-year data series for the entire period. A measure of the data coverage can be reached by

---

[19] Li, Squire, and Zou, 1996, connect this result to the capital market imperfection hypothesis.

Table 7.1. Gini Coeefficients for 23 OECD Countries, 1969–1992

	1969	1970	1971	1972	1973	1974	1975	1976	1977	1978	1979	1980	1981	1982	1983	1984	1985	1986	1987	1988	1989	1990	1991	1992
Australia								34.33		38.10	39.33	39.96					37.58	40.60			37.32	41.72		
Belgium											28.25						26.22			26.63				26.92
Canada			32.24		31.60	31.03	31.62		31.97				31.80	29.40	32.80	32.97	32.81	32.50	32.28	31.91	27.41	27.56	27.65	
Czech Rep.		22.50			21.01			20.71	19.37			20.67	23.92				19.86			20.07			24.60	24.51
Denmark								31.00					30.99						33.15					33.20
Finland		44.00							30.45	30.41	31.06	30.86	32.04	31.46	30.98	30.84								
France					30.62		43.00				34.85					34.91								
Germany										32.06			30.59		31.37	32.20								
Greece						35.11							33.29							35.19				
Italy						41.00	39.00	35.00	36.30	35.98	37.19	34.29	33.12	32.02	32.87	33.15		33.58	35.58		32.74		32.19	
Japan		35.50	36.90	33.40	32.50	33.60	34.40	33.90	33.70	32.90	33.90	33.40	34.30	34.80			35.90							
Korea, R.		33.30	36.01					39.10				38.63		35.70		34.54		33.64			37.60	35.00		
Luxembourg																	27.13							
Mexico						57.90			50.00							50.58					54.98			50.31
Netherlands						28.60			28.39		28.14		26.66	27.62	27.56		29.10	29.68	29.40	29.00	29.60		29.38	
New Zealand					30.05		30.04		32.95	31.90	34.79			33.93	34.10		35.82	35.53	36.45	36.58		40.21		
Norway					37.48			37.30			31.15					30.57	31.39		33.11					
Portugal					40.58							36.80											33.31	
Spain					37.11							26.79					25.19	26.00	25.79	24.42	25.91	36.76	35.63	
Sweden							27.31	33.12				32.44	32.54	30.66	30.06	31.83	31.24	31.72	31.65	32.22	31.33	32.52		32.44
Turkey					51.00														44.09					
UK	25.10	25.10	25.70	26.00	25.10	24.20	23.30	23.20	22.90	23.10	24.40	24.90	25.40	25.20	25.70	25.80	27.10	27.80	29.30	30.80	31.20	32.30	32.40	
USA	34.06	34.06	34.30	34.46	34.42	34.16	34.42	34.42	34.98	35.02	35.06	35.20	35.62	36.48	36.70	36.90	37.26	37.56	37.56	37.76	38.16	37.80	37.94	

Source: Deininger and Squire (1996a)

152

dividing the number of occupied cells (210) by the total number of cells (24 years × 23 countries = 552), which gives a coverage of only 38 percent. The average number of data points per country is nine, with a standard deviation of six.

Furthermore, some of the values reported by Deininger and Squire are highly inconsistent with those reported by other sources. Differences between values from different sources are to be expected; yet, in cases where there is a large difference between the value of Deininger and Squire and values widely consistent across alternative sources, the results from the Deininger and Squire data set must be questioned. For the Nordic countries, in particular, the values reported by Deininger and Squire tend to be ten points higher (on a scale of 1 to 100) than the consensus obtained from other sources. Table 7.2 shows a comparison of the values reported by Deininger and Squire with a selection of other sources. The differences for Sweden are particularly striking; those for Denmark and Norway are similar but slightly smaller. The differences in the case of Finland are smaller, but a thorough and comprehensive country study by Jantti and Ritakallio (1997) shows that inequality in Finland was stable in the 1980s, in clear contradiction to the evolution elicited from Deininger and Squire.[20]

What then? To assess the dynamics in the evolution of inequality, one needs a measure of changes in inequality through time. The questions we raise about the major source of inequality data, the World Bank, raises serious doubts about relying too heavily on the world's stock of Gini coefficients for this purpose. Nevertheless, it is not unreasonable to start by asking whether these data point in any particular direction, and if so, to where.

Table 7.3 illustrates the varied experience in the evolution of inequality across the OECD countries, as measured by Deininger and Squire. Some fairly plausible patterns do emerge. First, the countries that exhibited the highest levels of inequality in the first period (France, Portugal, Italy, Spain) are said to have become more equal throughout the period, with relative decreases in inequality ranging from 10 percent in Portugal to more than 30 percent in Spain. Italy, the United Kingdom, the Netherlands, and Japan have in common a U-shaped evolution of inequality, with the inversion point (from decreasing to increasing inequality) differing from country to country. Japan and the United Kingdom were the first to switch in the 1975–1980 period, followed by Italy and the Netherlands in the next period. Of the former, the United

---

[20] Further discussion of alternative measures of inequality, including rankings for all the major countries of Europe, can be found in Chapter 6.

Table 7.2. *Comparison of the Deininger and Squire (1996a) Gini Coefficients with a Selection of Other Sources for the Nordic Countries*

		73	75	76	77	78	79	80	81	82	83	84	85	86	87	88	89	90	91	92
Denmark	**D&S (1996)**			31.0					31.0						33.1					33.2
	LIS (1998)														25.7					24.0
	Burniaux et al. (1998)										22.9									
Finland	**D&S (1996)**				30.5	30.4	31.1	30.9	32.0	31.5	31.0	30.8			26.2				26.1	
	LIS (1998)														20.7				22.3	
	Burniaux et al. (1998)													21.2						
Norway	**D&S (1996)**	37.5		37.3			31.2					30.6	31.4	33.1					33.3	
	LIS (1998)						22.5												23.4	
	Burniaux et al. (1998)													23.4						
	Atkinson et al (1995)												22.5							
Sweden	**D&S (1996)**		27.3	33.1				32.4	32.5	30.7	30.1	31.8	31.2	31.7	32.2	31.3	32.5			32.4
	LIS (1998)								19.8						22.0					22.9
	Burniaux et al. (1998)		23.2																	
	Atkinson et al (1995)										21.6									
	Gustafsson et al. (1997)		21.3										22.0							

Notes: LIS (1998) is the Luxembourg Income Survey, an international data set. Burniaux et al. (1998) is a study for the OECD based on an individual questionnaire for each member country. Atkinson et al. (1995) is the result of an analysis for the OECD of data from the LIS. Gustafsson et al. (1997) is a country study based on national data.

Table 7.3. *Changes in Gini Coefficients for OECD Countries, 1970–1990*

	Relative Change				Absolute Change			
	Period 1 to Period 2	Period 2 to Period 3	Period 3 to Period 4	Period 1 to Period 4	Period 1 to Period 2	Period 2 to Period 3	Period 3 to Period 4	Period 1 to Period 4
	1970s	70s to 80s	1980s	All periods	1970s	70s to 80s	1980s	All periods
Australia	-	4.1%	1.4%	-	-	1.5	0.5	-
Belgium	-	-7.2%	0.8%	-	-	-2.0	0.2	-
Canada	-0.3%	1.4%	-3.8%	-2.8%	-0.1	0.4	-1.2	-0.9
Czech Rep.	-6.9%	6.1%	-7.1%	-8.2%	-1.5	1.2	-1.5	-1.8
France	-10.5%	-10.3%	-	-	-4.6	-4.0	-	-
Germany	4.7%	-2.1%	-	-	1.4	-0.7	-	-
Greece	-	-	5.7%	0.2%	-	-	1.9	0.1
Italy	-9.3%	-8.8%	2.6%	-15.1%	-3.7	-3.2	0.9	-6.0
Japan	-2.0%	2.7%	4.5%	5.2%	-0.7	0.9	1.6	1.8
Korea, R.	12.1%	-6.6%	-6.1%	-1.6%	4.2	-2.6	-2.2	-0.6
Mexico	-6.8%	-6.2%	8.7%	-5.0%	-4.0	-3.4	4.4	-2.9
Netherlands	-0.8%	-2.3%	5.8%	2.6%	-0.2	-0.6	1.6	0.8
New Zealand	7.9%	6.8%	6.6%	22.9%	2.4	2.2	2.3	6.9
Portugal	-9.3%	0.0%	-1.6%	-10.8%	-3.8	0.0	-0.6	-4.4
Spain	-27.8%	-3.0%	-2.0%	-31.4%	-10.3	-0.8	-0.5	-11.6
UK	-5.1%	8.7%	15.8%	19.5%	-1.3	2.1	4.1	4.9
USA	1.6%	4.3%	3.6%	9.9%	0.5	1.5	1.3	3.4

Source: Deininger and Squire (1996a).

Kingdom exhibited the strongest acceleration in the increase in inequality after switching occurs.[21] With the exception of New Zealand, the United Kingdom was the country in which inequality grew the most, by almost five Gini points.

New Zealand, Australia, and the United States exhibited a consistent pattern of increasing inequality. The increase in American inequality began in the 1970s and was the first to develop. Overall, the relative increase in inequality in the United States was 10 percent, second only to that of New Zealand and the United Kingdom. Czechoslovakia and Mexico showed an oscillating pattern over time, but the institutional setting for these countries was very different from the setting of all the others. In Canada and Belgium, the tendency was toward a decrease

---

[21] Note that in Table 7.3 the relative changes for the United States in the increasing periods are 8.7 percent, 15.8 percent, and 19.5 percent, compared with 2.7 percent, 4.5 percent, and 5.2 percent for Japan.

in inequality, with only one small increase between the periods for each country.[22]

Patterns and trends thus exist in the data, and they clearly lack the uniformity that would be implied by a simple, universal model of technological change affecting competitive labor markets around the world. Were that model correct, inequality should be rising or falling everywhere, according to the direction or strength of the skill bias. This is evidently not the case, even on the basis of the most standard data sets. Rather, there appears to be a wide variety of national experiences, with some dependence on initial conditions. This, in turn, suggests a pattern of macrodetermination, with national experiences differing because of differences in macroeconomic performance or because countries find themselves in different positions in a nonlinear structure. But we probably cannot distinguish between these alternatives without better evidence than we have.

7.4   Conclusion: Toward an Augmented Kuznets Hypothesis

How does the Kuznets hypothesis stand the test of confrontation with the Deininger and Squire data? Unfortunately, definite conclusions are not possible; if anything, these data simply differentiate the Anglo-Saxon economies, in which inequality rose most sharply, from the others. They provide little consistent evidence of a relationship between inequality and either income or the rate of growth. There are only three countries where the data coverage is adequate for a systematic comparison: the United States, the United Kingdom, and Japan. The evolution of inequality and income levels in these three cases in presented in Figure 7.3.

It seems clear that even if systematic relationships between growth and inequality exist and if there is any validity to these data, the patterns of the evolution of inequality in most of the OECD countries do not neatly fit the most simple Kuznets thesis. One has to deal with the raw fact that inequality has lately been rising, and quite sharply in the richest countries, as Figure 7.3 illustrates. Using the same data set, Ram (1997) finds for the developed countries a U-shaped relationship between inequality and growth rather than an inverted U; this is a hypothesis that

---

[22] Korea seems to show a distinctively different pattern, unlike that of any of the other OECD countries. Inequality in Korea witnessed a sharp increase from period 1 to period 2 of more than 12 percent, which was larger than the change suffered by the United States over the entire twenty years. This increase in the 1970s was followed by substantial decreases in the remaining two periods. This observed decrease more than compensated for the sharp growth in inequality in the 1970s, suggesting an inverted-U evolution of inequality over time for Korea.

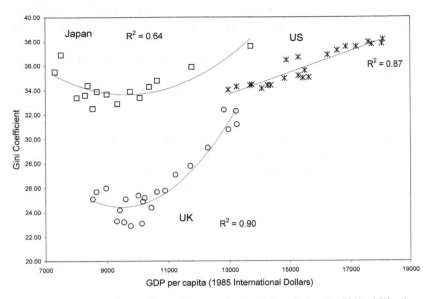

Figure 7.3.   Inequality and income in the United States, the United Kingdom, and Japan.

Harrison and Bluestone (1988) had already proposed for the United States in the late 1980s.[23]

The alternative of an *augmented* Kuznets curve, an inverted U that turns up for the small number of countries at the highest income levels, is consistent with the K-sector/C-sector framework of Galbraith (as set forth in Chapter 1 of this volume). Perhaps the original Kuznets hypothesis is best considered as valid for economies whose manufacturing sectors are principally engaged in the mass production of consumer goods – that is, all the developing countries and most of the industrial ones. But after a certain point, income inequality rises with growth in the highest-income countries simply because those countries have a manufacturing mix disproportionately weighted toward advanced and technologically monopolistic sectors.

In that case, inequality should decline with growth for most manufacturing economies, as Kuznets predicted. But it should rise for the few at the very top of the technology and investment pyramid, those that supply advanced capital goods to the rest of the world. Japan, the

---

[23] Another development, which we will not pursue here, consists of using measures of economic progress that go beyond per capita income (Vanhoudt, 1997, 1998).

United States, and the United Kingdom fall into this category; this could account for the upward slope of their income/inequality curves in Figure 7.3.

The challenge is to test this new Kuznets hypothesis over a wide range of countries and an adequate number of years. For this, the Deininger and Squire data will not take us very far; there is too little good data. But the interindustry Theil index of earnings inequality in manufacturing, introduced for the United States and Europe in Chapter 6, can be used instead. Our data set, for the OECD countries alone, permits us to double the number of observations available; more important, it provides a continuous series over time for all the countries included. Our measures of inequality for the years 1970 to 1992, plotted against GDP per capita in U.S. dollars for the same years, are presented in Figure 7.4.

Figure 7.4 also shows the result of the interpolation of a function where inequality is a cubic polynomial of income. From this simple procedure, we see that our suggestion of augmenting the Kuznets curve is, in fact, consistent with the data. While we do not claim that this test is in any way definitive, we do believe it opens the door to continued and expanded research on this problem.

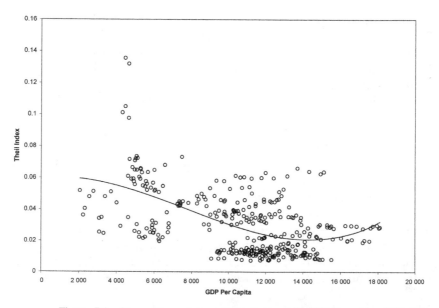

Figure 7.4. Inequality and income in nineteen OECD Countries (354 data points).

What then about the relationship between inequality and growth in developing countries? The chapters that follow expand our measurements of inequality to cover over seventy countries, including most of the manufacturing activity in the world. At this point, a limiting factor becomes the ability to obtain not timely and comparable measures of earnings inequality, but adequate measures of economic growth and time series that would permit adequate statistical controls for a comprehensive test of the relationship between growth and inequality. We will not get all the way there in this volume. But we do find the following:

- There appears to be a systematic negative relationship in the short run between inequality and economic growth in most developing countries. In contrast to the evidence just presented for the United States and the United Kingdom, strong growth reduces inequality in most developing countries. Crises and recessions, on the other hand, invariably increase inequality. This relationship is very well documented here for Latin America, and it becomes stronger where we have been able to improve the data coverage most significantly, as in the cases of Mexico and Brazil, where we have developed monthly observations of our inequality series.
- Populist and import-substituting governments tended to have better inequality records than export-promoting and liberalizing regimes, leaving aside the question of whether such policies are sustainable in the long run.
- Financial crises, particularly currency depreciations, increase inequality in most developing countries. They have little apparent effect on the hard-currency countries.
- Various forms of state violence, particularly coups d'état, are usually preludes to rapidly rising inequality. A significant exception is revolution, a rare event but with the decided effect of reducing inequality when it happens. Politics and political change, in other words, definitely do matter, not because they change the relationship between inequality and growth but rather because they tend to change, sometimes quite radically, the conditions under which growth and income equalization are pursued.

A full and final verdict on the relationship between growth and inequality will have to await the outcome of a larger research project. But we believe that the evidence we will present in the chapters to come strongly suggests that, in most industrializing countries, the relationship

exists almost as originally predicted: strong growth in urban manufacturing tends to reduce inequality except among the richest countries.
Readers of the chapters that follow will come away, we think, with a
renewed appreciation of the depth and durability of Simon Kuznets's
fundamental insight.

CHAPTER 8

Measuring the Evolution of Inequality in the Global Economy

James K. Galbraith and Jiaqing Lu

This chapter provides a summary of information in the UTIP data set on the evolution of industrial earnings inequality in the global economy. At this writing, the data set covers over seventy countries, with annual observations going back to 1972 in most cases and to 1963 in many. Our measure of changing inequality, based on the groupwise decomposition of the Theil statistic across industrial categories, appears to be a sensitive barometer of political and economic conditions in many countries, and the percentage change in this index appears to be meaningfully comparable across countries.

8.1   Measurement of Inequality Around the World

As the previous chapter made clear, the work of Deininger and Squire (1996a) has greatly advanced our knowledge of the state of research into income inequality around the world. By assembling a vast amount of past research, these authors have brought us as close as we are likely to get to having a comprehensive set of Gini and quintile estimates of the distribution of household or personal income across countries and through time. Yet, it is not enough to permit an authoritative examination of the effects of economic change on inequality in the world economy. Specifically, the effects of growth and globalization on wage inequality cannot be elucidated using these data, and, we argue, attempts to do so are likely to produce more perplexity than they are worth.

The first issue is conceptual. Gini coefficients typically are measures of household or personal income, not of annual earnings or hourly wages. This is an advantage for some purposes, because household income is the central concept for evaluating social welfare. But it is wages and earnings that bear the direct effects of the kinds of economic changes that have been of greatest interest to the profession: the effects of

161

technological change or of trade and globalization, for instance. Household incomes reflect these developments only indirectly. In addition, much variation in household income that may be due to changing sources of income, hours of work, labor force participation, and changing family structures must also be sorted out. A measure of inequality restricted to wages and earnings would better suit certain research problems of great interest to economists and policy makers, including those related to the effect of decisions about macroeconomic policy and trade regimes.

Then there are two major difficulties with the existing data. The first concerns comparability across countries. Gini coefficients are highly sensitive to underreporting of high incomes, and the distortion from this source differs to an unknown degree from one country to the next. (It may also differ across surveys within individual countries, where time elapses between surveys and the research methods and teams are not operating continuously.) And the bias may well be systematic: Countries with great inequalities are likely to have greater concealment of high incomes, greater tax evasion, and worse income accounting. Possibly for this reason, the Deininger and Squire (D&S) database suffers from unresolved anomalies, one might even say absurdities, such as ranking Spain as the most egalitarian country in Europe in the early 1990s or ranking the United Kingdom as more equal than Norway.

Finally, and most important for our purposes, analysis of economic change requires dense and consistent time series. Data must be available almost every year if valid comparisons with time series such as gross domestic product (GDP) growth or inflation are to be made. Yet, in too many countries, appropriate surveys of adequate quality on a consistent basis were simply never taken, and once a year is missing from the data set, it cannot be reconstructed. Indeed, existing measurements of inequality often combine multiple estimates of Gini coefficients for particular years with spotty or nonexistent coverage at other times. Restricting the data to series of acceptable quality on procedural grounds, a major D&S contribution, reduces the first problem but worsens the second. In the end, annual changes in inequality can be computed from these data for only a handful of countries.

The limitations of the D&S data for studies of the evolution of inequality through time are evident from Table 8.1, which shows the number of data points in a twenty-six-year period (1970–1995) for those countries for which more than three data points are available.[1] Only four coun-

[1] We thank Pedro Conceição for compiling this table and for permission to use it here.

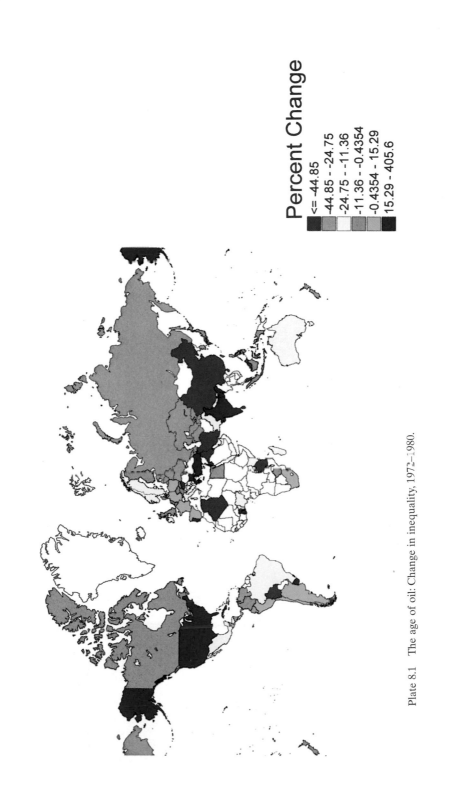

Plate 8.1   The age of oil: Change in inequality, 1972–1980.

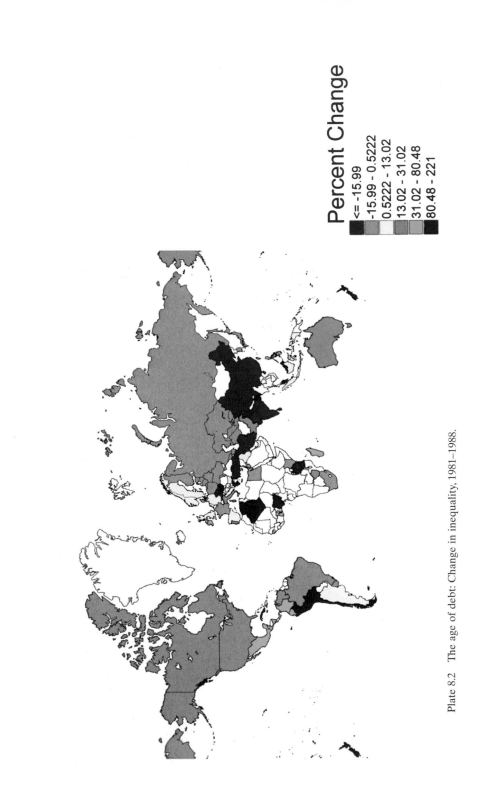

Percent Change

<= -15.99
-15.99 - 0.5222
0.5222 - 13.02
13.02 - 31.02
31.02 - 80.48
80.48 - 221

Plate 8.2   The age of debt: Change in inequality, 1981–1988.

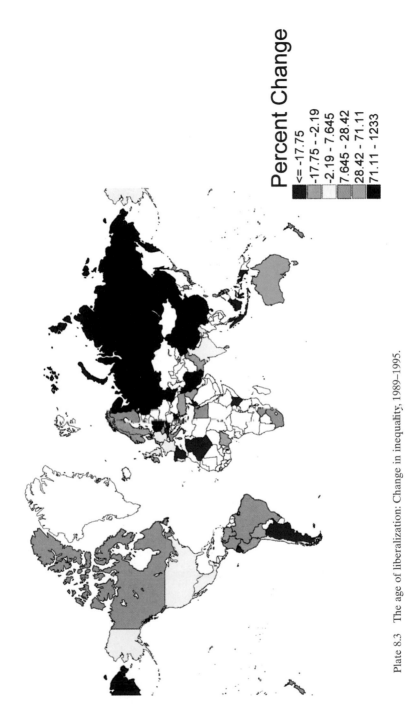

Percent Change

- <= -17.75
- -17.75 - -2.19
- -2.19 - 7.645
- 7.645 - 28.42
- 28.42 - 71.11
- 71.11 - 1233

Plate 8.3 The age of liberalization: Change in inequality, 1989–1995.

Average Cluster Distance

<= 98.71
98.71 - 106.6
106.6 - 119.8
119.8 - 155.1
155.1 - 183.1
183.1 - 280.3

Plate 8.4 Global inequality: Average degree of similarity.

Table 8.1. *Number of Data Points in the High-Quality Deininger and Squire (1996a) Data Set Between 1970 and 1995*

Australia	8	France	4	Norway	7	Taiwan	23
Bangladesh	8	Germany	5	Pakistan	8	Thailand	6
Brazil	14	Hungary	7	Panama	4	UK	22
Bulgaria	24	India	12	Peru	4	USA	22
Canada	17	Indonesia	9	Philippines	4	Venezuela	9
China	12	Italy	15	Poland	17		
Colombia	7	Japan	16	Portugal	4		
Costa Rica	8	Korea, R.	7	Singapore	6		
Cote d'Ivoire	5	Mexico	5	Spain	7		
Denmark	4	Netherlands	12	Sri Lanka	6		
Finland	10	New Zealand	12	Sweden	14		

Note: Only counries with more than three data points are shown.

tries show data for virtually every year, and most do not have data for even half of the years. And these gaps are irreparable. There is no way to construct Gini coefficients for countries and years for which adequate household sample surveys were never conducted in the first place.

8.2   The Theil Measure

Is there an alternative? Yes: a groupwise decomposition of Theil's T statistic (T′ hereafter) provides a useful alternative approach to measuring the *change* in earnings inequality within a single country and to comparing degrees of change across countries. Of the three major problems noted earlier, a T′ based on industrial payrolls solves the first and third and evades the second. Usefully for research on the structures of pay, T′ can be computed from payroll data. Those forms of income most likely to be underreported in household surveys, such as profits, interest, and off-the-books earnings, are simply not targets of the analysis. There may be problems of underreporting as some establishments escape notice, but larger establishments and hence most of manufacturing are likely to be covered routinely and accurately.

Most important, data for computing T′ reliably for earnings in manufacturing are available for long periods and in dense and consistent time series. Because T′ does not require rank-ordered income bins, grouped industrial payroll and employment data sets are an adequate source of raw material. These are available virtually everywhere; the exceptions are mainly in Africa and during short periods of war or revolution in other countries. For many countries, one can obtain useful data on a monthly basis, as Calmon et al. (Chapter 12) have done for Mexico and Brazil and as Galbraith and Garza Cantú have done for the United States (Chapter 4) and for Canada. Monthly data are perforce computed from higher-level categories and are volatile for many reasons, but by running a moving average through monthly series, one can obtain highly sensitive measures of changing wage and earnings dispersions.

The major deficiencies of the grouped Theil measure compared to the Gini coefficient are two. First, it is restricted to what is covered, and most countries report consistent data on payroll and employment only for a well-defined manufacturing sector. The informal sector, the services sector, the public sector, and agriculture, are all left out. But, as noted earlier, it is manufacturing that bears the brunt of technological change, of changing patterns of trade, of fluctuations in aggregate demand, and so on. And there is a reason why data on manufacturing are generally so much more widely available: Manufacturing establishments are comparatively stable, well-organized, well-defined operations with comparatively reliable bookkeeping. It is futile to complain about lack of measurements for other sectors, particularly in poorer countries, where instability and transience tend to prevail outside of manufacturing. And, for reasons to be discussed, we argue that changes in inequality within manufacturing are often, in fact, a good indicator of changes in other sectors.

Second, the Theil statistic has to be approached with extreme caution before being deployed to compare levels of inequality between countries. The level measure of T' depends, obviously, on the number of categories entered into the expression: The more subdivisions there are, the greater will be the between-group component of their differences. And while group structures – the industrial classification scheme – are likely to be maintained consistently from one period to the next within any one country, simply by force of bureaucratic inertia in many cases, there is no assurance that two different countries will classify their industries in comparable ways. Thus, differences in classification schemes, which are likely to be greater across countries than through time, favor the use of T' for evolutionary as opposed to comparative analysis.

On the other hand, there are certain data sets from which calculations of an interindustrial T' do appear to yield measures that are meaningful to compare across countries. The Organization of Economic Cooperation and Development's (OECD's) Structural Analysis (STAN) data set, for example, applies a single industrial classification scheme to all the industrial countries, and these countries are themselves sufficiently similar in their composition of employment that a ranking of the resulting Theil measures corresponds rather closely to the most sophisticated ranking of household income inequality in existence, those of the Luxembourg Income Studies (LIS). We have therefore deployed T' for level comparisons of OECD countries in Chapter 6 of this volume. While the care taken in computing the LIS Gini coefficients is incomparable, an advantage of our rough method is that it is very inexpensive. Annual series for every OECD country can be computed for an outlay of a few hundred dollars.

One other methodological reservation bears mentioning. The Theil statistic is a weighted measure of earnings dispersion, with the weight of each group depending on its proportion of total employment. In general, we find that the evolution of T' in practice depends mainly on changes in payrolls, reflecting changes in relative wage rates; changes in employment structure are usually a slow-moving source of variations in T'. But this is not always the case: Sometimes major upheavals occur, and changes in our measure then reflect changing employment structures. This issue takes on importance from time to time because the relationship between changing inequality within manufacturing and changing inequality in the rest of the economy can depend on the types of changes in pay and employment that are taking place.

The measurement of inequality that we present is, in effect, a chain-linked index of earnings dispersion, updated annually for changes in the structure of employment as well as changes in relative per capita earnings. It reflects changes both in relative wage rates per se and changes in employment structures. In most cases, this variable weighted measure is the appropriate gauge of changing industrial earnings inequality overall precisely because it accounts for changes both in average earnings and in the structure of employment.

A limited exception occurs during periods of sharp employment change of a certain kind, particularly industrial job losses associated with globalization. If job losses are concentrated among low-wage and/or part-time workers, while job gains occur among both low-paid ordinary services and relatively high-paid producers' services, then the change in a variable-weighted T' may understate the rise in inequality overall. As workers disappear into unemployment or low-wage services, the relative weight of low-wage workers in manufacturing declines, along with their wages, and a diminished manufacturing sector retains an artificial aspect of stable pay dispersion.

This problem seems to be serious only for a handful of high-income countries, though it appears to be especially significant for the United Kingdom. Our data show an apparently low rate of inequality increase for the United Kingdom compared with the United States, in contrast to other work that finds very large relative increases in inequality in the United Kingdom.

In such cases, it is possible to distinguish between inequality caused by rising relative wage differentials and inequality caused by changing patterns of employment by computing an index whose employment weights are fixed to a base-year employment structure. Differences in the change between a variable and a fixed-weighted statistic can illustrate the comparative extent to which the two forces are at work in any particular nation. The difference between increases in inequality in the United States and the United Kingdom narrows when one compares fixed-weighted indices – even though the rise in earnings inequality in the United States remains larger. If this is correct, then a reasonable interpretation of the still larger increase in *total income* inequality in the United Kingdom, revealed in a number of studies, may be that sharper increases occurred in nonwage income among the wealthy and sharper cutbacks in social welfare programs than was the case in the United States.

Allowing for subtleties of this kind, for occasional irregularities in the data,[2] and for the other methodological qualifications mentioned earlier, it seems clear that the use of the change in T′ to estimate changes in the overall distribution of earnings in a country expands substantially the available measures of the evolution of inequality in pay. When compared to the difficulties involved in acquiring acceptable Gini coefficients, we believe these numbers are as plutonium is to isotope separation: cheap, available, easily processed, and effective. It is a bit surprising that these calculations have not already become a standard part of the inequality literature. Though the data need to be treated with caution, it seems clear that the added information is significant and that availability of dense, reliable time-series coverage far outweighs the disadvantages of limited coverage of nonmanufacturing sectors and other occasional problems.

Indeed, for the most part, increasing or decreasing inequalities in pay rates in manufacturing, which dominate movements of T′ in practice, are likely to reflect comparable increases or decreases in inequality in the larger economy. The reason for this is quite simple. Steelworkers (for instance) are everywhere and always more highly paid than shirt makers. When the gap between the pay of steelworkers and that of shirt makers

---

[2] France and Belgium are the two identified problem cases, both in the early or mid-1970s. Galbraith, 1998c, provides an explanation. We would also not lean heavily on the measurements for countries with minuscule industrial sectors, such as El Salvador, Honduras, Kenya, or Madagascar.

widens, that is usually not due to forces specific to those two industries, but instead is part of a larger process – in which, say, surplus labor is driving down relative wages in shirt making and also in other low-wage occupations. Because these include both manufacturing and low-wage service occupations, the forces increasing inequality within manufacturing are likely to resemble those operating on, say, the differential between engineers and cleaning women in the services sector. In this case, T′ is quite a robust social indicator; manufacturing is not isolated from the forces affecting pay in the economy at large. Gaining clear view of what happens in manufacturing is a little like looking out of a small window at the sky: One cannot see the whole thing, but it is usually enough to detect changes in the weather.

8.3   Computing T′ from Industrial Earnings Data

Industrial earnings data are ubiquitous. Virtually every country performs an industrial classification of its manufacturing establishments, and most countries collect basic information on total employment and total payrolls on at least an annual basis, with exceptions only in the poorest nations and those afflicted by severe political instability or war. In the various phases of this work, we have employed the following major data sources:

- The Annual Survey of Manufactures for the United States, which provides annual information on U.S. industries by Standard Industrial Classification (SIC) for 1958 1992. This data set is distinctive in that it permits us to calculate the inequality of hourly wage rates for production workers in manufacturing; full details are presented in Galbraith's *Created Unequal.*
- The OECD STAN database, which provides three- and four-digit International Standard Industrial Classifications (ISIC) data on annual earnings for about forty industries in twenty-two countries for 1970–1992, with incomplete recent extensions up to 1995. These data form the basis of the analysis in Chapter 6 of the present study.
- The Economic Commission for Latin America and the Caribbean (ECLAC) data set on industrial structure, which provides twenty-nine industrial (ISIC) categories for eight Latin American countries – Argentina, Brazil, Chile, Colombia, Jamaica, Mexico, Peru, and Uruguay – for 1970–1995. Galbraith and Garza Cantú's work on Latin America in Chapter 11 is based mainly on these data.

- The United Nations International Development Organization (UNIDO) Industrial Statistics database, with up to twenty-nine ISIC categories for 173 countries; annual coverage varies but begins for many countries as far back as 1963. The present chapter provides the first formally published results from this rich source of industrial earnings and employment data.
- Finally, Lu has computed inequality by region and by industry for 1985–1996 in the People's Republic of China from data in the 1997 *China Statistical Yearbook*.

The basic evolution-of-inequality calculations from the STAN, ECLAC, and UNIDO data sets are presented in Figures 8.1 through 8.5. At the present writing, we include twenty-one countries from inside and outside the OECD, seventeen countries in Asia, fourteen South American and Caribbean nations, nine countries in Africa, and six European nonmembers of the OECD.[3] Where countries are represented in more than one data set, we chose the series that appears to be of higher quality, which usually means STAN over the other two because of the finer industrial classification scheme. ECLAC and UNIDO appeared to be working from essentially the same numbers for Latin America; however, data going back to 1963 are available in the UNIDO series for many countries, and this is an obvious advantage. In all, we currently have continuous inequality time series for more than seventy countries, including many for which previous inequality computations have been restricted to a bare handful of widely separated years.

8.4   Summary of Main Trends

Industrial earnings inequality throughout most of this period rose comparatively little in Central and Northern Europe and actually declined in a number of smaller, mostly social democratic countries as well as in Japan. In a subset of southern and Atlantic countries in Europe, notably the United Kingdom, Italy, and Portugal, inequality declined in the 1970s but then rose in the 1980s. In the United States, inequality rose from the early 1970s on; the patterns in Mexico and Canada resemble those in the United States, but with less movement in the 1970s and more in the 1980s.

---

[3] Korea, a late-joining OECD member, is presented with other Asian countries even though the Korean data come from the STAN. Meanwhile, Ireland, a founding OECD member, is listed with European outsiders because the data for Ireland come from UNIDO.

Inequality rose in most of Latin America and the Philippines during this period, dramatically in some places and at certain times. In just a few Asian countries, inequality declined, and quite sharply, from the late 1980s on – often after having risen in the early part of the decade. In the People's Republic of China, inequality fell during the first decade of reforms after 1978 but rose again from 1989 through 1994, with an especially sharp increase in 1993; this striking finding is paralleled in data for Hong Kong and Macau.

In the Soviet Union, earnings inequality seems to have declined in the 1960s and to have remained unchanged from that point until the country collapsed; the usual caveats about Soviet data naturally apply, and we note that the story for other forms of income in the Soviet Union may have been quite different. Following the collapse of the Soviet Union, inequality in Russia unquestionably soared.[4] In Eastern (Central) Europe, inequality was also held constant throughout most of the period under study, but it rose sharply when communism collapsed in the early 1990s.

We have data for nine highly disparate countries in Africa: Nigeria and Algeria, where inequality seems to follow the price of oil; Egypt, where earnings compression in the early 1970s was followed by rising inequality in the 1980s; South Africa, where inequality rose sharply in the early 1970s and again following the end of apartheid rule in the early 1990s; Ghana, which experienced drastic increases in inequality according to these measures; Zimbabwe, where inequality fell following liberation and has yet to return to colonial levels; and Madagascar, Kenya, and Tanzania. In Iran, inequality fell sharply following the revolution, only to rise again in the early 1990s. In Iraq, a decline in inequality during the Iran–Iraq War was followed by a large increase in the wake of the Gulf War.

There are many stories in these data. Galbraith and Garza Cantú (Chapter 11) have examined in detail the trends in inequality in Latin America from 1970 to 1995, linked to the patterns of political change. Inequality rose following military coups in Chile, Argentina, and Uruguay (see Chapter 10). But inequality also rose following the introduction of postmilitary "liberal" regimes in Argentina (Alfonsin) and Peru (Belaunde Terry) and in the course of austerity and liberalization in Mexico (López-Portillo, de la Madrid). Stabilization plans tended to arrest the rise in inequality in Brazil and in Mexico but not to reverse past increases (see Chapter 14). In Peru, the extreme instability

---

[4] The proportionate increase in interindustry earnings inequality in Russia compared with the Soviet Union is by far the largest in the world, albeit from a very low base.

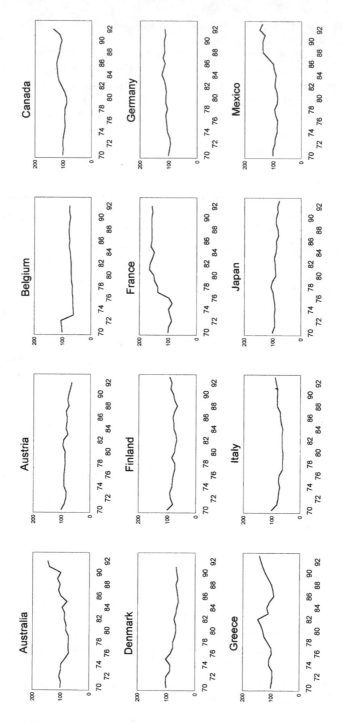

170

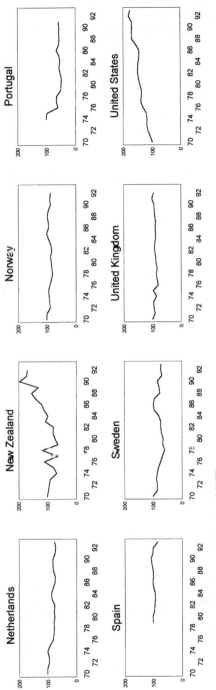

Figure 8.1. Inequality in the OECD.

171

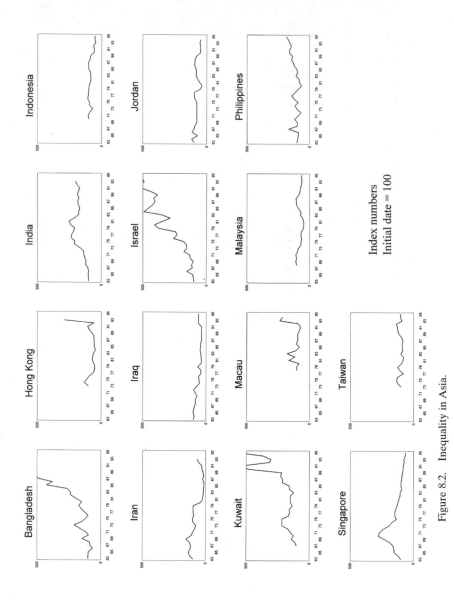

Figure 8.2.   Inequality in Asia.

172

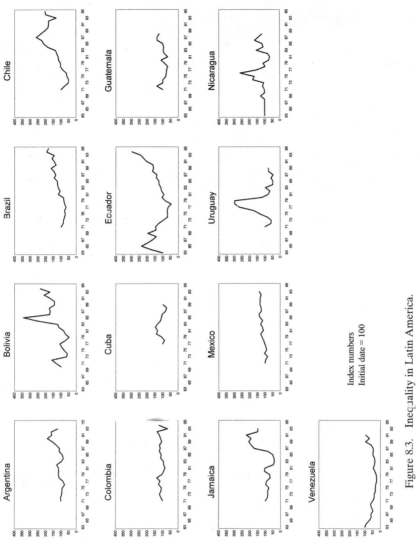

Index numbers
Initial date = 100

Figure 8.3.   Inequality in Latin America.

173

174   Galbraith and Lu

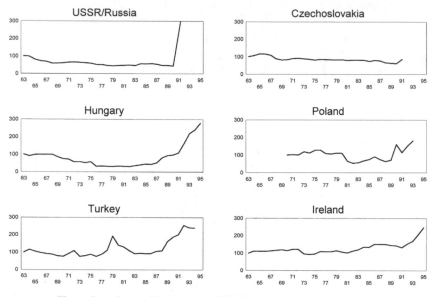

Figure 8.4.   Inequality in Europe (UNIDO data set).

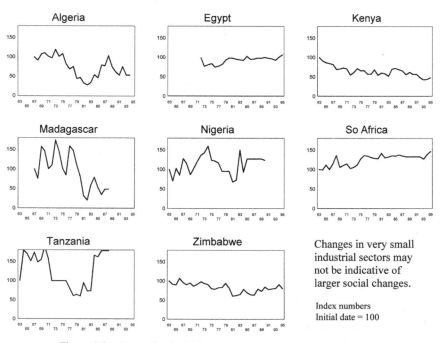

Changes in very small industrial sectors may not be indicative of larger social changes.

Index numbers
Initial date = 100

Figure 8.5.   Inequality in Africa.

surrounding the failed stabilization efforts of Alan Garcia is evident, as are the harsh consequences of the Fujimori liberalizations. Colombia, Venezuela, and Jamaica are also covered in this work.

From preliminary work on the comparative role of employment and wage shifts in the evolution of inequality in developing countries, it seems that almost all countries that liberalized their trading regimes experienced significant increases in raw earnings inequalities. Of these, a small number – Malaysia and Indonesia notably – achieved sufficient increases in higher-wage employments so that overall inequality actually declined in the late 1980s and 1990s. In a few other cases – for instance, Korea and the Philippines – changes in the structure of employment partly offset rising inequality in pay.

In many other countries – Egypt is an example – the rise in inequality is a combination of rising earnings inequality and a worsening distribution of jobs. This appears to be due to declining relative employment in high-wage sectors as import-substituting regimes eroded, without replacement by high-wage exports. Within the OECD, both patterns are evident, but overall fluctuations tend to be less. New Zealand is a leading OECD case of rising wage inequality that was not offset by favorable shifts in employment, whereas in Germany total inequality rose less than would have been the case without employment shifts toward the high-wage sectors.

8.5   Globalization, Growth, and Inequality

Many countries compressed their wage structures in the 1970s, but most saw rising inequality in the 1980s. Of these, only a few succeeded in reducing inequality in the 1990s. The United States experienced consistently rising inequality in annual earnings from the early 1970s through the 1980s, though with hourly wage rates it appears that the rise in inequality peaked in the early 1980s (see Galbraith's *Created Unequal* for details on this point). Other countries generally joined the movement toward higher inequality later on, and it is useful to try to summarize the patterns at the global scale.

Color plates 8.1 through 8.3 provide summary measures of changes in inequality in map form for three periods chosen to emphasize major developments and turning points in recent global economic history. Plate 8.1 (page 176 and preceding page 161) covers the years 1972 to 1980: the years of two global oil shocks and energy crises. The map reveals a striking differentiation in movements of inequality during this time. The major capitalist consuming nations react to the energy shocks with contractionary policies that led to recessions in the United States and in

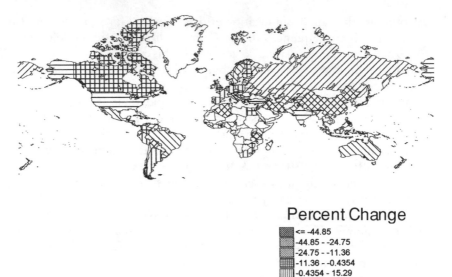

Percent Change

■ <= -44.85
▨ -44.85 - -24.75
▦ -24.75 - -11.36
▤ -11.36 - -0.4354
▥ -0.4354 - 15.29
▤ 15.29 - 405.6

Plate 8.1   The age of oil: Change in inequality, 1972–1980 (*see 4-color map preceding Chapter 8 p. 160*).

Europe, as well as in India and Argentina, which experience the greatest increases in inequality in these years. But the producers, here represented most vividly by Iraq, Iran, Algeria, and a few others, show sharply declining internal inequality as the oil boom makes them rich. It is a striking pattern in which the low-wage manufacturing workers in the oil countries gain ground.

Plate 8.2 (page 177 and preceding p. 161) shows the pattern of change in the years 1981 to 1988: the years of debt crisis and oil bust. Inequality continues to rise in the United States. But now other countries experience much sharper inequality increases, particularly along the Pacific coast of Latin America, where debt and financial crises hit exceptionally hard. The oil boom countries become the victims of the oil bust, and inequality rises sharply, for instance in Nigeria; exceptions are Iran and Iraq, which spend the decade locked in war. In a world where inequality is rising almost everywhere, the major exceptions are China and India, which are the two large developing countries most successfully isolated from the world financial system in these turbulent and unhappy years.

Plate 8.3 (page 178 and preceding p. 161) reports the changes in inequality in the years 1989 to 1995: the years of global liberalization and

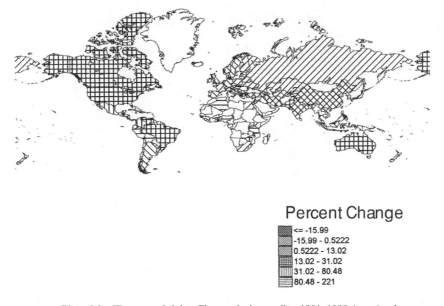

Percent Change

▓	<= -15.99
▨	-15.99 - 0.5222
░	0.5222 - 13.02
▤	13.02 - 31.02
▥	31.02 - 80.48
▦	80.48 - 221

Plate 8.2   The age of debt: Change in inequality, 1981–1988 (*see 4-color map preceding Chapter 8 p. 160*).

the collapse of communism in Europe. The figure is now dominated by rising inequality in the formerly communist countries, including most dramatically the case of Russia, where inequality explodes. But China also experiences sharply rising inequality at this time, as do most countries on the periphery of the formerly communist world: Iran, Iraq, Turkey, and Korea among them. Even Finland, which suffered a sharp depression following the collapse of its Soviet markets, shows rising inequality in these years. These are the years of global liberalization; from the standpoint of a measure of internal inequality, they are not a pretty sight.

Speaking broadly of the entire period, countries that are rich and strongly social democratic generally succeeded in controlling their wage structures throughout most of this period comparatively well, irrespective of their patterns of trade. This is also true of India after the shocks of the early 1970s; though poor, India remained aloof from global capital markets until comparatively late. Germany, the Scandinavian countries, the Netherlands, Austria, and Denmark are notable examples of stable or declining inequality or of increases in inequality that remain modest by historical and international standards. In some of these cases, favorable employment shifts offset rising wage differentials, but in others, such

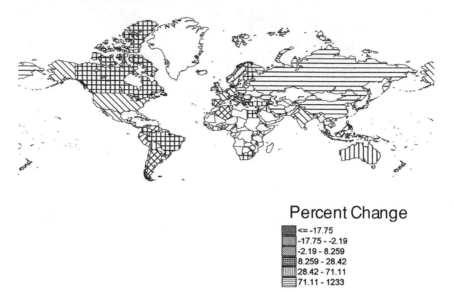

Percent Change

▓	<= -17.75
▨	-17.75 - -2.19
▤	-2.19 - 8.259
▦	8.259 - 28.42
▥	28.42 - 71.11
▬	71.11 - 1233

Plate 8.3   The age of liberalization: Change in inequality, 1989–1995 (*see 4-color map preceding Chapter 8 p. 160*).

as Austria, overall inequality declined continuously as interindustry differentials were compressed.

Throughout the period, developing countries that liberalized and globalized were subjected to larger swings in inequality than countries that did not; one may contrast India in the 1980s, for instance, with Argentina (which liberalized following coups against Peronism in the 1970s) or the Philippines. In most cases, identifiable liberalizations were followed by rising inequality in wages. Just a few liberalizing countries managed to compensate for an increase in raw wage differentials with large increases in relatively high-wage employment – Malaysia and Indonesia seem to be the main cases[5] – as well as Korea in the middle to late 1980s, though overall inequality increased in Korea in the early 1990s. Almost everywhere else, the effects of liberalization appear to be associated with rising inequality, and the issue is only whether the redeployment of jobs moderated or actually worsened this trend.

Given that earnings inequality was rising worldwide, this result is hardly surprising: Liberalizing countries found themselves forced to conform to a global pattern. But it leads to a profound conclusion. It

[5] This is evidently not the case of Singapore, which appears to have experienced persistent wage compression.

would appear that export-led modernization is inherently a zero-sum game for income distribution in developing countries. That is, improving employment distributions in one country lead to not especially creative destruction and worsening inequality in others through the redistribution of jobs. In a liberalized and globalized world economy, only a general compression of earnings structures can create an environment where equalization prevails on the global development scene. This the world economy has not seen since the 1970s.

8.6   A Cluster-Analytic Approach to Economic Systems and Performance

As a final exercise, Figure 8.6 presents a cluster analysis of the coevolution of earnings inequality across sixty countries in our data set for which the time series are adequately long. Details of the algorithm are presented in Chapter 16. The figure aligns countries according to the similarity of the movement of wage inequality from year to year in percentage terms between 1971 and 1995. Strong geographic and developmental patterns are evident in the figure, including the clustering of the richest OECD countries on the center-left, along with such cases of nonglobalization as India and the old Soviet Union, and with a striking clustering of the unstable cases on the right side. Smaller-scale geographic affinities in the evolution of inequality are apparent throughout the figure. We note in passing the comparative wage stability of the enduring communist countries and their affinity to the developed capitalist ones in the evolution of inequality. We think this is real, but we caution that our runs of data for China and Cuba are short, and unrecorded events earlier in the period could have upset our picture.

Figure 8.6 shows a striking divide between countries that maintained reasonable control of their wage structures and those that did not. It also illustrates just how extreme fluctuations and, for the most part, increases in inequality have been for some countries of the Third World. War and revolution obviously play a role in the high fluctuations on the right side of the diagram (viz., Israel, Iran, Iraq, Kuwait, Nicaragua, Poland, and Peru). We are also struck by the suggestion that emerges again here that the price of oil (affecting Iran, Iraq, Nigeria, and Kuwait) and the collapse of the competitive position of natural textile fibers (affecting Peru, Bolivia, Uruguay, New Zealand, and Bangladesh, among others) may have played major roles in the havoc experienced by more than a few of these countries. Immigration is no doubt also a major consideration in such smaller countries as Israel and Kuwait.

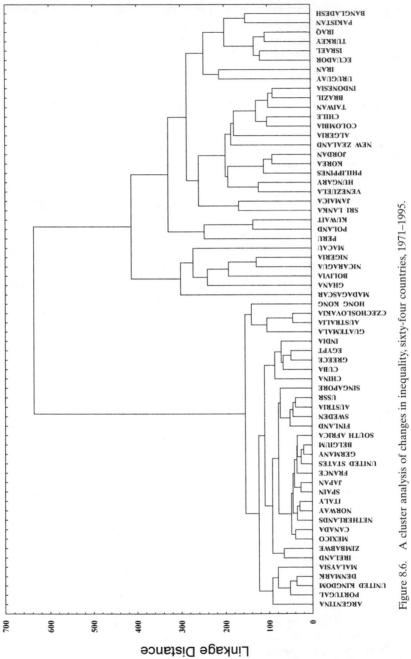

Figure 8.6.   A cluster analysis of changes in inequality, sixty-four countries, 1971–1995.

180

Plate 8.4 (page 182 and preceding page 161) presents this information in another way: as a map showing the *average degree of similarity* in the movement of pay inequality in every country for which we have data compared to every other country. This map answers the question: Which countries have inequality experiences that most resemble those of the world as whole? Countries with high degrees of intersimilarity are shown in red, and the scale fades to orange, yellow, green, and blue to indicate greater and greater dissimilarity in the behavior of inequality between any given country and the rest of the world.

Naturally, countries with low volatility in our inequality index are more likely to resemble each other, in this respect, than those with higher volatility. Note which countries these are: the industrialized and democratic members of the OECD. Countries on the periphery of the OECD club, such as Mexico, Egypt, and South Africa, come in next (alongside the once artificially stable but now radically unstable former Soviet Union[6]). Beyond these cases, the record becomes increasingly erratic until one arrives at war-torn Iran and debt- and terror-torn Bolivia and Peru, the countries with the greatest sustained instability on our record.

8.7   Conclusions

The major conclusion of this chapter is that industrial data sets can greatly enhance our knowledge of the evolution of earnings inequality in manufacturing worldwide and are therefore a valuable resource in an effort to understand the effects of economic globalization. While it remains possible for wealthy and determined countries to keep control of their wage structures, our analysis shows that the predominant recent trend in inequality worldwide has been decisively up. Liberalizations have almost always made inequality worse; only a few developing countries escaped by upgrading their employment structures, and this is a feat that necessarily only a few can achieve.[7] The experience of the 1960s and early 1970s was quite different; in those years, many countries reduced inequality and many more held their wage structures stable.

Because our measures are drawn from several different data sets, they cannot be readily used to compare levels of inequality across countries.

---

[6] Data for the Soviet Union are through 1991 only in this map.

[7] We applaud the work of Rowthorn and Kozul-Wright, 1998, who criticize the simple-minded view that openness produces more rapid growth per se. Our point, building on theirs, is that in an open world, national performance will be influenced by global conditions. Countries, of course, also retain the right to restrict their degree of openness, but this is easier for large countries than for small ones.

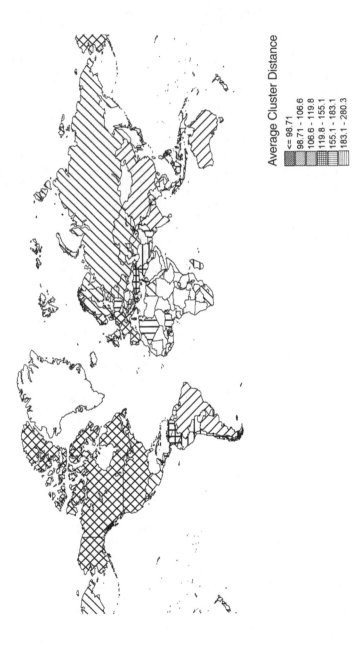

Average Cluster Distance

<= 98.71
98.71 - 106.6
106.6 - 119.8
119.8 - 155.1
155.1 - 183.1
183.1 - 280.3

Plate 8.4 Global inequality: Average degree of similarity (*see 4-color map preceding Chapter 8 p. 160*).

We are therefore not able to answer that oft-asked question, is equality good for growth? However, this evidence does point, in a loose way, toward an answer to the inverse question. In most countries, growth is good for equality; indeed, strong growth appears to be an indispensable prerequisite for equalization. Conversely, the weak growth in most industrializing countries in the 1980s was an inequality disaster.

It does not seem to matter greatly whether growth is achieved through import substitution or the rapid growth of high-wage exporting sectors. The problem is that the rapid growth of high-wage exports is an inequality solution open to only a few countries at any one time. It follows that a reduction in inequality globally will require either a return to import substitution and nationally based wage structures or to a substantially higher pace of world economic growth.

And, to be sure, higher growth globally can be achieved only if led by the comparatively successful, stable, and wealthy nations of the global center and the international financial institutions that they control. It cannot be achieved by liberalizing reform of small nations on the periphery.

We think that this policy conclusion, so contrary to the conventional view that each country is responsible for its own performance in the global economy, flows inevitably from a global look at the evolution of inequality. It is, indeed, remarkable and perplexing that in our age of global economic relations, so little analysis has so far been devoted to the global determinants of national economic performance. We hope that our demonstration of the computability of statistics measuring the year-to-year evolution of inequality worldwide will contribute to an effective globalization of economic policy research and so help to lay the groundwork for a truly global approach to the great policy problems of growth, employment, and incomes equalization.

Appendix: Notes on the United States and United Kingdom Cases

We find that T' constructed from either the Annual Survey of Manufactures or the STAN for the United States is highly correlated with a measure of the Gini coefficient for household income, based on the Current Population Survey (CPS), for the years 1970–1992. However, our measure of T' for the United States rises more rapidly than the CPS series in the 1970s and less rapidly in the 1980s; indeed, T' stabilizes in the mid-1980s. The divergence in the 1970s may have occurred because wage incomes grew more unequal in that decade, while nonwage

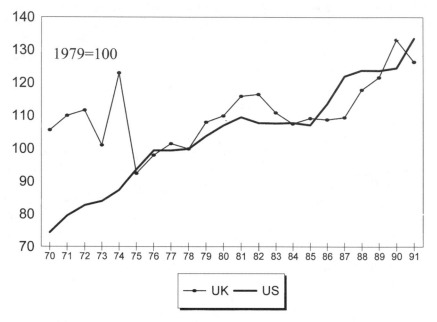

Figure 8.A1.   Inequality in the United States and the United Kingdom: fixed-weighted Theil indices.

incomes actually contributed to a reduction in household income inequality through the expansion of social security and other entitlement programs in those years. In the 1980s, on the other hand, a huge rise in interest incomes flowed mainly to wealthier Americans, so that nonwage incomes worked to increase inequality.

In the case of the United Kingdom, several colleagues have noted that our measure of wage dispersion shows less increase since 1979 than other measures, notably the Gini coefficient for inequality of household incomes, and that the rise in inequality in the United Kingdom is more nearly comparable to that in the United States than our data show. We believe there are two explanations for this. First, our variable-weighted T′ deviates from the fixed-weighted measure for the United Kingdom but not for the United States. When a fixed-weight T′ is substituted, the measured rise in wage inequality in the United Kingdom approximately doubles, from 8.6 to 16.9 percent, compared to 26 percent for the U.S. series. Second, we believe that the dispersion of nonwage incomes probably grew much more in the United Kingdom than in the United States after 1979: the Thatcher regime was much harsher on the welfare state than that of Ronald Reagan, partly because Reagan never controlled both houses of Congress. Thus, a measure of inequality based on household income will grow more rapidly in this period in the United Kingdom, compared to a measure based on wages. Figure 8.A1 presents a comparison of fix-weighted T′ measures for the United States and the United Kingdom.

CHAPTER 9

Economic Regionalization, Inequality, and Financial Crises

James K. Galbraith and Lu Jiaqing

In this chapter, we examine the comovement of macroeconomic variables, similarities, and dissimilarities of industrial structure, as well as patterns of similarity and dissimilarity in the movement of inequality in manufacturing earnings. This information can illuminate the degree of economic integration across countries in a region, and it can highlight important differences between Europe and Asia. We then examine the relationship between financial crisis and the movement of inequality. We show that crises typically generate increases in inequality, but more so in less developed countries and more so in regions that are more liberal in their policy regimes.

9.1   Introduction

In this short chapter, we examine the comovement of macroeconomic variables, similarities and dissimilarities in industrial structure, and the movement of inequality in manufacturing earnings, on which we have annual information for much of the global economy over the past thirty years. We argue that this information can illuminate the degree of economic integration across countries in a region and that it can highlight important differences between Europe and Asia. We then examine the relationship between financial crisis and the movement of inequality.

9.2   Macroeconomic Comovement and Regionalization

Was there an Asian crisis? Or again, was there an *Asian* crisis? Was the financial crisis that swept across the Pacific Rim in the summer of 1997, with a cascade of stock market crashes, currency devaluations, and regime changes, notably in Indonesia, specifically *Asian, reflecting distinctive characteristics of the Asian region?* Or is it better characterized in some other way, more illuminating of the relationships between the once rapidly growing economies of the Pacific Rim and those of the advanced industrial world?

It is normal that a sequence of financial crises is identified, in news accounts and ordinary conversation, by the large region in which it occurs. It is something else again, however, when financial decisions begin to be made on such a basis, when "tequila effects" emanate from Mexico to the rest of Latin America or "bamboo effects" from Thailand to the rest of southern Asia. And the matter becomes grave for economists when the spread of financial crisis itself becomes evidence of a common pattern of policy mistakes, so that the "Asian crisis" becomes grist for an ideological campaign against the once admired and once feared "Asian development model." For such a campaign to be viable, the model itself has to have existed and in the countries to which it is ascribed.

One way to approach this question dispassionately is to examine the comovement of major macroeconomic variables across national economies. If similar macroeconomic patterns reflect similar economic structures, then regional financial analyses may be appropriate. But if, on the other hand, the regionalization of macroeconomic performance turns out to be entirely superficial, *perhaps even an artifact of the financial markets themselves*, then reading meaning into the comovement of macrovariables can be disastrous. Two such variables, the growth of real gross domestic product (GDP) and the rate of change of inequality in manufacturing earnings, are, we think, especially illuminating. They reveal the difference between a superficial and a deep or structural similarity in neighboring economies.

The method of cluster analysis can be applied to the rates of change of any commonly observed time-series variable to derive a pattern of comovement of that variable across countries and through time. The distance matrix computed in the course of such analyses is a useful source of information about international patterns of similarity and dissimilarity. And maps based on that distance matrix can help to reveal regional patterns.

Such a map is presented in Figure 9.1. It shows, for France, the pattern of relative similarity of GDP movements for the period 1972–1995 for other countries in the data set, divided into six classes of roughly equal number. The numerical scale shows the Euclidean distance between paths of GDP growth: Smaller numbers indicate a greater degree of similarity in the performance of this indicator over time. A clear regionalization of GDP growth is apparent: France forms part of a European/Organization of Economic Cooperation and Development GDP growth cluster to which few other countries belong. The use of

Figure 9.1. Similarity of patterns of GDP growth in the world economy, 1972–1995, with France as the reference case.

Cluster Distance

0 - 8
10 - 13
14 - 17
19 - 22
23 - 25
26
27 - 31
33 - 40
186 - 231
307 - 371

7000   0   7000   14000   Miles

188

other OECD countries as the point of reference yields broadly similar results: They are all more similar to each other than they are to countries in other parts of the world.

Figure 9.2 presents similarity of GDP growth to Singapore, which for GDP growth may be taken as characteristic of the Asian region. Again, a distinct pattern of regionalization appears. Almost uniquely in the world economy, the Asian countries show high growth into the 1990s. As with the European case, this finding is robust with respect to the choice of reference country within the region. There is an Asian GDP growth cluster. The question is: does it mean anything? In particular, does it indicate an underlying structural similarity between the economies of the Asian region?

From the common similarity of GDP growth rates, one might be tempted to infer that Asia now resembles Europe – an integrated regional economy. But common sense warns otherwise. While the European countries have long (and bloody) histories of competitive industrialization and a pattern of progress toward trade and now monetary integration that goes back to the 1950s, industrialization in Asia is comparatively new and there is little basis for thinking that economic integration has more than begun.

A direct, though crude, way to examine industrial integration in Asia is simply to look at the composition of exports of the economies of the region. Table 9.1 provides this information for eight countries in 1996. Many of the countries – Korea, Malaysia, the Philippines, Singapore, and Thailand – show strong concentrations in electronic products. Unless they are eating each other's semiconductors, this suggests that rather than intraregional integration, what we have here is competition for the markets of the advanced countries, notably the United States and Japan. Indonesia is predominantly an energy exporter at this time.

Another useful and revealing way to visualize the difference between the Asian rim and the OECD is to compare the patterns of evolution of inequality in manufacturing wages. In the case of a highly integrated region, two factors dictate close conformity in the movement of inequality through time. The first is a broadly similar distribution of employment across industries, so that external shocks and technological developments affect countries in similar ways. The second is the combination of integrated labor markets and relative factor price equalization in intraregional trade.

We are able to offer such a comparison, thanks to the data set described in the preceding chapter. This data set exploits the decomposability of Theil's T statistic and the ubiquity of information on payrolls

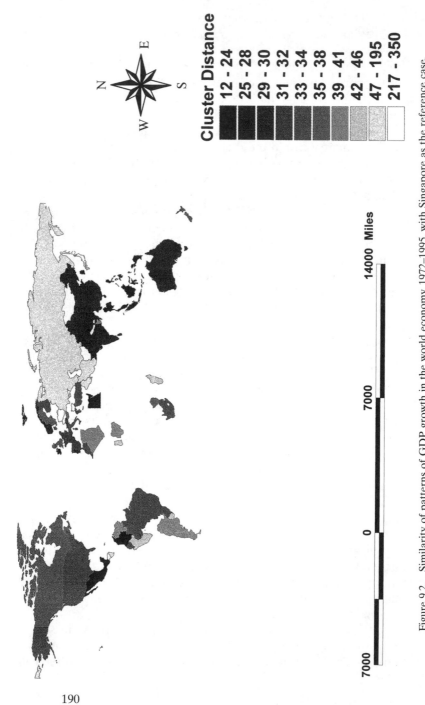

Cluster Distance

12 - 24
25 - 28
29 - 30
31 - 32
33 - 34
35 - 38
39 - 41
42 - 46
47 - 195
217 - 350

7000   0   7000   14000 Miles

Figure 9.2.   Similarity of patterns of GDP growth in the world economy, 1972–1995, with Singapore as the reference case.

190

Table 9.1. *Major Exports of Selected Asian Countries, 1996*

China		Hong Kong		Indonesia		Korea	
Footwear	4.70	Articles of Apparel	10.31	Petroleum/Crude Oil	10.38	Valves/Transistors, Etc.	13.34
Baby Carriage/Toys, Etc.	4.30	Women/Girl Clothing	8.60	Natural Gas	8.08	Passenger Cars, Etc.	7.01
Articles of Apparel	4.22	Valves, Transistors, etc.	7.85	Veneer/Plywood, Etc.	8.01	Ships/Boats, Etc.	5.49
Men's/Boys' Wear Woven	4.20	Men's/Boys Wear	7.11	Footwear	4.41	Manmade Woven Fabrics	4.84
Women's/Girl's Clothing	3.86	Watches and Clocks	5.65	Natural Rubber/Latex, etc.	3.85	Gold, Nonmonetary	4.09
Telecomm. Equipment	3.10	Office Equipment Parts	4.82	Copper Ores/Concentrates	3.51	Computer Equipment	3.63
Computer Equipment	2.44	Telecomm. Equipment	3.94	Heavy Petroleum Oils	3.02	Telecomm. Equipment	3.40
Cotton Fabrics, Woven	1.94	Women/Girl Wear, Knit	3.88	Fixed Veg. Oils, Not Soft	2.67	Electrical Equipment	3.05
Headgear, etc.	1.90	Cotton Fabrics, Woven	2.99	Man made Woven Fabrics	2.31	Heavy Petroleum Oils	2.84
Petroleum/Crude Oil	1.85	Jewelry	2.72	Men's/Boys Wear	2.27	Flat Rolled Iron/Steel	1.70

Malaysia		Philippines		Singapore		Thailand	
Valves/Transistors, Etc.	17.92	Valves/Transistors, Etc.	29.84	Computer Equipment	18.46	Valves/Transistors etc.	5.21
Office Equipment Parts	6.03	Office Equipment Parts	8.17	Valves/Transistors, Etc.	15.80	Computer Equipment	5.09
Computer Equipment	5.26	Computer Equipment	4.53	Office Equip. Parts.	7.56	Natural Rubber/Latex, Etc.	4.36
Telecomm Equipment	5.07	Telecomm Equipment	3.12	Heavy Petroleum Oils	7.55	Crustaceans, Mollusks	4.28
Articles of Apparel	4.60	Articles of Apparel	2.78	Telecomm Equipment	4.93	Office Equipment Parts	4.16
Fixed Veg Oils, Not Soft	3.93	Fixed Veg Oils, Not Soft	2.77	Special Transactions	2.48	Footwear	3.83
Petroleum/Crude Oil	3.92	Women/Girl Clothing	2.54	Electrical Equipment	2.09	Rice	3.46
Radio Broadcast Receiver	3.55	Electrical Distrib. Equip.	2.35	Electric Circuit Equipmt.	1.98	Preserved Fish/Shellfish	2.82
Sound/TV Recorders Etc.	2.78	Mens/Boys Wear, Woven	1.92	Radio Broadcast Receivers	1.53	Telecomm Equipment	2.72
Veneer/Plywood, Etc.	2.67	Fruit/Nuts, Fresh/Dried	1.70	Television Receivers	1.44	Plastic Articles NEC	2.18

Percentage of total exports.

and employment by industrial category to compute annual time-series estimates of the interindustry change in inequality of industrial earnings, dating back at least to 1970 for over seventy countries. Conceição and Galbraith (Chapter 15) explore the properties of this measure and argue that under general conditions it is likely to be a reasonable index of the change of inequality in manufacturing earnings as a whole.

Figure 9.3, again using France as the reference case, shows that the predicted intraregional conformity does indeed characterize Europe and also the rest of the OECD (e.g., North America and Japan). Compared to movements of inequality in the rest of the world, the rich countries resemble each other more than they do any others.

But such comovements of inequality do not characterize the Asian region at all. Figure 9.4, using Singapore once again as the reference case, illustrates. The Asian countries, by and large, present highly diverse patterns of change in wage structures; they do not resemble each other, on average, more than they resemble other countries elsewhere in the world. The pattern of Singapore itself is one of rigid wage structures and job upgrading leading to declining inequality. That of the Philippines is one of rising inequality following the political crises and liberalizations of the 1980s. Korea has a stormy history of rising and falling inequality whose industrial basis is explored in Galbraith and Kim (Chapter 13). And Indonesia and Malaysia experienced equalizations in the 1990s, which appear to have been due to rapid growth in employment in the construction and export sectors, but not equalization of wage rates.[1] Figure 9.4 illustrates the nonregional character of inequality movements in Asia (Figure 8.2 presented the underlying time series for the Asian countries.)

Without moving to sweeping inferences at this stage, we note that these measurements do point to a preliminary synopsis of the Asian development experience leading up to the crisis. First, it seems reasonable to infer that all the Asian countries experienced common factors of rapid external demand growth and rapidly growing foreign direct and portfolio investment. This was financial euphoria, founded on a shallow sense of geography that itself fueled an ongoing convergence of GDP growth rates. In this way, we can understand the continuation of rapid GDP growth as a whole through the mid-1990s, and also the common experience of real estate and commercial office building booms so evident in the major urban centers of the region at this time.

[1] As a rule, the Asian countries share Singapore's characteristic of resembling Japan (and the OECD) on this measure more than they resemble each other; there is thus a hub-and-spoke character to the evolution of inequality in the region.

Figure 9.3. Similarity of changes in industrial earnings inequality, 1972–1995, with France as the reference case.

193

Figure 9.4.   Similarity of changes in industrial earnings inequality, 1972–1995, with Singapore as the reference case. Note the lack of regional similarities in Asia.

Cluster Distance

- 66 - 71
- 72 - 76
- 77 - 84
- 86 - 90
- 91 - 98
- 107 - 137
- 140 - 151
- 153 - 169
- 172 - 185
- 187 - 272

7000   0   7000   14000   Miles

On the other hand, the dissimilarity of inequality movements suggests to us that this common pattern of export and investment growth masked fundamental dissimilarities of three kinds. First, there were dissimilarities in income level and manufacturing penetration, so that an export and building boom might have comprised a disproportionately larger share of economic activity in Bangkok or Djakarta than, say, in Singapore or Seoul. Asian development, even if it was fundamentally of one kind – state-directed and export-promoting – occurred in waves, and at any one moment, latecomers did not resemble the earlier cases even if they were following a similar track.

Second, the countries were not in fact evolving along similar lines. There were and are differences in industrial structure; for instance, no other Asian country has emulated Korea's emphasis on heavy industrialization, itself partly designed to meet that nation's unique security threat. For this reason, external shocks to, say, textile or food prices or prices in the semiconductor industry might have very different impacts on wages in the Phillippines than in, say, Malaysia.

This point is illustrated in Figure 9.5, which shows the evolution of a measure of diversity or specialization in industrial development over time. The measure is a Herfindahl index, a common measure of concentration, computed here as the sum of squared shares in industrial employment of each of twenty or so two-digit International Standard Industrial Classification (ISIC) categories. Because the ISIC categories are themselves designed to represent the industrial structures of the most advanced countries, a Herfindahl index built around these categorizations will be typically lower for diversified and richer countries and higher for those countries that are specialized, usually in lower-wage, primary-sector industries. And the index for any given country will decline as it diversifies or rise as it specializes in particular industrial sectors.

As Figure 9.5 reveals, the Asia region shows great diversity in this measure of industrial change. Certain countries – for instance, Korea and China as well as Indonesia and Hong Kong – show considerable declines in the measure, indicating rapid diversification of industrial structure. Others, notably Malaysia and Singapore, show strong movement in the opposite direction. Still others – the Philippines – show little evidence of change in this measure. Taiwan shows comparatively small movements, first in one direction and then in the other.

Third and finally, there is an almost complete lack of integration of industrial and construction labor markets, except perhaps for the partial interlinkage of Malaysia, Singapore, and Indonesia. For this reason, relative factor price equalization need not and in fact did not occur.

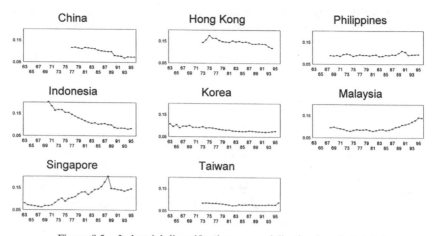

Figure 9.5.   Industrial diversification or specialization in selected Asian countries, as measured by the Herfindahl index, applied to ISICs.

The next question is, how, if at all, did the dissimilarity in industrial structure contribute to the crisis? The difficulty that differences in industrial structure pose for the development of financial instability concerns essentially asymmetries of information across small-country banking systems. If a German banker wishes to invest in the Netherlands, the similarity of industrial conditions, integration of labor markets, and other similarities in the underlying situation of the two countries lead to a high level of confidence that the banker can, in fact, judge the Dutch situation correctly. Moreover, if something does go wrong in the Netherlands, the German banker is very likely to survive simply because the exposure of a large-country bank in a much smaller country will rarely be sufficiently large in itself to threaten the large-country bank.

But if a Korean banker wishes to invest for the first time in Indonesia, he is likely to know from direct experience in Korea very little that is useful for judging the Indonesian scene. Any number of things can go wrong that will be, from the Korean point of view, unforeseen. External shocks, speculative attacks, differences in the growth rate of demand across industries, developments in the internal labor market, and consequent political events in Indonesia will all be essentially unpredictable on the basis of Korean experience. And if the Korean banker is operating on the misleading impression, conveyed by common high GDP growth, that Korea and Indonesia are working from a similar development playbook, then there is the risk that the Korean bank may become dangerously, even fatally, overexposed in the Indonesian market.

Something like this seems to have happened. And the lesson of over-investment across Asian banking systems suggests to us that financial integration across highly dissimilar developing countries without under-lying integration of the economies themselves is per se a dangerous proposition. Very large Western banks, backed by lenders of last resort, may well survive the carnage of a severe financial shock in much smaller places. But national banking systems like that of Korea that become exposed elsewhere in their own region as a result of financial dereg-ulation run the risk that they will become prime vectors for the transmission of financial shocks from far away back to their home country.

9.3   Effects of Financial Crises on Inequality

The next issue our data set enables us to examine is the relationship between financial shocks and industrial earnings inequality.

There is, of course, no reason in orthodox economics to expect any such relationship: Why should an external macroeconomic shock have distributional effects? But in practice, financial shocks resulting in capital flight and currency devaluations for developing countries do have such effects, along the lines of causality laid out by Yotopoulos (1996) in his important book on exchange rate parity and the development process. Low-wage workers suffer more than relatively high-wage workers, and inequality increases. In Chapter 12 we report month-to-month changes in earnings inequality for Mexico, and the three large devaluations of modern times stand out as precipitators of substantial increases in the inequality series.

We find that the effect of financial crisis on inequality is quite general. Using a data set of crises compiled by Kaminsky and Reinhart (1996), in which financial crisis is defined as a weighted average of exchange rate changes and reserve changes, we have identified thirty-four distinct financial crises in the countries and during the time period covered by our analysis. The mean increase in inequality in the two-year period immediately following such a crisis is 16.2 percent, compared with 3.2 percent in years during which crises did not occur. This difference is highly significant using both a t-test ($p < 0.007$) and a nonparametric Kolmogorov–Smirnov test ($p < 0.05$).

Interestingly, there appear to be substantial differences in the responsiveness of wage structures to crisis across countries. In Europe, inequality rose following crises only 46 percent of the time, and the rises are greatest in two fairly peripheral countries, Turkey and Iceland. Denmark, Finland, Norway, and Spain experienced a sequence of crises without increased inequality thereafter. In Latin America, at the other extreme, crises raised inequality 73.5 percent of the time; only Argentina reacted to crises with falling inequality. Asia, perhaps not surprisingly, is a middle case: Crises raised inequality there 62.5 percent of the time. Table 9.2 presents this evidence.

9.4   Conclusions

Comovement of GDP growth in Asia did not occur because of fundamental similarities in economic policy or in the stages of economic development across countries but rather in spite of very large differences. To judge from similarities in industrial structure or comovements of inequality, Europe and the OECD are much more integrated internally than is Asia. Asian comovement of GDP is thus perhaps best seen as a demand phenomenon affecting a hub-and-spoke system in which the low-income Asian economies grew first by supplying diverse products to high-income countries and later through real estate and office construction booms.

Second, once Asian countries liberalized their financial systems, financial crisis in Asia was a greater risk than in Latin America, and in both regions was a greater risk than in Europe or the OECD countries, because diversification of Asian financial institutions into other Asian markets opened them to systemic risks that they could not assess properly and against which they were not properly protected. Diverse economies can each fail in a variety of ways, yet when one fails, the financial cross-linkages can cause severe problems for, and ultimately capital flight from, all the others. We do not, of course, offer direct evidence here for this proposition, but we think it is broadly consistent with other known facts about the evolution of the Asian crisis.

Third, crises tend to raise inequality. But they raise it more in the most deregulated labor markets and less in more highly regulated ones. Thus, financial crises have had worse effects on Latin American workers than on Asians and worse effects on Asians than on the organized and politically powerful workers of the OECD. Whether this ordering will hold true when data from the latest round of crises come in remains to be seen. But we think it points to a fundamental fact about the advanced countries that proponents of structural adjustment plans for developing

Table 9.2. *Currency Crises and Changes in Income Inequality*

Latin America		Changes in Theil Indices (%)	Europe		Changes in Theil Indices (%)	Asia		Changes in Theil Indices (%)
Argentina	71–72	1.99	Denmark	70–71	2.93	Indonesia	78–79	(3.02)
	75–76	15.89		73–74	(0.03)		82–83	1.72
	80–81	11.24		79–80	(5.76)		86–87	2.12
	82–83	(13.49)	Finland	72–73	3.19	Malaysia	75–76	(0.81)
	86–87	18.90		82–83	3.85	Philippines	69–70	21.70
	88–89	22.40		91–92	(4.24)		83–84	(10.77)
	89–90	(15.49)		92–93	8.02		84–85	4.55
Bolivia	82–83	5.43	Norway	73–74	1.51		85–86	19.75
	83–84	112.42		77–78	(4.89)		Increase	62.50%
	84–85	35.24		85–86	(6.54)		Decrease	37.50%
Brazil	82–83	4.36	Spain	82–83	(2.60)			
	86–87	7.17		91–92	(2.31)			
	89–90	9.51		92–93	(16.06)			
	90–91	10.20	Sweden	77–78	(10.13)			
	91–92	(9.07)		81–82	4.67			
Chile	71–72	(34.23)		82–83	0.38			
	72–73	(5.36)		92–93	(3.37)			

Table 9.2. (cont.)

Latin America		Changes in Theil Indices (%)	Europe		Changes in Theil Indices (%)	Asia	Changes in Theil Indices (%)
	73–74	27.12	Turkey	70–71	22.02		
	74–75	4.82		79–80	(26.80)		
	75–76	36.82		93–94	(0.76)		
	82–83	38.33	Iceland	74–75	15.32		
	83–84	13.52		77–78	4.31		
Colombia	82–83	17.65		83–84	40.11		
	84–85	11.75		84–85	(6.27)		
Mexico	76–77	7.04		Increase	46%		
	81–82	10.25		Decrease	54%		
	82–83	(10.83)					
Peru	76–77	42.26					
	87–88	153.44					
Uruguay	71–72	(0.92)					
	82–83	(51.17)					
Venezuela	83–84	7.79					
	86–87	(0.24)					
	88–89	65.81					
	Increase	73.50%					
	Decrease	26.50%					

nations tend to overlook: namely, that it is the rich, advanced, and successful economies that have the best-paid workers, the most stable wage structures, and the strongest forms of insulation from economic shocks, including financial shocks.

We do not think this is entirely accidental.

CHAPTER 10

Inequality and State Violence:
A Short Report

James K. Galbraith and George Purcell

This chapter presents a brief review of the relationship between various forms of state violence–including war, revolution, civil violence, and coups d'état–and a measure of inequality of manufacturing earnings in countries around the world over the period 1960 to 1995. We find evidence of several systematic relationships, of which the strongest and most striking is that coups precede a long period of rising inequality with a very high probability.

10.1. Introduction

This chapter asks whether there exist systematic relationships between levels of state violence and changes in economic inequality in countries around the world. The question is, of course, quite natural. Entire lexicons exist that describe economic relationships in terms that evoke violence; exploitation, dependency, unequal exchange, and class struggle are but prominent examples. And the case histories of war, revolution, repression, and coups d'état are loaded with what seem – transparently – to be efforts either to rectify gross inequalities or to impose them.

Yet from the standpoint of an empiricist interested mainly in the search for patterns in data, substantial obstacles stand in the way of definite observations. First of all, there is the difficulty that reliable measures of *short-term change* in economic inequality, measures that are both consistent and consistently available, particularly in countries that have been wracked by violence, have not existed. Second, there is the problem of arriving at a consistent *categorization* of types of violence, so that one may define the predicted effect of each type on economic inequality and vice versa. Third, there is the problem of developing consistent and comparable *data* across countries and through time on levels and types of violence.

202

In what follows, we first describe the first problem and our efforts to solve it. We then tackle the latter two challenges, constructing a taxonomy of the major types of violence that have occurred from 1960 to 1996. We then offer a preliminary assessment of the relationship between economic inequality and one relatively standard type of violence, for which twenty-seven cases exist in our data set, namely, the coup d'état.

10.2. Measuring the Evolution of Inequality

Most recent comparative studies of economic inequality have been based on one of two data sources: the Luxembourg Income Studies (LIS) and the compilation of quintile income distributions and Gini coefficients by Deininger and Squire of the World Bank.

The Luxembourg data are not designed for historical work. Their emphasis is on acquiring detailed information on population characteristics at each time of survey. In most countries, only a few LIS observations exist, and those few papers that work with LIS data over time have been restricted to making comparisons between distributions observed at just two or three widely separated dates. The LIS studies also have so far emphasized the relatively rich, peaceful, and politically stable industrial world, so that this source is unlikely to contain much information on the relationship between economic inequality and state violence.

At first glance, the World Bank data set might seem more promising. It covers most of the countries of the world, and in many cases it spans long periods of time. But on closer examination, it, too, is virtually unusable for detailed analysis of historical episodes. Deininger and Squire find that only a very small number of available Gini coefficients are of acceptable quality; only a handful of countries have as many as half a dozen usable coefficients in thirty years (see Chapter 7). This lack of short-term coverage means that the effects of some particular episode – a revolution or a war, say, let alone a financial crisis or a devaluation – usually cannot be disentangled from the larger flows of history that pass between observations.

Our approach draws instead on the work of Galbraith and Lu (Chapter 8), supplemented by that of Galbraith and Garza Cantú (Chapter 11) and that of Conceição and Galbraith (Chapter 15), who have worked together to build a dense and consistent data set measuring annual *changes* in the dispersion of earnings across industrial categories in manufacturing sectors. The emphasis in these data is on changes rather than levels, on employee earnings rather than family incomes, and the analysis is restricted to the manufacturing sector. These limitations are more than outweighed by the fact that restricting ourselves in this way permits us to measure the movement of inequality almost every year, for countries comprising the overwhelming part of world product, and in many cases to register observations in times of war and revolution when the normal civilian activities of census and survey-taking are generally suspended, as well as for countries like Iran and Cuba, for which household surveys are in any event few and far between.

For the purposes of this chapter, we use a three-year rolling average of changes in inequality, which has the advantage of allowing us to interpolate over small gaps in the underlying data sets. In the case of Iran, for example, we can substitute a two-year average for the period 1978–1980, filling in the missing year of 1979 (when the revolution occurred). A three-year average also provides some flexibility in associating particular episodes of state violence, where the decisive event may not always be the one at a date given in the historical record, with movements of inequality in wage structures.

10.3. Characterizing and Categorizing State Violence

We have no firm theory to guide our efforts to categorize the types of state violence to which people and nations are periodically subjected. Some are fairly clear-cut. Conventional scholarly definitions exist for war, which is generally defined as a protracted conflict between regular military forces across national frontiers (Singer and Small, 1968). Some fuzziness emerges only in rather arbitrary measures of intensity, most particularly Singer and Small's requirement that for a conflict to be declared a war requires over 1,000 battle deaths.

The idea of revolution means the complete overthrow of a ruling elite (Dogan and Higley, 1998). Some events typically called revolutions, such as the dissolution of the Soviet Union in 1990, do not qualify because the actual change in leadership was quite small. Revolutions are rare; only four examples occur during the time covered by our data set: Portugal in 1974, Nicaragua and Iran in 1979, and (more controversially) Zimbabwe in 1980. Levels of violence differed in each of these cases; Portugal's revolution was nonviolent, while that of Zimbabwe ended in a negotiated solution. The revolution in Nicaragua was won by force of arms and that in Iran by a violent popular uprising. All four revolutions enjoyed wide popular support at the beginning, and all embodied a drive for social reform.

Coups d'état are somewhat harder to keep track of, particularly in countries where military regimes are endemic. Coups do not result in a complete turnover of the elites; typically, one small group or faction displaces another. And coups are not revolutionary in the social sense: They do not mobilize the population or bring on waves of social change. We define a coup d'état as the takeover of state power by organized elements of a state's own military forces, often, though not always, accompanied by violence, and generally with an intent to bypass or dismantle existing constitutional forms. We do not distinguish between left- and right-wing coups; overwhelmingly, coups in modern times are right-wing in character. We have identified twenty-seven such episodes in the countries for which we have inequality measures.

Other forms of state violence include insurgencies, civil war, martial law, dirty war, proxy wars, state terrorism, and conditions of endemic and continuing violence such as those in the Middle East. South Africa, Israel, Turkey, Colombia, and many other countries are examples. We leave these for later investigation, mainly because they vary greatly in scale and intensity from case to case. Also, it is unclear whether these cases will necessarily intersect strongly with the manufacturing sectors of the countries in question. In big countries, civil violence may often be a phenomenon of the hinterlands and may be isolated from the experience of the cities; the 1995 uprising in Chiapas, Mexico, is a useful example.

10.4. Examples of Revolution, War, and Civil Violence

Revolutions are fought to rectify injustice. As the experience of France in 1789 established, they often prevail against regimes that are trying to save themselves by reducing injustice but that cannot manage to do so quickly enough. Or so a history sympathetic to the *ancien regime* often maintains.

The experiences of our four clearly identified revolutions are shown in Figure 10.1. In each case, the revolution accomplished, to some degree, what it promised to accomplish. In each case, we observe a reduction of inequalities in pay, beginning during or just before the revolution and accelerating sharply as it took hold.

The revolution in Iran shaded quickly into war with Iraq, while that in Nicaragua came under the intense pressure of the *contra* war. But the two experiences in the war following the revolution were evidently quite different. Nicaragua quickly reversed its revolutionary inequality reductions. In Iran, in contrast, inequality remained at revolutionary levels for a decade, rising only with the partial liberalization of the early 1990s. Difference in the two cases that might account for this – differences in wealth, the internal and external balance of power, and ideology – are not far to seek.

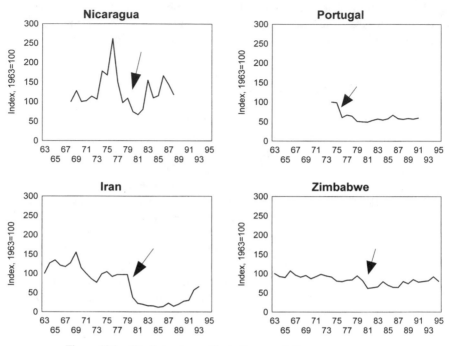

Figure 10.1.   Declining inequality in four revolutions

Figure 10.2 presents the contrast between Iran and Iraq. Both countries export oil and so were immeasurably enriched by the first oil crisis in 1973. A critical difference between them, however, was that in Iraq inequality declined sharply following the oil boom: Incomes of low-paid Iraqis rose more rapidly than those at the top of the scale. In Iran, this did not happen until 1979. Interestingly, the proportionate reduction in inequality in Iran following the revolution was only moderately greater than in Iraq after 1973, though much more sudden and violent. In the 1980s, both countries experienced prolonged mobilization that kept inequality low; inequality increased once hostilities ended (in 1988). Both countries experienced rapidly rising inequality in the 1990s; as the graph shows, Iraq's experience after the Gulf War was traumatic.

War is often the end game for military governments. Two examples from our data set are given in Figure 10.3: Greece at the end of the colonels' government in 1974 and Argentina following the Falklands/Malvinas debacle of 1982. In both cases, military governments collapsed and were replaced by classically liberal, politically conservative regimes, that of Constantine Karamanlis in Greece and that of Raul

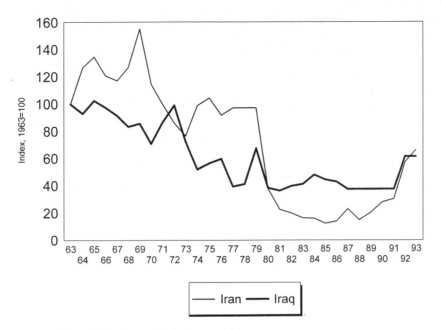

Figure 10.2. Inequality in Iran and Iraq.

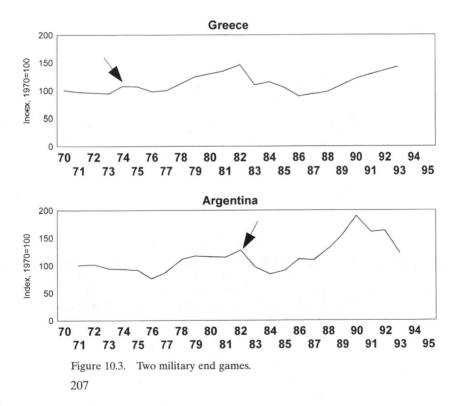

Figure 10.3. Two military end games.

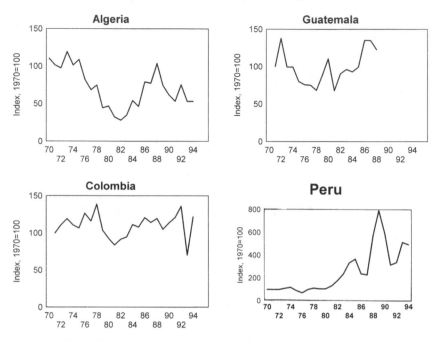

Figure 10.4.   Inequality in four countries with prolonged civil violence.

Alfonsín in Argentina. In both of these cases, inequality rose under the successor government until it was replaced by a regime substantially to its left. This happened in Greece with the return of the Socialist Andreas Papandreou in 1980 and in Argentina with the election of the Peronist Carlos Menem in 1986.[1]

Civil violence is harder to quantify. In Figure 10.4, we present a series of four countries where levels of violence were endemically high during recent years: Peru, Algeria, Guatemala, and Colombia. It may be that the difference in the inequality records of the first two cases and the second two can be explained by the nature of the civil violence each experienced. That of Peru and Algeria reached the cities; that of Guatemala and Colombia generally did not. But a deeper analysis will have to await a substantially more detailed historical treatment of events in these countries; unfortunately, the shadowy character of much civil violence also makes it difficult to track effectively in the historical record.

[1] We leave additional analysis of other cases, including the India–Pakistan war of 1971, for a later date.

10.5.   An Analysis of Coups d'État

Coups d'état, on the other hand, tend to be discrete historical events with
specific characteristics and identifiable dates. Table 10.1 lists our twenty-
seven cases. Figure 10.5 shows the canonical case of Chile, where inequality declined sharply throughout the 1960s and up to 1973, when the
military took power in a bloody uprising that suppressed democracy for
seventeen years. Inequality, as measured in our data, rose promptly and
continuously, accelerating sharply with the financial crisis of 1982.

Is this a general pattern? Figure 10.6 presents the average percentage
change in our inequality measures over the twenty-seven coups for each
year from five years before the coup until five years afterward. The figure
shows, we think, quite a striking result. Coups typically follow the emergence of a government or policy environment that results in a sharp
reduction in inequality. In the five years following the coup, inequality
rises. This is the mechanism of violent repression.

We caution that the standard deviations around each of the yearly
averages in Figure 10.6 are high. Figure 10.7, therefore, gives corrobo-
rating evidence in the form of a count of cases. Each bar measures the
excess of positive changes over negative changes during the year relative to the coup year in question. Again, the pattern is striking: there

Table 10.1. *Coups d'Etat*

Country	Year
Bangladesh	1975
India	1975
Iraq	1968
Turkey	1980
Nigeria	1966, 1975, 1984, 1985
Argentina	1976
Chile	1973
Peru	1975, 1992
Uruguay	1973
Bolivia	1971, 1978, 1979, 1980
Ghana	1966, 1972, 1979, 1981
Pakistan	1977
Algeria	1992
Madagascar	1975
Guatemala	1982
Ecuador	1968, 1972

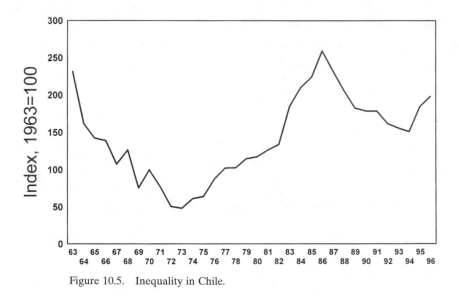

Figure 10.5.   Inequality in Chile.

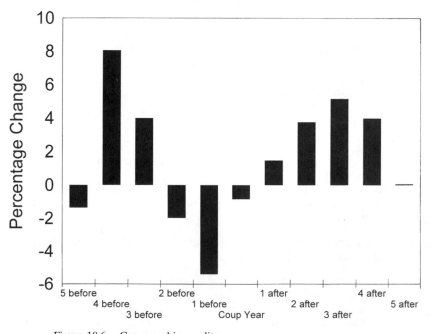

Figure 10.6.   Coups and inequality.

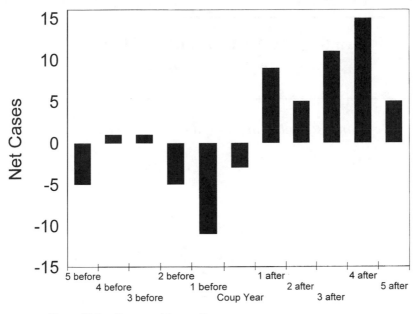

Figure 10.7.   Coups and inequality.

is a preponderance of inequality reduction before a coup d'état and a preponderance of inequality increases afterward.

10.6   Conclusion

We believe we have shown a promising connection between two phenomena that intuitively and theoretically should be considered connected: inequality and state violence. We have also shown that it is possible, in principle, to measure the movement of inequality across a wide variety of national settings in ways that do appear to be sensitive to social and economic developments, of which state violence is, of course, only one extreme manifestation. Some reasonable generalizations can be drawn. Generally speaking, inequality rises during civil violence and following coups d'état. It falls during revolutions. And the effect of wars on inequality appears to vary in individual cases; protracted wars such as that between Iran and Iraq require mobilization of the population, which in turn requires significant leveling of the wage and income structures. Other, smaller and shorter wars need not have this effect; typically, the short wars that spell doom for ineffective military governments have been followed by rising inequality.

CHAPTER 11

Grading the Performance of Latin American Regimes, 1970–1995

James K. Galbraith and Vidal Garza Cantú

For most of Latin America, the 1970s were a decade of growth, though with political upheaval in Argentina and Chile. The 1980s were a disaster. The 1990s saw economic reform, liberalization, a return to democracy, and financial turmoil. This chapter reviews the three decades as one piece through an analysis of the evolution of earnings inequality from year to year in eight major Latin American countries and one Caribbean nation. We find that changes in earnings inequality are a sensitive indicator of slump, repression, political turmoil, civil war, natural disaster, and – on the positive side – occasional periods of growth and stability in Latin America. Indeed, almost the whole recent history of Latin America can be summarized in the movement of industrial inequality statistics.

11.1   Introduction

This chapter focuses on the relationship between industrial earnings inequality and the political history of Latin America. First, we offer a word on the data and the method used to construct a measure of the movement of industrial earnings inequality for each of the countries under study. Second, we investigate the relationship between political regimes and changes in earnings inequality for each of the countries, including orthodox and heterodox stabilizations and the transition from closed to open trading systems. Third, we examine the relationship between economic growth and our measurement of inequality and present the report card for each of the regimes of the countries studied. Conclusions stressing policy implications complete the chapter.

11.2   Data and Methods

The United Nations Economic Commission for Latin American and the Caribbean (ECLAC/CEPAL) maintains a detailed industrial data set on the major Latin American economies, including total payrolls and employment for twenty-eight industrial sectors for each year from 1970 to 1995. Wages in each case are expressed in constant 1985 U.S. dollars. The countries included are Argentina, Brazil, Chile, Colombia, Jamaica, Mexico, Peru, and Uruguay, along with incomplete data for Costa Rica that we did not use. In addition, we have data for Venezuela from a separate data source, the Industrial Statistics database of the United Nations International Development Organization (UNIDO). Together, the countries represented include 394 million people (85 percent of the region's population) and 91.2 percent of the region's total GDP between 1970 and 1994.

Our measurement of the change in earnings inequality within each country is the change in the between-group component of the groupwise decomposition of the Theil statistic, or T' (Theil, 1972). Typically, this is based on a decomposition of average earnings per employee into ECLAC's twenty-eight industrial groupings.[1] Because these groups cover almost all manufacturing employment, the movement of this statistic through time generally reflects the changing dispersion of earnings in the manufacturing population taken as a whole (Chapters 2 and 16 provide technical details). In this way, computations of T' usefully augment traditional sources of information about earnings inequality, particularly those generated by the common theoretical base of household expenditures surveys to produce time-specific Gini coefficients.[2]

11.3 Political Regimes and the Evolution of Earnings Inequality in Latin America

In this section, we review the political regimes in each country and the major political and policy turning points, in conjunction with changes in the dispersion of industrial earnings. Figure 11.1 shows the movement of inequality, as measured by our data set, and the dates of each change of government in the nine countries.

Argentina

Argentina is characterized by large increases in inequality during the past twenty-five years, alternating with modest reductions under

---

[1] Some exceptions should be noted. The case of Uruguay represents twenty-seven industries (excluding industry ISIC 372); that of Jamaica represents twenty-six industries (excluding industries ISIC 372 and 385); and that of Peru represents twenty-six industries (not including ISIC 354 and 372).

[2] Deininger and Squire's data set of Gini and quintile measures of inequality do not reveal any systematic pattern of change in inequality for Latin America.

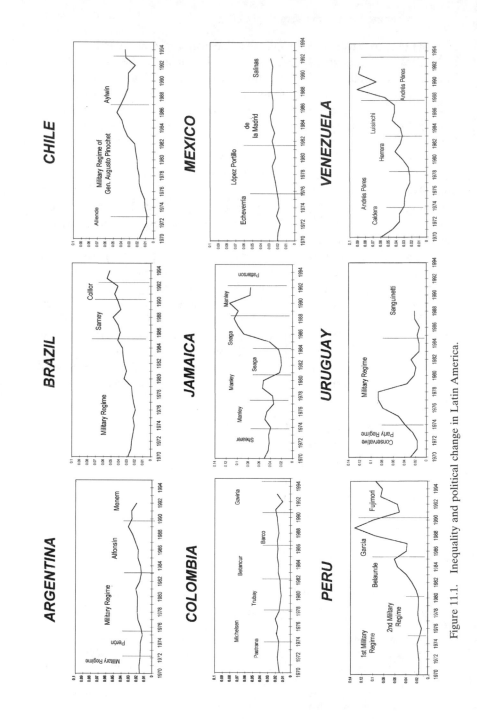

Figure 11.1.   Inequality and political change in Latin America.

214

Peronism. Inequality declined during the Peronist government of the early 1970s, grew sharply during the military government that followed the overthrow of Isabel Peron in 1976, and then fell during the period of renewed opposition to the military in the early 1980s, leading up to the Falklands war, which produced the collapse of military rule in 1983. After a brief respite, however, inequality surged during the first civil government of President Raúl Alfonsín – a development evidently associated with the economic crisis that ended the Alfonsín government in 1989. President Carlos Menem was able to reduce the trend of inequality after 1989, but earnings inequality in Argentina remains high by its own historical standards.

Brazil

Brazil presents a second example of military–civilian transition during the 1980s. In Brazil's case, the military regime that began in 1964 produced a period of high economic growth. In 1971, General Medici presented the First National Development Plan, aimed at achieving 8 to 10 percent annual economic growth and development of the northeast and the Amazon area, especially by means of road construction and redistribution of land. These expansionary policies were associated with decreasing inequality from 1970 to 1976, according to our measurement. At the end of 1976, the international oil crisis hit this oil-importing nation quite hard; inequality began to rise. The collapse of lending to Brazil deepened the inequality crisis in 1982. A devaluation of 30 percent was necessary in 1983. Brazil began to enjoy strong economic growth again in 1984 and 1985, but at the price of triple-digit inflation in 1984.

In an indirect election in January 1985, the electoral college selected Tancredo de Almeida Neves for president and Jose Sarney for vice president, but President-Elect Neves died from the effects of an illness before he could assume office. In March 1985, Vice President Sarney was inaugurated as Brazil's first civilian president since 1964. After Sarney took office, economic expansion and inequality reduction took place, but only briefly; crisis returned with a severe increase in inequality in 1987–1988. During 1989, the government suspended debt payments and began spending as new elections were coming; an improvement in inequality occurred that year.

On March 15, 1990, after winning the elections of December 1989, Fernando Collor de Mello was inaugurated. But Collor's economic plans quickly failed, and as the economy declined, inequality rose. Evidence of corruption was traced to the highest levels of government, and in September 1992, the Brazilian Congress voted to begin impeachment proceedings against Collor. Minutes after the Senate opened the impeachment trial on December 29, 1992, Collor resigned and Vice President Itamar Franco assumed the presidency. President Franco was a weak political figure, and so was his administration. Economic growth and industrial production continued to decline, inflation rose, and income inequality worsened during 1993. While the ECLAC data set conveys some of the flavor of these developments, monthly measures reported in the next chapter capture them more vividly.

Chile

Inequality in Chile shows a reduction during the Allende years, a constant increase in inequality during the Pinochet regime with a big spike from 1982 to 1986, and some improvement thereafter. Inequality declined somewhat under the civilian regime of Patricio Aylwin, but as in Argentina and Brazil, civilian governments were unable to restore the social situation of the premilitary period even if they were inclined to do so.

Between 1970 and 1972, inequality declined in Chile. It was a time of rapid growth, rising minimum wages, and greatly increasing real wages, especially for the poor. However, the resistance to these policies and their international unsustainability produced a backlash that led to the savage coup of September 1973. Under the military government of Augusto Pinochet, Chile embarked on radical free market policies combined with the elimination of minimum wages and the harsh repression of organized labor. Not surprisingly, inequality increased. The slump of 1982 and the following years made the situation seriously worse. It was only in 1985 or 1986, following partial stabilization of the international situation, that inequality in Chile appeared to begin to recover slightly. Inequality, however, remained high as Pinochet ceded power to the Christian Democrats in 1990. As in Argentina, the transition to civilian rule brought with it a reduction in inequality, but only briefly, and never came close to restoring the egalitarian earnings structures of the period before the military coup.

Colombia

Our measure of inequality for Colombia reveals the most stable behavior of wage dispersion in our sample. This is perhaps not surprising: Colombia has pursued stable and successful policies almost continuously throughout this period and has enjoyed comparative political stability as well despite its ongoing civil war. Colombia is the only Latin

American country that has repeatedly showed positive real gross domestic product (GDP) growth during the entire period of this study. Doubtless, the fact that Colombia relies almost entirely on primary-sector products for export earnings has also helped maintain relative equality of industrial earnings; the industrial sector is small, and there has never been a question of export-led industrialization in Colombia.

Jamaica

The data allow us to compute an inequality measurement for only one Caribbean country, Jamaica. During the 1970s, inequality remained relatively stable in this small island state, despite the transition to a progressive government under Michael Manley early in the decade. The 1980s were characterized first by a sharp decrease in inequality during the first term of Prime Minister Edward Seaga and then by a rebound of inequality in his second term from 1984 to 1988. As Manley returned to power in 1989, an unstable economy delayed the decline in inequality until 1991.

After a campaign marked by considerable violence, Jamaica's first general election since independence was held on February 21, 1967. The Jamaica Labour Party (JLP) won, and Hugh Lawson Shearer was elected prime minister when his chosen predecessor died shortly after the election. Shearer's main policy was to continue the fast pace of economic growth pushed by the export of natural resources. Our measure captures a small decrease in wage inequality between 1970 and 1972. In the election of carly 1972, the People's National Party (PNP) obtained its first major victory, and Michael Manley was sworn in as prime minister. Manley based his winning campaign on the "politics of participation," and once in office he embarked on a number of social reforms. Censorship was eliminated, and many restrictions on civil liberties were lifted. The new government pursued a program, largely successful, to wipe out illiteracy. But although Manley's regime had promising beginnings, economic problems undermined most of his social programs. Our measurement tracks a drop in inequality for Manley's first year of government in 1973 and 1974.

But then inequality rose in 1975, with a slight recovery in 1976 as elections came close. During the crucial elections of 1976, there was virtual political warfare between the PNP and the opposition JLP. Manley's PNP won overwhelmingly. In 1977, the government assumed majority ownership of the bauxite mines, which had been foreign-owned. Inequality declined in 1977. However, the economy did not recover, and a rise in violence led to Manley's defeat in the 1980 election. The new prime minister, Edward Seaga of the JLP, had to contend with the widespread destruction of Hurricane Allen as one of his first acts in office. The economy performed well at first, and its recovery translated into a sharp reduction in inequality in 1981 and 1982. In 1984, the electorate returned Seaga for another four years.

Despite success in the political arena, problems for Seaga began to mount soon after he was elected for a second term. In 1985, they became unmanageable, and strong measures were taken to reduce and rationalize government expenditures. As the economy worsened, a dramatic increase in inequality of the wage structure occurred. Despite some economic recovery in 1987 and 1988, the electorate unseated Seaga in February 1989 and restored Manley. Manley was succeeded by Percival Patterson in 1992.

Mexico

For Mexico, the 1970s were a decade of macroeconomic adjustment. President Luis Echeverria took office in a crisis of legitimacy in 1970 following the 1968 protests and the Tlatelolco massacre; the bitter flavor of that episode had pressured the government to incorporate minority and also, to some extent, radical opposition groups in government. This explains the selection of populist policies during Echeverria's regime. Among these policies were substantial increases in minimum wages and the pegging of the exchange rate to the U.S. dollar. Mexico continued to grow in this period, and inequality fell. But difficulties in the balance of payments inevitably forced a retrenchment, which came during the first three years of the administration of President José López Portillo. Inequality increased during this time. But with the rise in oil prices and the discovery of huge new oil reserves, Mexico abandoned austerity and was able to expand greatly. This growth produced a slight decrease in inequality in 1980.

However, growth collapsed in 1982. President Miguel de la Madrid introduced a harsh stabilization program; inequality rose again, through 1985 according to the data in Figure 11.1, and particularly sharply when Mexico reduced its tariffs and signed the General Agreement on Tariffs and Trade (GATT) in 1986. Late in 1987, an orthodox-heterodox economic program was announced, the Pacto de Solidaridad Económica. This program helped stabilize prices, and inflation fell in that year and the next. Carlos Salinas de Gortari took office, late 1988 and continued the Pacto vigorously. He was able to make a debt service arrangement in 1989, bringing confidence to the economy, which grew steadily between 1989 and 1994. Unchanging inequality, but at historically high levels, is the pattern for the Salinas years. As in the case of Brazil, readers are advised to look also at the monthly measures reported in Chapter 12.[3]

Peru

Peru illustrates the extreme case of how economic and political upheaval can raise inequality in the wage structure. Peru displayed a stable trend in inequality during the two military regimes in the 1970s. In 1981, after President Fernando Belaunde Terry returned the government to civilian rule, inequality began a meteoric rise, which continued until President Alan Garcia briefly but unsuccessfully tried to force it back down. There followed an economic and political explosion, leading to Alberto Fujimori's administration, under which inequality, after first declining somewhat, once again began to increase.

Unique in Latin America, Peru was ruled by left-wing military governments from 1968 to 1980; during this time, the wage structure remained quite stable. Civil elections held in May 1980 returned Fernando Belaunde Terry to the presidency; he embarked on a major liberalization. The economy deteriorated quickly, mainly because of the following: (a) an increase in imports due to Belaunde's free-market policies, (b) lower world prices for Peru's major export commodities, (c) high international interest rates on the nation's growing foreign debt, (d) a devastating El Niño weather phenomenon in 1982–1983 that severely affected fishing and agriculture, and (e) the rise of the guerrilla movement of the neo-Maoist Shining Path (Sendero Luminoso) and the Tupac Amaru Revolutionary Movement. Prices rose a staggering 3,240 percent between July 1980 and June 1985. Our measurement for inequality maps very clearly the overall economic behavior of Peru during the first half of the 1980s: a consistent and sharp increase in inequality.

In 1985, a young and charismatic opposition candidate, Alan Garcia Perez, was elected president. Populism came into power with him. Garcia's main policy was an expansion of aggregate demand. To combat inflation he launched a stabilization program, the Inti Plan, changed the currency to the inti from the devalued sol, and introduced a multiple exchange rate with nine different rates while tightening control of financial intermediaries. Our measurement of inequality shows a sharp decrease for 1986 and a small reduction in the next year. In 1987, the

---

[3] In this chapter, Calmon et al. use another data set covering the period 1968–1998. They show that Mexican inequality rose sharply in 1995 as the peso collapsed once again.

president announced two striking plans: that Peru would pay no more than 10 percent of its export earnings toward a nearly $14 billion foreign debt and a law to nationalize commercial banks, completing public control of the financial system. As economic activities contracted and GDP fell dramatically in 1988, the Inti Plan failed to control inflation. Confidence in the president collapsed. A huge increase in inequality came in 1989 and 1990.

Alberto Fujimori was elected president in 1990. He began a difficult set of policies to regain domestic and international confidence, the most salient being the start of strong liberalization policies. Exports began to recover by the end of 1990, led by the primary sector. Oil exports grew as Petroperu, the national oil company, was partially concessioned to private investors. Increased direct foreign investment was achieved during 1991, and private investment and private consumption expanded as the economy recovered and GDP grew in 1991. Our measurement for inequality shows a reduction in 1991 and stabilization in 1992, though at very high levels. Economic recovery followed: In 1994, Peru registered the highest GDP growth of all Latin America, 12.7 percent, mostly fueled by the expansion of exports and private investment. We observe an increase in inequality for 1993 followed by a slight reduction in 1994, echoing the behavior of GDP growth.

Uruguay

With a new constitution in 1966 and a conservative civilian government until 1973, Uruguay was unable to control inflation and production fell. This pattern intensified as the urban guerrilla group called the Tupamaros began a violent attempt to bring about a socialist revolution. The government was unable to control the urban uprising and allowed the military to take over. The military defeated the Tupamaros but then took over the government in 1973, acting with extreme force against civilian opponents. In the economic arena, the effects were felt as censorship, suspension of civil political activity, and dissolution of unions were designed not only to control the people but also to force a new economic outlook on them. Our measurement of wage inequality shows a decrease in 1971 and 1972 but then a spectacular increase after the military seized control from 1973 to 1976. Also from 1973 to 1977, interests rates were held high, and both domestic and external debt soared. In 1978, policies changed: Emphasis was placed on lowering inflation, and a mandatory system of wage indexation was introduced. This was successful in bringing inequality down. Positive economic growth was achieved in 1980 and 1981, and inequality continued to fall at this time.

Julio Maria Sanguinetti, a conservative, was elected president in 1984. His great achievement was the reestablishment of full democracy and human and civil rights. In the economic arena, he continued to implement the adjustment program, increasing taxes to strengthen public finances and social security. In 1986, the effects of the adjustment plan were felt; lowered inflation and an external balance equilibrium helped increase the economic output of Uruguay. This relative success of economic policies translated into a slight decrease in inequality for 1986. In 1987, Uruguay reduced trade tariffs to a historic low. The effect on inequality was perceived as an increase in the trend in 1987 and a slight rise in 1988. In November 1989, Sanguinetti's party lost the election against the liberals, and Luis Alberto Lacalle became president in 1990.

Venezuela

Following the patterns of oil-exporting countries, Venezuela experienced a decreasing trend in inequality during the 1970s. Increasing inequality followed as international recession and debt crises occurred and as Venezuela's stabilization plans failed.

As Venezuela's oil and iron ore industries began to boom in the early 1970s, economic expansion began and continued throughout the decade. President Rafael Caldera of the Christian Democratic Party was elected in 1968. In the early 1970s, Venezuela took majority ownership of foreign banks, nationalized the natural gas industry, and declared a moratorium on the granting of oil concessions. This pseudonationalism transferred the benefits of growth to the working classes, and earnings inequality decreased sharply during the years of the Caldera government. In 1973, Carlos Andres Perez Rodriguez was elected. He represented a continuation of Caldera's policies, although he did not come from the same political party. Andres Perez promptly moved to nationalize the iron ore industry in 1975 and the entire petroleum industry in 1976.

In the three years after 1973, the price of oil quadrupled and Venezuela benefited greatly; oil industries represented almost 90 percent of the export goods for this country. Inequality declined vigorously throughout the Perez regime. Luis Herrera Campins was elected president in 1978. During the 1980s, however, economic growth stopped, a steady increase in inflation began, and exports declined. Unemployment became a major concern. The effect on inequality is clear: Our measure increased sharply in 1980–1981. Then, as newly elected President Jaime Lusinchi took office in 1984, he adopted strong austerity measures to slow capital flight and encourage lenders to reschedule foreign debt; the latter was accomplished in 1985. Inequality was relatively stable in 1986 and 1987, but as the economy tumbled in 1988 following the oil bust of the mid-1980s, inequality soared. The electorate returned former President Carlos Andres Perez to office in the December 1988 elections. But the second Perez administration could not replicate the inequality reductions of the first.

11.4   Grading the Performance of the Latin American Regimes

Figure 11.2 shows our measure of inequality along with the level of real GDP (in constant U.S. 1985 dollars) for each country in Latin America. The shaded areas represent time spans when inequality increases and GDP growth declines. It seems clear, above all, that slumps in Latin America increase inequality in wage and earnings distributions. Periods of very strong growth reduce inequality, generally speaking, and periods of weak but positive growth have ambiguous effects. In other work based on monthly data (see Chapter 12), we found a close association between the movement of per capita GDP growth and industrial earnings inequality for Brazil and Mexico. The present findings, while based on less precise annual measurements, are fully consistent with this picture.

Table 11.1 presents correlation coefficients relating the percentage change in inequality to the growth rate of real GDP per capita for each country through time from 1971 to 1995. The correlations are invariably negative, and though in certain cases they are weak, in others, notably Argentina, Colombia, and Peru, they are quite strong. Taken together, they tend to support the hypothesis of a Kuznets relationship between GDP level and inequality in Latin America in the short run: strong progress toward higher GDP reduces inequality and vice versa (see Chapter 7). These correlations are consistent with the intuition that when GDP growth exceeds population growth, inequality declines, and conversely. However, a full analysis of the economic determinants of changing inequality for Latin America lies well beyond the scope of this chapter.

Yet we believe it is useful to attempt a general evaluation of the performance of Latin American governments during the quarter century for which we have data. Our motivation in this instance is not econometric; we have only our own perceptions of history and our reading of the graphical relationship among inequality, growth, and regime change with which to justify the exercise. Still, we believe that fair-minded and knowledgeable observers of Latin American history will agree: There is a striking tendency for inequality to rise during orthodox and liberalizing governments, particularly military regimes, and for inequality to

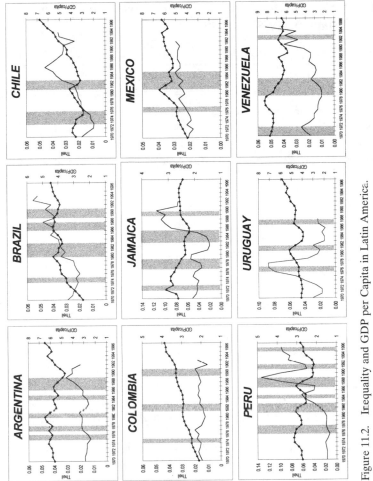

Figure 11.2. Irequality and GDP per Capita in Latin America.

Note: Primary Y-axis shows the Theil statistic. Secondary Y-axis shows real GDP per capita in 1985 U.S. dollars (darker line). Shadow areas indicate periods of declining real GDP per capita.

Source: Author's calculations from data supplied by ECLAC and UNIDO; GDP per capita is from the World Bank.

Table 11.1. *Correlation Between Real Economic Growth Rate and Changes in Inequality in Latin America, 1971–1995*

Argentina	Brazil	Chile	Colombia	Jamaica	Mexico	Peru	Uruguay	Venezuela
-0.26	-0.23	-0.08	-0.16	-0.08	-0.16	-0.44	0.08	-0.42

Source: Author's calculations, real GDP data as reported by the Inter-American Development Bank.

decline, at least briefly, under populist, protectionist, and heterodox regimes.

On the assumption that economic growth and increasing equity are both socially desirable goals, interesting questions can be posed: Which governments during this tumultuous period best achieved both goals in tandem? Which government performed worst on both criteria? And are there governments that succeeded in producing growth without equity or equity without growth?

We used the data reported in Figure 11.1 to provide an answer in the following highly simplified way. For each year in which GDP growth is positive and inequality falls, we assigned a positive point. For each year in which inequality rose and GDP fell, we assigned a negative point. Growth with rising inequality and recession with declining inequality were each assigned a score of 0. Then we divided the sum of the points obtained by the number of years each regime was in power. This produces an index that can vary from −1 to 1. Table 11.2 summarizes the grades of each of the Latin American regimes from 1970 to 1995.

Overall, populist regimes come off well in the scaling we offer here. High scores go to Echeverria in Mexico, the Peronists in Argentina, Andres Peres in Venezuela, the early military regimes in Peru, and Allende in Chile. Right-wing military regimes and liberalizing democrats, such as Alfonsín in Argentina and Belaunde Terry in Peru, do badly. High scores for several other postmilitary regimes, such as those of Aylwin in Chile and Menem in Argentina, reflect very high starting levels of inequality and do not produce a return to the differentials of the premilitary era. And on the whole, it seems clear to us that the recent performance of Latin American regimes has been substantially and systematically worse than it was in the earlier years of our period.

Obviously, this analysis is severely limited in important respects. We do not allow for the vagaries of external events over which Latin

Table 11.2. *Grade Report on the Latin American Regimes*

Country	Period	Regime or Government	Grade
Argentina	1970–1973	Military Regime (General Levingston)	0.00
	1973–1974	President Juan Domingo Peron and	0.67
	1974–1976	President Maria Estela Mtz de Peron	
	1976–1983	Military Regime (Generals Videla, Viola, and Galtieri)	0.00
	1984–1989	President Raúl Alfonsín	–0.33
	1990–1995	President Carlos Saúl Menem	0.67
Brazil	1964–1985	Military Regime	0.27
	1986–1990	President José Sarney	0.00
	1991–1992	President Fernando Collor de Mello	0.00
	1993–1995	President Itamar Franco	0.50
Chile	1971–1973	President Salvador Allende	0.33
	1974–1989	Military Government under General Augusto Pinochet	0.00
	1990–1994	President Patricio Aylwin	0.60
Colombia	1971–1974	President Misael Pastrana	0.50
	1975–1978	President Alfonso Michelsen	0.50
	1979–1982	President Julio Cesar Trubay Ayala	0.50
	1983–1986	President Belisario Betancur	0.50
	1987–1990	President Virgilio Barco	0.25
	1991–1994	President Cesar Gaviria	0.33
Jamaica	1969–1972	Prime Minister Hugh L. Shearer	1.00
	1973–1976	Prime Minister Michael Manley	–0.50
	1977–1980	Prime Minister Michael Manley	0.00
	1981–1984	Prime Minister Edward Seaga	0.25
	1985–1988	Prime Minister Edward Seaga	–0.25
	1989–1992	Prime Minister Michael Manley	0.75
Mexico	1971–1976	President Luis Echeverria	0.50
	1977–1982	President José López Portillo	–0.17
	1983–1988	President Miguel de la Madrid H.	0.17
	1989–1994	President Carlos Salinas de Gortari	0.75
Peru	1968–1975	1st Military Regime	0.40
	1976–1980	2nd Military Regime	0.20
	1981–1985	President Fernando Belaunde Terry	–0.20
	1986–1990	President Alan Garcia	0.00
	1991–1995	President Alberto Fujimori	0.20
	1996	President Alberto Fujimori	0.00
Uruguay	1968–1973	Conservative Party	0.00
	1974–1984	Military Regime	0.09
	1985–1990	President Julio Maria Sanguinetti	0.17
Venezuela	1969–1973	President Rafael Caldera	0.33
	1974–1978	President Carlos Andres Perez	0.80
	1979–1983	President Luis Herrera Campins	–0.40
	1984–1988	President Jaime Lusinchi	0.40
	1989–1993	President Carlos Andres Perez	0.20
	1994–1995	President Rafael Caldera	0.00

Note: Regimes with dates falling outside the range of this study are weighted solely on the basis of available data.

governments had no control, such as the oil shocks. And we do not address the intertemporal sustainability of regimes of different kinds, a critical question. Obviously, some populist policies were reversed because of untenable declines in the external account (Echeverria in Mexico) or a failure to cope with wage pressures leading to inflation (Garcia in Peru). In other cases, internal and external resistance led to the violent termination of populist experiments, notably that of Allende in Chile. It would be foolhardy to cite the evidence offered here in support of the case that certain policies "work" while others "fail."

Nevertheless, we believe that a broader lesson does emerge, in a tentative way, from this evidence and analysis. It is that for much of the period under examination the political coloration of the government did affect the short-run performance of the economy. Populist governments set out to achieve reductions in inequality and achieved them, while military governments with the opposite objectives also achieved their goals. Policies did matter. This conclusion is perhaps likely to be surprising only to economists, and only those of a certain stripe. And it may not continue to hold in the Latin America of today, characterized by very open economies and weak democracies with few of the economic powers of twenty years ago. But we believe it is a useful reminder of how things once were in the not-so-distant past.

CHAPTER 12

The Evolution of Industrial Earnings
Inequality in Mexico and Brazil

Paulo Du Pin Calmon, Pedro Conceição,
James K. Galbraith, Vidal Garza Cantú, and
Abel Hibert Sanchez

In this chapter, we use industrial data to derive estimates of the pattern of change
in wage inequality in Mexico and Brazil. Using the group decomposition of
Theil's T statistic, we present monthly changes in the dispersion of industrial wages
for Brazil (1976 through 1995) and for Mexico (1968 through 1998). Both
countries show increases in wage dispersion over time, and we find a strong
negative correlation with the rate of real economic growth. Other things being
equal, the later Brazilian heterodox stabilization plans seem to have reduced
inequality in the short run.

12.1   Introduction

A great many things have been written about inequality on the basis of
evidence that may charitably be described as thin. As the recent work of
Deininger and Squire (1996a) makes clear, the measurement of household and personal income inequality for most countries has been sporadic and of uneven quality.[1] Even where these authors judge the data
to be of acceptable quality, the number of observations is generally too
few to permit useful time-series analysis. Over the quarter century from
1970 to 1995, Deininger and Squire find only fourteen acceptable estimates for Brazil and only five for Mexico.

This chapter presents measurements of change in the dispersion
of industrial wages for Brazil from 1976 through 1995 and for Mexico
from 1968 through 1998. For both countries, we present *monthly*
series. Our measures are constructed by applying the groupwise decomposition of Theil's T statistic (Theil, 1972) to wage data grouped by
industry, yielding estimates that we believe to be reasonable measures
not of the level, but of the *change*, in inequality of manufacturing wages
through time.

---

[1] This issue is discussed in detail in Chapter 7.

Our concern is with changes for the straightforward reason that changes are precisely measurable from aggregated industrial data sets and levels are not. Many casual observers doubt this, believing that the movements of an "interindustrial" measure of wage dispersion are likely to convey information that is quite different from what one would observe in microdata. In fact, this is not generally so. Because each individual is a member of some group, changes in the dispersion of individual earnings necessarily affect the dispersion of the means of groups to which individuals belong. For classification schemes meeting some basic conditions of coverage and consistency through time, the between-group component of a Theil index therefore will covary closely with the unobservable movement of the whole distribution (Chapter 15, this volume). The advantage of industrial classifications is merely that they are widely available and generally reliable.

Both countries show increases in wage dispersion over time. Both Brazil and Mexico experienced dramatic increases in inequality following the 1982 debt crisis and, in Mexico's case, again in the crises of 1986 and 1994. For both countries, the change in wage inequality shows a strong negative correlation with the rate of real economic growth; inflation has little effect except insofar as growth crises are also inflationary in both countries. This finding suggests partial corroboration of the Kuznets hypothesis relating inequality to growth on the assumption that both countries are on the downward-sloping portion of the inverted U curve.

Brazil displays evidence that certain measures of heterodox stabilization – measures that typically combine fiscal restraint with lower interest rates, monetary reform, and incomes policies – work to reduce inequality in the wage structure. This is true of the more recent Brazilian stabilization plans but apparently not of the earlier ones. Whether it is also true of the mixed orthodox-heterodox Pacto de Solidaridad Economica in Mexico beginning in December 1987 is harder to say. On the other hand, purely orthodox austerity policies – those that combine fiscal and monetary restriction while eschewing incomes policy – clearly increase inequality because they dramatically reduce growth and increase unemployment.

12.2   Previous Work on Inequality and Growth

Kuznets (1955) first attempted to relate economic growth to inequality in the context of economic development. Exploring the historical relationship of income distribution and per capita output, Kuznets proposed an inverted U curve: that high growth in early development increases inequality, with the relationship taking the opposite form as broadly based industrialization is achieved. Hirschman (1964) proposed a model to account for the Kuznets conjecture: that "unbalanced growth" characterizes early development and implies a trade-off between equity and growth, while the balancing out of industrialization in later stages implies equalization.

These perspectives assume that there is a causal relationship running from growth to income distribution. This causal direction has been reversed in more recent models. In Aghion and Bolton (1994) and Perotti (1993), the inverted U curve arises due to imperfections in the capital market: The rich and the poor have different patterns of investment that, in the initial stages of development, benefit mainly the rich. But as growth occurs due to this investment, the poor have more and more opportunities and returns to investment increase for poorer people; thus, trickle-down prosperity generates equalization eventually. More recently, Galor and Tsiddon (1996) have developed a general equilibrium model in which growth and inequality are both endogenous; endogeneity is achieved by considering human capital alongside physical capital markets.

Early empirical explorations (Paukert, 1973; Ahluwalia, 1976) provided confirming evidence of the Kuznets conjecture, as did the works of Adelman and Robinson (1989) and Brenner, Kaelbe, and Thomas (1991). Ahluwalia (1976) provides the essential framework, which amounts to fitting a quadratic form to cross-sectional measures of income level and inequality. But because Fields (1980) exposed the sensitivity of the conclusions to the particular statistical method used to test the hypothesis, a large array of contradictory results have appeared. Anand and Kanbur (1993) show that if the Kuznets hypothesis is tested using regression, the functional form determines the conclusion. We therefore doubt that there is much to be gained from pursuing cross-sectional analysis of the Kuznets hypothesis, though the Deininger and Squire data set will no doubt provide fuel for such studies well into the future. Ram (1997) is an example: Using data only from nineteen developed countries, this study finds a U curve rather than an inverted U.

There is a wider literature that has attempted to explain the movement of inequality through time, but it remains substantially *microeconomic* in character and centered on the developed economies. The North American literature in this area is now vast; in a useful survey, Lawrence (1996) has concluded that slow economic growth is the major single cause of rising inequality in the United States; but Lawrence does not refer to Kuznets.

Brazilian studies of income distribution tend to follow those of the United States in emphasizing human capital and education differentials (see Fishlow, 1972, and Langoni, 1973). Yet time-series estimates of changes in inequality in Brazil are sporadic. In a major step forward, Almeida Reis and Barros (1989) obtained a full Theil estimate for the years 1976–1986 from the Pesquisa Nacional de Amostra a Domicilio (PNAD), with a sample of over 50,000 workers. Their series shows inequality falling during the high-growth period through 1981 and rising afterward with the arrival of the International Monetary Fund (IMF) in Brazil, austerity policies and the debt crisis.[2] Similar arguments have been made about Mexico, though with an even greater shortage of hard evidence; Aspe and Beristain (1984) attempted a heroic "first estimate of the evolution of inequality in Mexico" with data for only three years.

12.3   The Measurement of Change in Inequality from Industrial Data: Methods and Sources

Our general approach follows the work of Theil (1972), who demonstrates that his T statistic can be decomposed into the sum of between-group and within-group dispersion for any partition of the data into mutually exclusive and exhaustive groups. An ordinary table of average wages by sector or industry is such a partition; hence, data from this source can be used to compute a lower-bound Theil estimate, which we call T'. Such a decomposition cannot be achieved with a Gini coefficient or an Atkinson measure of inequality. It is uniquely a feature of generalized entropy measures, as Shorrocks (1984) has proved.

With only a few groups covering thousands of workers apiece, the proportion of wage dispersion that is between groups, and therefore measured by T', is only a small part of total wage dispersion. But because T' converges to T as decomposition into larger numbers of groups proceeds, the change in T' or ΔT' must necessarily converge to ΔT. It is possible to construct artificial examples in which the two series move in opposite directions, but even a small amount of disaggregation usually seems sufficient to get the direction of movement right. Moreover, because industrial groupings are not wholly arbitrary, but rather tend to segment workers into categories that are internally homogeneous and stratified by wage level, the between-industries components of T contain more information than they would if classification were arbitrary. Thus, con-

---

[2] More recently, the Instituto Brasileiro de Geografia e Estatistica (IBGE) has published Gini statistics based on the PNAD for the years 1983–1995, omitting 1991 and 1994, when no survey was conducted. These calculations appear to show rising inequality in the middle and late 1980s, with some decline in 1995.

vergence of T′ to T and of ΔT′ to ΔT will be more rapid under an industrial than under an arbitrary grouping.

It follows that the time series of a lower-bound Theil estimate constructed from data grouped by industrial sector can serve as a reasonable approximation of the movement of a broader measure of wage dispersion, including the unobserved within-group dispersion. The particular advantage of this approach lies in the ability to construct dense time series estimates, even on a monthly basis. Because errors in data collection and fluctuations due to calendar irregularities and natural events tend to offset each other from one month to the next, moving averages of monthly series can be used to obtain the underlying trends.

In the case of Brazil, we have data of apparently high quality from the Instituto Brasileiro de Geografia e Estatistica (IBGE) from January 1976 through December 1995. The data cover average wages on a monthly basis for seventeen major industrial sectors.[3] The data are weighted by monthly employment. Experiments with computing a fixed-employment-weighted Theil measure showed that the practical difference between the two series is confined to the period from 1982 through 1984, when the relative employment of industries with wage rates near the middle of the dispersion declined sharply. In this situation we are inclined to trust the variable-weighted measures.

Mexico presented a greater data challenge. In the end, we developed a continuous between-group Theil measure for Mexico derived from three distinct sources of data: a monthly survey of wages and earnings in 129 four-digit Standard Industrial Classification industries from the Instituto Nacional de Estadística Geografia e Informática (INEGI) for the years 1987 through 1995, an index of earnings in nine major sectors, from the Labor Information System for the Manufacturing Sector of the Banco de México for the full period from 1968 to 1988, and an index from INEGI for earnings in the same nine sectors from 1995 through February 1999. The overlap between index values and actual earnings measures in 1987–1988 and 1995 permitted us to reconstruct the underlying earnings measures for 1968–1986 and 1996–1998.

12.4 Time-Series Measurements of Inequality for Brazil and Mexico

Figure 12.1 shows our estimate of monthly changes in wage dispersion for Brazil. The figure shows a slight decline in inequality in the late 1970s,

---

[3] Because errors in data collection and fluctuations due to calendar irregularities and natural events tend to offset each other from one month to the next, moving averages of monthly series are likely to be an especially robust approximation of underlying trends.

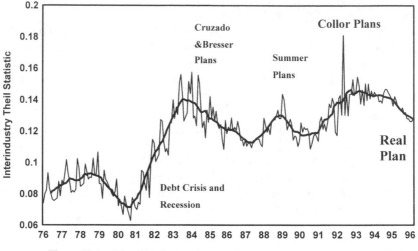

Figure 12.1.   Monthly changes in manufacturing earnings inequality for Brazil, 1976–1995.

followed by a sharp increase in the early 1980s. Inequality in the Brazilian wage structure then stabilized from 1985 through 1987, bumped up again in 1988, stabilized, bumped up sharply in 1992, and finally stabilized again in 1994–1995. Some years show a severe sawtooth pattern in the dispersion of wages from month to month, whereas in other years within-year variation is virtually absent. The thick line is a twelve-month moving average of the raw monthly series.

Figure 12.2 presents our monthly measure of wage inequality in Mexico, again with a moving average of the same series superimposed. The measures show wage compression in Mexico from 1970 through 1976, a bump-up in the mid-1970s that was offset by the end of the decade, another rise in the early 1980s, and then a pattern of sharply rising inequality from 1984 through 1989. This upward movement was briefly arrested in 1989–1990, the early period of the Pacto, but resumed in 1991. The series makes a further sharp jump in 1995, with the Chiapas rebellion and the peso crisis.[4]

Our measures of the evolution of inequality can be deployed to evaluate the relationship between inequality and economic growth. As noted

[4] A T′ computed from Mexico's submissions to the STAN for 1970–1992 shows a similar pattern, except that the STAN data place the largest rise in inequality in the crisis of 1986 and less emphasis on the crisis of 1982.

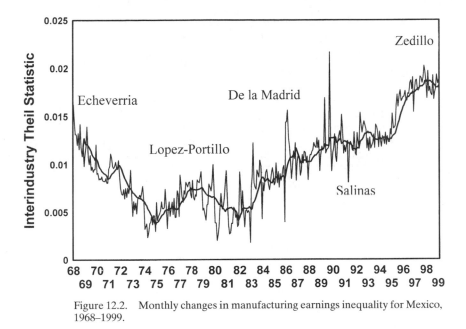

Figure 12.2.   Monthly changes in manufacturing earnings inequality for Mexico, 1968–1999.

previously, Kuznets long ago postulated that such a relationship would exist: positively sloped in the early stages of development and negatively sloped later on. Mexico and Brazil are middle-income countries. And so, on the Ahluwalia (1976) estimates of where the turning point occurs, the Kuznets hypothesis suggests that the *change* in inequality and the *change* in economic growth will be negatively related in Mexico and Brazil.

High inflation, frequent changes in currency, and political instability bedevil the collection of long time series on macroeconomic matters for Brazil. We present evidence on only two annual variables: the growth rate of gross domestic product (GDP) and a measure of inflation plus a constant term measuring the trend. In addition, we include a dummy for the five years when Brazilian inflation exceeded 1,000 percent per annum, partly on the grounds that such inflation measures tend to be unreliable. Hyperinflation also may have had different structural effects on the economy than "regular" Brazilian inflation in the range of 200 percent.

The results are presented in Table 12.1; the dependent variable is the annual average change of our raw monthly series. There is a strong upward constant trend in Brazilian inequality, as the intercept term reveals. Nevertheless, the data show that the growth rate of real GDP is

Table 12.1. *Regression Analysis of the Change in
Theil Measures of Inequality in Brazil: 1977–1995
(N = 19)*

Variable	Beta	t statistic
Intercept (trend rate of change)	12.5	4.51*
Growth rate of real GDP	−0.83	5.19*
Rate of inflation	0.38	1.27
Hyperinflation (inflation > 1,000%)	−0.67	2.16

Notes: R^2, 0.65; Durbin-Watson, 1.56.
Dependent variable: year-to-year changes in the average
monthly inequality measure.
Asterisk indicates significance at the 0.01 level.

a dominant determinant of the movement of inequality in Brazil about
this trend. There is also weak evidence that hyperinflation may compress
the Brazilian manufacturing wage structure.

It is clear that the change in GDP has a strong linear association with
changes in inequality in Brazil, with an *R* value of −0.73, and of −0.91 if
just three outliers – 1977, 1978, and 1982 – are excluded. Figure 12.3 presents a summary of this result and illustrates the need for strong positive growth in Brazil – generally speaking, above 3 percent per annum
at least if inequality is not to increase.

Inflation is not a significant determinant of changing wage dispersion
in Brazil on a year-over-year basis. However, we find that inflation does
affect the within-year variation of inequality in Brazil; those sawtooth
patterns are produced by hyperinflation. A final regression exercise in
Brazil tests for effects on inequality of the various stabilization programs:
the Cruzado and Bresser plans, the two Plans Verao (Summer Plans), the
two Collor plans, the transition to the Real Plan, and the Real Plan itself,
beginning in July 1994.[5] Our specification is very simple: we suppose a
rising trend for inequality in Brazil and a negative relation of real GDP
change to inequality, as the previous regression suggests; We then ask
whether the stabilization plans reduced inequality once the movement
of GDP was controlled for.

The results are presented in Table 12.2. Coefficients on the earlier
plans are not significant; though these plans clearly affected inflation,

[5] We exclude only the so-called Cruzado II plan of November 1986 because it was merely
a reindexation of prices and not a true stabilization plan.

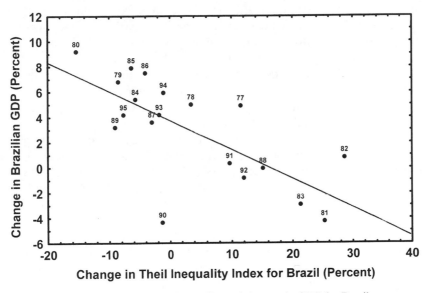

Figure 12.3.   Changes in inequality and changes in GDP for Brazil.

Table 12.2. *Regression Analysis of Stabilization Plans in Brazil; Dependent Variable: Measure of Inequality (N = 239)*

Variables and Stabilization Plans	Beta	*t* statistic
Trend	3.67	23.59*
GDP	−0.222	15.53*
Cruzado	−0.017	0.49
Bresser	0.034	0.87
Verao 1	−0.034	1.15
Verao 2	−0.136	3.79*
Collor 1	−0.308	8.89*
Collor 2	−0.668	12.33*
Transit to real	−0.476	11.23*
Real	−0.593	11.63*

Notes: R^2: 0.86.
*Coefficients significant at the 0.01 level.
Durbin-Watson before Cochrane-Orcutt correction: 1.24.

they did not alter trend inequality. The later stabilization plans did affect inequality independently, however, and the Real Plan is notable for combining inflation stabilization and inequality reduction. Unfortunately, the Real Plan was implemented from a base of extremely high inequality even by Brazilian standards. Moreover, if our estimates are correct, it will not prove strong enough to withstand the secular trend toward rising inequality in Brazil unless it is accompanied by strong per capita income growth for a sustained period of time.

In Mexico, the years 1970 through 1976 were a time of strongly pro-labor and high-growth policy under the administration of President Luis Echeverria; significant wage compression was the result. Crisis, however, erupted in the years following the oil shocks, producing rising inequality under President Lopez Portillo until, in the late 1970s, Mexico announced that it had discovered vast new reserves of oil. Then it was off to the races again, but only briefly: The debt crisis of 1982 rudely ended the reverie of oil-based prosperity. Under President Miguel de la Madrid, Mexico struggled with the debt crisis and responded by opening to the North and signing the General Agreement on Tariffs and Trade (GATT); the result was a vast increase in inequality. President Carlos Salinas, taking office in late 1988, presided over an economy whose wage structure was no longer entirely locally determined. The Salinas years saw high but comparatively stable inequality; under Ernesto Zedillo, inequality rose sharply at first, but then declined in 1996 and 1997.

Table 12.3 presents a regression model for Mexico using annual averages of our monthly data. We estimate the change in inequality as a function of the Mexican inflation rate and the Mexican real growth rate. The results account for about half of the variation in the change of T' for

Table 12.3. *Regression Analysis of Change in Theil Inequality Measures: Mexico, 1971–1993 ($N = 23$)*

Variable	Beta	t statistic
Intercept	21.3	2.54*
Rate of real GDP growth	−0.72	3.87*
Inflation	−0.08	0.43

Notes: R^2: 0.46; Durbin-Watson: 1.77
Dependent variable: year-to-year changes in the average monthly inequality measure.
Asterisk indicates significance at the 0.01 level.

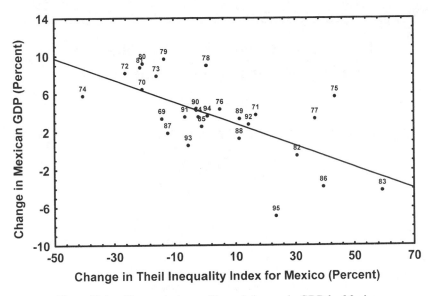

Figure 12.4.   Changes in inequality and changes in GDP for Mexico.

Mexico. Clearly, the GDP effect is very strong: Higher growth reduces inequality in Mexico, as Figure 12.4 illustrates. The inflation variable is not significant in the multiple regression.

Mexico and Brazil thus appear to conform to the downward-sloping portion of the Kuznets curve. More rapid growth, roughly corresponding to positive economic growth per capita, reduces inequality; real GDP growth below the rate of population growth tends to increase it, and recessions are inequality disasters. There is no particular reason in these data to suspect that the trade regime per se matters. If liberalized trading regimes could produce high rates of growth – as they did, for example, in Asia until mid-1997 – they would reduce inequality. The problem is that both Mexico and Brazil have experienced low growth following liberalization. To put it another way, liberalization in Latin America has failed to deliver the high rates of growth that had previously been achieved under less liberal trading regimes.

CHAPTER 13

The Legacy of the HCI: An Empirical Analysis of Korean Industrial Policy

James K. Galbraith and Junmo Kim

While much has been written on the successes and failures of industrial policies, systematic evaluation of their effects remains difficult. This chapter presents an approach based on a combination of cluster and discriminant analysis applied to time series of the rate of change of average wages by industry. We apply this approach to a Korean data set that may be one of the most comprehensive national archives of industrial and occupational wage data in the world. Our approach permits quantitative assessment of the legacy of Korean industrial policy and helps to show how Korean development has depended both on government and on the market.

13.1   Introduction

Governments and markets both exist. And while enthusiasts of markets have contested the role of government in development, and vice versa, it seems more realistic to accept that both play roles. The important questions are therefore: What roles? Through what channels? And to what extent? A sensible way to advance this discussion is to present an empirical indicator that can show the legacy of policies and other factors that have contributed to industrial and economic growth, and thereby approach the issue of the role of the government and the market. This chapter presents a combination of cluster and discriminant analysis applied to time series of average wage change by industrial category in order to assess the balance of government and market forces in Korea, with the Korean Heavy and Chemical Industrialization (HCI) as the prime example.

From 1971 to 1991, the Korean economy changed dramatically, in part because of a massive industrial policy. Our goal is to contribute something to the literature assessing this experience. First, we will present a brief overview of the literature on the role of government in industrialization, highlighting the government–market dialectic. Second, we will review the history of the HCI policy, which was surely one of the grandest efforts at national industrial transformation, relative to the size of the underlying economy, ever undertaken. Third, we will introduce the methodology and data employed in this research, followed by a discussion of the results.

13.2   The Government and the Market in the Literature

The study of state intervention in stimulating industrialization is not a completely new idea. Historically, mercantilism served the same goal, so that Adam Smith's critique of Elizabethan practices can perhaps be called an early analysis of industrial policy (Smith, 1776). More recently, Alexander Gerschenkron's (1962) historical analysis depicts how, in the late nineteenth century, German government-backed industrial banks commanded industrialization.

A new element from the 1980s was a more refined theory of the state. Katzenstein (1978) discusses strong and weak states, and, following him, Johnson (1982, 1987) focuses on bureaucracies and bureaucrats. Still more refined discussions have analyzed government–business relations, developing the statist argument that in certain countries, notably Japan, these relationships make government industrial policy and government leadership over industries meaningful (Samuels, 1987). One type of government–business relationship takes the form of *reciprocity*; Amsden's (1989) idea was to find the reciprocal relationships that, she argues, have existed between big business and the Korean government since the 1960s.

Against statism, an alternative construction has focused on the market, arguing that Korea's development track can be explained in neoclassical terms (Patrick and Rosovsky, 1976; Westphal, 1978; Hugh, 1985, 1988). Scholars in this tradition have argued that the main impetus behind Korean development has been private business investment demand, private savings, and a well-educated workforce operating in market-oriented environments. These authors are not unaware of the role of government; they simply put more weight on market factors, believing that market mechanisms rather than state policies have been decisive.

With two conflicting ideas, research has developed in several directions. One has provided deep investigation into specific industrial policies. This approach has yielded a comprehensive vision of how actual government support was provided to firms and of how government and firms interacted with each other (Okimoto, 1989). One case study of the Japanese computer industry, for instance, shows that government not only provided financial support for a startup of the industry, but also created demand to make the investment worthwhile (Anchorduguy, 1988).

A second stream of research has attempted to link the state and market traditions, for example by describing government as the management of a quasi-market system (Wade, 1990). Other examples in this second stream have refined the description of industrial policy in Korea, with a systematic and persuasive presentation of data (Leipziger, 1987). These authors have opened their eyes clearly to the Korean context. Whereas earlier statist authors had ignored serious crises that Korea's HCI experienced after the two big pushes (1973–1974 and 1978–1979), this fact is well treated in some of the later studies, notably those of Auty (1992, 1994), who has described the lagging performance of the HCI sectors in Korea as "the maturation of the HCI sectors."

Still, the existing literature on HCI suffers from insufficient empirical support. Approaches generally based on statism tend to overemphasize the role of government, as a focus on the historical development of a specific policy must inevitably do. Approaches rooted in the neoclassical development paradigm tend similarly to minimize the importance of the government's role; this is again a function of the paradigm rather than of the evidence. Indeed, both sorts of studies tend to provide little analytical support for their positions, offering instead raw data and largely leaving it to the reader to assess what the numbers actually may mean. What is missing is an analysis that can begin to "weigh up" the burden of the evidence. For that, we need not only data but also method; this the present study attempts to supply.

13.3   A Brief History of the HCI Initiative

After successfully implementing its first and second economic development plans, the Korean government officially launched the ambitious HCI in 1973. By that time, however, much of the groundwork for the HCI had been laid (Pack and Westpal, 1986; Enos and Park, 1987; Haggard, Cooper, Collins, and Kim, 1994), including the Pohang Iron and Steel Company (POSCO), construction of which started in 1968, with the first phase completed in 1973.

Under HCI, six strategic industries were selected for major support: steel, nonferrous metal, shipbuilding, electronics, machinery, and the chemical industries (Government of the Republic of Korea, 1976; Office of the Prime Minister, 1978). These industries required a huge scale of investment, and government industrial policy was a crucial element in the undertaking; no one has argued that it would have happened otherwise (Stern, Kim, and Perkins, 1995).

The essence of industrial policy under the HCI was financial support, though more conventional measures such as tax incentives and the provision of industrial parks were also included in the policy package. New financial institutions, such as the National Industrialization Fund (NIF), were specifically created for the HCI (Leipziger, 1987; Kim, 1990), while commercial banks, virtually under the government's control until the early 1990s, played major supporting roles.

The NIF, created in 1974, lent about two-thirds of its portfolio to HCI's industrial projects, which enabled the purchase of domestic machinery and ships and the construction of facilities. The Korea Export-Import bank also served the HCI's promotional goal of the Korean government by providing deferred payment loans to foreign buyers. Other financial institutions specially designed to promote the HCI include the Machinery Localization Fund and the Plant Localization Fund.

With intensive promotion, production of HCI products increased; more important, the proportion of HCI products among total exports of Korea also increased: from 4.8 percent in 1970 to 13.1 percent in 1983 and to 30 percent in 1995 (Bank of Korea, 1971, 1984, 1995). Yet, despite these indicators, many economists have described the HCI as a policy failure. Above all, the HCI policy has been criticized for misallocating subsidized credit to excessively large-scale industries, with resulting inefficiency in the overall allocation of resources (Kwack, 1984; Leipziger, 1986; Rhee, 1987). The favor given to HCI sectors reflexively reduced industrial resources that light industries could have received. Thus, when the impact of the second oil shock came, the effects on the industrial base were dire. More basically, economists have raised fundamental questions about the efficacy and meaning of sectoral policy (Krueger and Tuncer 1994). These critics argue that while the necessity for infant industry protection can be admitted, subsequent targeting of industries always reduces the competition that will bring efficiency and fosters rent-seeking behavior of firms (Frischtak, 1989).

Macroeconomists have also criticized the HCI, citing effects on inflation, the trade deficit, and debt accumulation. Instead of using stabilization measures, the Korea's government launched the HCI at the moment of inflationary pressures from the oil shock and demand pressures from the recycling of world income toward the Middle East (Auty, 1992). The HCI push thus worsened trade deficits at a critical time, leading to a major increase in Korea's external debt. Korea's debt was increased from 3.9 billion U.S. dollars in 1973 to 8 billion U.S. dollars in 1976 (World Bank World Debt Tables, 1988–1989). This early burst is largely attributable to HCI investment to sustain growth through the first oil shock – though, of course, the much larger growth of Korean external debt in the late 1970s and early 1980s, up to $46 billion by 1985, had more complex causes.

As the critiques set in, policy headed toward liberalization. From the standpoint of industrial policy, this meant a reduction of incentives given to the HCI sectors. The preferential interest rate system, which favored the HCI, ended in 1982 (Cho, 1988). Interest rate differentials between large and small firms were reduced or eliminated. The Korean government reduced restrictions on interest rates and prices, five formerly public banks were privatized, and the government hoped to increase the savings rate through financial reform. The interest rate advantage of the HCI over light manufacturing industries, which was about 3 percent in the period between 1974 and 1979, was reduced to approximately 1.6 percent between 1980 and 1984 (World Bank, 1987).

As the HCI case shows, government industrial policy can be powerful and yet inefficient and can be regarded as either a success or a failure, depending on the theoretical orientation and the time frame that specific authors may take into account. In the most recent evaluations, it seems that the reputation of the HCI initiative may be making a comeback. With almost two decades gone by since the initial pushes, the HCI sectors are today the locomotives of Korea's export growth. In 1995, HCI-related products made up almost 30 percent of all exports, *excluding* the electrical and electronics sectors. When one includes the electrical and electronics sectors that were also targeted as part of the HCI promotion, HCI products made up almost 64 percent of total Korean exports in 1995 (Bank of Korea, 1995). But even this will not prove to be the final word. It is equally possible to argue that patterns of world demand, rather than decisions about domestic supply and therefore the market rather than the state, was in some ultimate sense responsible for this most recent reversal of fortune.

13.4   Methodology and Data

Our study is based on a different premise: that the market and the state are inseparable but that it is possible to assess the relative effects of particular policies with some precision if one approaches the analytical task in a systematic way, and this should enable us to cast some light on issues of efficiency and rent sharing. We are interested in the *relative performance* of industries in Korea, specifically the performance of those that were HCI-targeted compared to those that were not, and with the forces through time that affected and differentiated the relative performance of industries. The first question, then, is how can we measure industrial performance?

Our theoretical idea is that workers earn industry-specific labor rents (Katz and Summers, 1989), and these comprise a significant part of the pay packet (Blanchflower, Oswald, and Sanfey, 1996). As Galbraith and Calmon (1990, 1994, 1996) have pointed out, this implies that *change* in wages must reflect the *changing* relative performance of industries; hence, it should be possible to infer changes in relative industrial performance from changing wage patterns. Thus, a pattern of steadily rising *relative* wage rates in a group of industries can be taken as a marker of rising rents in that sector. Because we know that the HCI sectors were heavily subsidized through financial channels, and that the HCI sectors expanded rapidly in consequence, the interesting question becomes: Did these subsidies generate industry-specific rents that show up in differentially increased wages specifically for the HCI sectors? This would be a fairly sure sign of inefficiency and resource misallocation, though it would not necessarily bear on the criticisms and defenses of HCI on other grounds.

In the case of a developing country like Korea, and particularly one where union activity was savagely repressed under an authoritarian government, one might argue that the case for the existence of industry-specific labor rents is less plausible than in developed countries. We doubt this: Manufacturing industries even in repressive developing countries pay substantial wage premiums over agricultural labor, even though they could in principle easily replace their workforces with new recruits. In any event, the proposition is testable. If patterns of industry-specific wage variation can be found, that is a sign that industry-specific labor rents existed. (We shall see that in fact a major source of interindustry wage variation is associated with changes in the flow of aggregate investment.)

More generally and on closer examination, that the Korean case should exhibit labor rents is not so surprising. In Korea, industrialization had already substantially reduced the importance of agriculture by the early 1970s; by the end of our data series in the early 1990s, Korea was a full-fledged industrial economy by any standard. Moreover, it is a fairly general pattern that unions emerge after labor rents become substantial, not beforehand. (See, inter alia, the discussion of interwar American unionization in Ferguson and Galbraith (Chapter 3, this volume)). We take the sharp rise in unionization and organized labor activity in Korea in the 1980s – after unions had been effectively and brutally repressed during the 1970s – as a sign that the flow of industry-specific labor rents had by that time risen to very substantial levels. The questions, then, are what caused labor rents to rise and to what extent the cause can be traced to the HCI policies.

We employ the year-to-year change in average wages by industry as our indicator of industrial performance and the variation of industry-specific labor rents. This particular use of changing wage rates deserves a word of defense. On a theoretical level, we believe wage changes are a more reliable index of rent variation than even varying profit rates might be. Capital markets clear, and labor markets do not; therefore, profit rates tend to equalize across industries, and wage rates tend not to. Industrial performance differentials should therefore not be expected to show up in profits, except as a very short-run disequilibrium phenomenon. Due to provisions of tax law, moreover, incentives to misrepresent profits are much greater than are incentives to misrepresent average wage rates. Wage rates surely move only in part with industry rents; but in contrast with profit rates, we do expect them to covary systematically with the performance- or rent-earning characteristics that we are fundamentally interested in.

There is also a pragmatic issue. Average wage data by industrial classification are available in time-series format, both for Korea and for many other countries, and this creates possibilities for the use of statistical techniques to group industries by patterns of wage performance and then to analyze the forces causing variation in performance between groups. Our techniques require the existence of consistently measured information for every industry and every time period. We would be happy to have a measure of industrial performance that is more sensitive to interindustry performance differentials – Galbraith's (1998a) use of U.S. data on total compensation (in effect, value added) per production worker hour is an example – but in Korea, wage rates are available and they will have to do.

In this analysis, we use the Occupational Wage Survey (OWS) collected and published by the Ministry of Labor in Korea in 1971–1991 as our principal data source. The OWS covers approximately 18 percent (1971) and 29 percent (1991) of the total economically active, nonagricultural population in Korea, including both manufacturing and service industries. The sampling frame used in this survey is all workplaces that hire more than ten workers. Due to the systematic and comprehensive sampling frame, we expect that the data set harbors reliable information on the interindustry patterns of wage movement in Korea. With appropriate techniques, combining cluster analysis on the patterns of wage change to determine the group structure of industries with discriminant function analysis to determine the patterns of difference between groups through time, we expect to extract that information. In other words, we expect to develop a chromatography of factors that affected relative industrial performance, to assess the comparative importance of those factors, and to classify them as originating principally with the market or with the state.

Cluster analysis is a numerical technique that classifies objects (industries) based on the similarities found in their characteristic variable (Lorr, 1983; Aldenderfer and Blashfield, 1984) – rates of average wage change in the present study. In actual calculation, we construct an $N \times P$ matrix **A**, in which $A(i,t)$ represents the annual wage change of industry i in year t. Each row, a profile of an industry, contains P annual rates of change of average wages for the industry. Similarity between paths can be determined by means of a conventional Euclidean distance measure in a P-dimensional space. We deploy a hierarchical agglomerative clustering method designed to yield compact clusters (Ward, 1963). Ward's method has the advantage that it maximizes between-group variance and minimizes within-group variance at each step in the clustering.

As a first step, then, we deploy differing patterns of annual percentage wage change as an industry classification scheme. Compared to the conventional scheme of industry classification, such as the Standard Industrial Classification (SIC), this new classification scheme shows the similarity of industries according to their patterns of wage change (industrial performance) through time. Industries are similar if the forces of history have affected them in similar ways and different to the degree to which they responded differently to those forces in the past. The use of percentage rates of wage change as a classification variable also has technical advantages in the application of cluster analysis, because these data are unit-free and therefore the resulting clusters are invariant with respect to changes in the scale of measurement.

Once clusters have been determined, the purpose of performing a discriminant analysis is to find out the factors that yielded the clustering pattern. Each discriminant function, denoted as F, can be understood as a function that expresses a force underlying the pooled wage variation across industries (Morrison, 1969; Klecka, 1980; Tatsuoka, 1988; Galbraith and Calmon, 1990, 1996). From the discriminant analysis, we get several canonical roots of the discriminant function, otherwise known as eigenvectors of a matrix of between-group variations standardized by the within-group variations. From among them, we can select statistically meaningful ones according to the value of the associated eigenvalues. Roots with smaller eigenvalues have less discriminating power. These canonical roots are matched with real-world economic data series in the later stage of this research.

13.5   Findings

Figure 13.1 presents the results of our cluster analysis, whereby we reduce thirty-nine original categories to a small number of homogeneous and distinct large groups. The tree diagram, which depicts in a compact way the comovement of wage change for every pair of industries, clearly suggests a four-group structure, even allowing for a somewhat higher degree of within-group variation in the group on the left of the diagram compared with the other three. Table 13.1 lists the members of the four groups.

Group 1 includes Machinery, Transportation Equipment, Primary Iron and Steel, Metal Assembly, and Other Chemical – all HCI or closely related – plus other mining, paper, business service, and beverage categories, which are arguably related in regard to either inputs or chemical process. We will take this sector as embodying the main sector-specific results of the HCI policy, with one exception to be noted subsequently. It is already indicative of the power of HCI policy in this period that the members of the HCI group have a distinct and common pattern of wage change (industrial performance). This tells us that the HCI policy was largely unitary; it affected almost all of the designated sectors in similar ways.

Group 2 we identify as a labor-intensive, low-skilled sector. It includes Textiles, Apparel, Other Manufacturing, Wood Cork, Print, Electrical

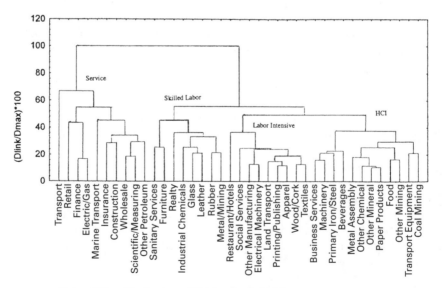

Figure 13.1.   Cluster tree of thirty-nine industries.

Table 13.1. *Cluster Table: Member Industries in Each Cluster Group*

Group 1 HCI Concentration	Group 2 Labor Intensive/Service
Machinery	Textiles
Transportation Equipment	Apparel
Primary Iron and Steel	Other Manufacturing
Metal Assembly	Wood Cork
Other Chemical	Print
Coal Mining	Electrical Machinery
Other Mineral	Social Services
Other Mining	Restaurant/Hotel
Business Services	Land Transportation
Beverage	
Paper	

Group 3 Skilled Labor	Group 4 Service Industry Concentration
Glass	Wholesale
Leather	Retail
Rubber	Electricity/Gas Utilities
Furniture	Finance
Industrial Chemicals	Insurance
Metal Mining	Construction
Realty	Marine Transportation
Sanitary Services	Transportation Related
	Personal Services
	Scientific Measurement
	Other Petroleum

Machinery, and three service categories: Social Services, Restaurant Hotel, and Land Transportation. Group 3 is primarily a skilled-labor manufacturing sector covering Glass, Leather, Rubber, Furniture, Industrial Chemicals, Metal Mining, and the small service categories of Realty and Sanitary Services. Of these sectors, one, Industrial Chemicals, was a targeted HCI sector; it is the only specifically targeted sector to fall outside of our Group 1. Group 4, finally, captures the remainder of the service sectors: Wholesale, Retail, Electricity/Gas Utilities, Finance, and Insurance, plus several transportation sectors, science, petroleum, and construction. On the whole, we consider that the cluster analysis is informative. Because it succeeds in dividing Korean industrial structure along lines that appear broadly to reflect factor intensities of production, we are led to believe that patterns of industry-specific labor rents did vary over this period in ways that systematically reflect the changing relative fortunes of different types of industry.

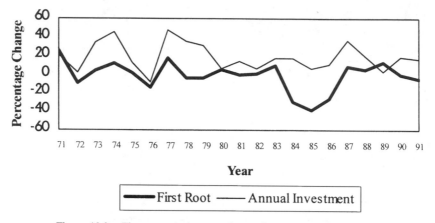

Figure 13.2.   First canonical root and gross investment in Korea, 1971–1991.

Next, we report a discriminant analysis based on the grouping structure provided by the clustering. Three canonical roots were extracted; however, only the first two of them are statistically significant. Between them, these two roots account for 89.5 percent of between-group variations in wage change over our time frame (1971–1991), with the first accounting for 72.5 percent and the second adding the remaining 17 percent. With this information in hand, the next step in analysis was to find macroeconomic data series that match these two roots.

The first root matches well with the annual change in gross investment during the same time. Figure 13.2 illustrates the comovement of the two series, one of them drawn from the national income and product accounts and the other artificially constructed from wage data. This suggests to us that the single major force affecting comparative industrial performance and wage rates in Korea is *macroeconomic*: the movement of aggregate investment and the business cycle.

The economic intuition behind the finding that macroeconomic fluctuations cause differential performance across industries is straightforward, though at variance with the competitive model. In an economy characterized by degrees of market power and scarce factors of production, we would expect to find that labor rents fluctuate with aggregate investment demand. Moreover, when demand is strong, rents should be concentrated in those sectors with the greatest concentrations of scarce factors (capital and skilled labor) and political and market power.[1] The

---

[1] This finding is consistent with evidence for the postwar United States, as argued in Galbraith, 1998a.

HCI sectors enjoyed high capital intensity, greater than average political and market power, and a skilled labor force. One is therefore not surprised to find them scoring above average on the first root.

On the other hand, as the scatterplot of canonical scores in Figure 13.3 shows, HCI industries do not score as highly as the skilled-labor industries of Group 3. These industries – which except for industrial chemicals were not HCI targeted – show greater responsiveness to the flux of aggregate investment than do most of the HCI industries. The industries, on the left of the diagram, that show weak wage responsiveness to aggregate investment are the labor-intensive manufacturing sectors that are especially vulnerable to labor-saving innovation and the services sectors that do not enjoy capital rents. Moreover, because aggregate investment over this period as a whole was strong, the scatterplot has an upward tilt, and we can see that the behavior of aggregate investment in Korea had a distinctly cumulative effect on the distribution of industrial wages between 1971 and 1991. We note – it is not surprising – that this effect originates entirely during the first half of the sample, that is, during the time of the HCI pushes. Aggregate investment added nothing to interindustry wage differentials after 1982.

The appropriate inference, we think, is that *any* policy raising aggregate investment in Korea would have had approximately similar effects on the industrial and wage structures. Conversely, the HCI policy can be said to have worked through this channel *only* to the extent that HCI raised *aggregate* investment. To the extent that HCI *did* raise aggregate investment, investment rose not only in the HCI sectors themselves, but

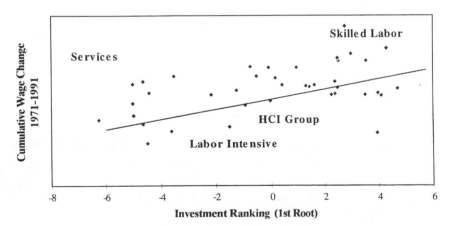

Figure 13.3.   Scatterplot of the first canonical root and cumulative wage change in Korea (1971–1991) showing the approximate location of the major groups.

also in the non-HCI sectors that rely on skilled labor. It is the general
rise in investment, and not the channeling of investment to the HCI
sectors specifically, that accounts for the positive effect of this first canonical root on the structure of Korean industrial wages.

The second canonical root of the discriminant function, though it
accounts for only 17 percent of the between-group variations, is equally
telling because it effectively does isolate the HCI sectors from the rest
of the Korean economy. Figure 13.4 illustrates the distribution of canonical scores, showing clearly the position of the HCI sectors on the right
side of the diagram and of virtually everything else on the left. A second
feature of the figure also stands out. In contrast to Figure 13.3, which is
clearly upward sloping, the distribution of scores in relation to cumulative wage performance in Figure 13.4 is flat. (If one divides the sample
in 1982, it is also flat in both subperiods separately.) This force clearly
differentiates the HCI sectors from the rest of the economy during this
period, but it does not lead directly to higher wages on that account
alone.

Figure 13.5 presents the time-series comparison of the canonical coefficients of the second root with the variable that best matches it. This is
the "uncovered interest parity," or the London Interbank Offer Rate
(LIBOR) minus the depreciation of the Korean won during the time
period – a depreciation that typically had to be covered by high domestic interest rates. The uncovered interest parity is thus a measure of the

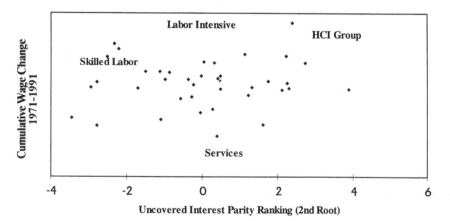

Figure 13.4.   Scatterplot of the second canonical root and cumulative wage
change in Korea (1971–1991) showing the approximate location of the major
groups.

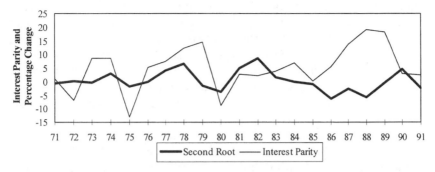

Figure 13.5. Second canonical root and uncovered interest parity in Korea (1971–1991).

relative tightness of monetary policy in Korea as it applied to firms that were obliged to borrow on open domestic credit markets. Thus, the fact that the HCI sectors score high on this root and all others score low suggests that the HCI sector was successfully insulated from domestic monetary fluctuations. It is also noteworthy that this correspondence – the advantage of the HCI sectors during spells of credit restriction – is quite tight in the 1970s but much weaker in the 1980s, when the HCI policy ended and financial markets underwent liberalization.

What does this linkage imply for the study of industrial policy in Korea? From the existing literature on Korea's industrialization, it is well known that the government rationed capital in the form of policy loans (Amsden, 1989; Wade, 1990; Cho and Cole, 1992; Stern, Kim, and Perkins, 1995). On this point, different theoretical approaches nearly agree. In a society where capital is a scarce resource, access to capital is an advantage. Even clearer is the advantage that comes from low and fixed-rate policy loans for targeted industries in comparison with conventional loans based on market rates for nontargeted sectors.

During its massive and ambitious drive to industrialize, and especially during the big push of the HCI in the 1970s, the Korean government offered preferentially low – but, more importantly, stable – interest rates to the new heavy and chemical industries. Government statistics and previous academic works have presented the different interest rates given to the HCI sectors and how much capital was allocated to them as against other sectors (Bank of Korea, various years; Leipziger, 1987, vol. I; Government of Republic of Korea, 1976; Stern, Kim, and Perkins, 1995). Our analysis shows the impact of that policy treatment on the HCI sectors. The other side of the HCI coin was a reflexive underemphasis on light industries and service industries. This has been discussed in earlier studies (Kwack, 1984; Rhee, 1987). While heavy and chemical industries were able to rely on long-term, fixed-rate capital for their equipment, light industries and service industries had to depend on short-term capital. Our analysis clearly illustrates the source of this weak position. Light industries, such as apparel and textiles, and service industries, such as wholesale, real estate, and sanitary industries, score much lower on the uncovered interest parity ranking.

What we find, interestingly, is that on balance this differential impact was not enough to generate a sustained net surplus in the HCI sectors, as that would have shown up as a differential cumulative wage gain and therefore as an upward-sloping scatterplot. In other words, whereas the existence in the wage structure of roots corresponding both to aggregate investment and to credit subsidies clearly indicates the presence of labor rents in Korea, the HCI credit subsidies were not a sustained source of such rents. One possible interpretation is that periods of easy domestic credit, overall, were sufficiently frequent and important to offset substantially the pecuniary advantages that the HCI sectors were offered in hard times. Taken together with the evidence of the first root, this finding suggests that HCI policies were effective in raising aggregate investment, but that the credit subsidy element of these policies was not channeled directly into an inefficient and wasteful rise in relative wages.

Thus, the movement of domestic credit proves to have been perhaps the key determinant of the effect of industrial policy in Korea, not so much because the government provided cheap capital to industry, but because it insulated preferred sectors from the fluctuations of the domestic interest rate after the policy loans were made. That, of course, only leads to a second question: What is the value of being insulated from domestic credit fluctuations when on the whole (as in the early 1970s) domestic credit conditions were not particularly tight?

We think the answer to this conundrum provides the key to the HCI policy, which lies in the value of ex ante stabilization per se for the industrial mix. Insofar as heavy industries with their large capital requirements demand a credible promise of macro and credit stability before they can even begin to contemplate investing on a large scale, the essence of heavy investment in small countries is the artificial provision of stability. Small developing countries have historically found it very difficult to launch such industrialization without outright state ownership and the disadvantages of bureaucracy, politics, and inertia that such ownership entails. Korea's solution was to guarantee financial stability ex ante to large private corporations and thus achieve a balance between private-sector flexibility and public-sector responsibility. In this way, the HCI can be said to have fundamentally guided the structure of Korean economic development, even though it conferred no measurable pecuniary surpluses either on the industries themselves or on their workers – even though the net benefits (or losses) from the policy were distributed over the economy as a whole.

In sum, our argument leads to the following narrative interpretation. During the early 1970s, interest rates were low in Korea, in part because of a worldwide climate of low interest rates, in part because of a tolerance for inflation by Korean policymakers and in part because Korea became a magnet for Middle Eastern capital flowing back from Korean construction firms working in the Middle East after the oil shock. In this environment, with capital relatively cheap, it was not overly difficult for policymakers to launch the HCI. Indeed, it is hard to imagine that it could have been launched under any other conditions. But by the same token, the drama of the HCI initiative itself is overstated, because what was involved was simply a promise of differential stability, not a fixed commitment to any particular reallocation of resources.

If there was a drama, perhaps it lay in the willingness of the HCI industries to believe the commitment. But firms did believe it. They drew the conclusion that they had been offered a no-lose proposition. More investment would lead to a bigger empire, more political power, and more economic income in the long run. If markets did not develop in the short run, products could be sold at a loss and losses would be covered. No doubt, the dual-use character of the HCI in the context of Korea's security situation contributed mightily to this understanding. In sum, what was transformed, above all, was the attitude of HCI firms toward capital risk, as a result of which they made irrevocable commitments they would never otherwise have dared to undertake.

The real test of the HCI initiative, on the other hand, appears to have come later in the 1970s, when international events drove up interest rates both internationally and in Korea. This began in the aftermath of the oil shock as tight monetary policies raised interest rates in the United States. In Korea, with HCI underway, the effects of tighter credit conditions were bifurcated, and the cost was paid in the very high interest rates that had to be charged to the non-HCI sectors. Obviously, the HCI industries withstood the shock relatively well; they were insulated by their strong financial protection from the state. The macroeconomic implications that took the form of a great increase in Korea's external debt, as previously noted, were in part the consequence of this success: The policy sustained the rate of investment in Korea and prevented a contraction in response to the oil shock that would otherwise have occurred. During this period, the effect of HCI on the aggregate rate of investment took the form of sustaining investment rates that might otherwise have collapsed while putting off, through debt accumulation, the accounting that eventually struck in the 1980s.

As events unfolded, financial market liberalization brought an end to the HCI period, and the relative interest rate advantages of the HCI sectors declined. By that time, however, the industrial character of the Korean peninsula had been changed and the pattern of development had been set. That which followed had the advantage of the capital sunk in the HCI during its heyday. It seems to us pointless to speculate on whether average Koreans might have been better off under some alternative allocation of resources. Had the HCI not been in place, the result would not have been an alternative path to full employment. It would have been a marked cutback in fixed and long-lived capital investment.

13.6   Conclusion

We have attempted to present the legacy of Korean industrial policy legacy from an empirical angle not explored by previous scholarship, with a view toward isolating the main channels of policy and assessing their comparative importance. By pursuing a cluster/discriminant analysis based on time series of industrial wage change, we are able to reach some tentative conclusions in this regard: first, that HCI policy worked mainly *through* its effect on the aggregate rate of investment in Korea and, second, that it achieved this effect mainly by promising ex ante stabilization of the financial conditions for investment, in effect transferring interest rate risk from the companies to the state. In focusing on the empirical evidence that leads us to emphasize these macroeconomic and financial aspects of industrial policy, we can claim that we have moved the assessment of industrial policy one step forward.

Our analysis, we should stress, provides no definitive answer to the counterfactual question, would Korea have been better off without the HCI? We do not see how any objective analysis can seriously tackle such a question. But we do point to a dynamic stabilization and buffering role for industrial policy that may be harder to criticize on efficiency grounds than the traditional arguments turning on the microefficiency of resource allocation would allow. Given the goal of heavy industrialization, the specific mechanisms of the HCI seem to have achieved it in ways that helped to stabilize the Korean macroeconomy through a period that might otherwise have seen a developmental crisis, and the fact that the crisis was deferred for eight years surely counts to the policy's credit. The fact that during those years sustained labor rents can be traced only to aggregate investment, and that credit subsidies were not large enough to generate wage-raising surpluses in the HCI sectors, also suggests that they were not excessive relative to the task they accomplished.

CHAPTER 14

Inequality and Economic Development: Concluding Reflections

James K. Galbraith

In a recent book on the determinants of economic growth, Robert Barro (1997) argues that global capitalism is characterized by *conditional convergence*: Poorer countries tend to grow more rapidly and thus to catch up with their developed neighbors and trading partners, *provided* that they equip themselves with appropriate institutions and policies. Barro points to significant statistical associations between schooling, public health, and democratic political institutions, on the one hand, and subsequent periods of strong economic growth on the other. He also argues that economic development tends to yield progress toward democracy over time.

Barro's work may be questioned on many empirical grounds. His data are heterogeneous and sometimes obscure, involving efforts to assign quantitative measures to qualitative phenomena (why, for instance, is South Africa's "index of democracy" three times higher than Tanzania's for 1975?). His casual remark that "non-democratic places that experience substantial economic development tend to become more democratic. Examples are Chile" (p. 61) suggests a perhaps tenuous grip on modern political history. And one can't help noticing that his predictions of high-growth "winners" for the period 1996–2000, including South Korea, Thailand, the Philippines, and Hong Kong, have been overtaken by the Asian crisis and its aftermath. Decidedly, statistical prediction in economic development can be a dangerous affair.

Still, in the abstract and at the most general level, there is a strong case for Barro's basic point. The prospects for economic growth do depend on institutional conditions. Poor countries can – and do – develop, sometimes, when the conditions are right. The questions are: What institutions? What conditions?

The answer of many economists like Barro emerges from their prior commitment to the economics of human capital, to free-market institutions, and to the ideology of minimal government. In general, Barro confines his attention to *domestic* institutional variables. He looks for the effect of education on growth, for instance, and finds that countries with stronger advanced education tend to grow more rapidly, other things being equal. While this is neither surprising nor objectionable, it does raise a question: How did the universities get there? Through weak governments or strong ones? And how do such preconditions for growth as long life expectancies come about, if not through public health and literacy investments that themselves require an effective system of schools?

These interdependencies suggest that it is not adequate to treat social institutions as independently observed exogenous facts. Rather, one needs a unifying theme of a deeper kind. One needs to explain why some poorer countries develop conditions suitable for the creation of growth-favoring institutions and others do not and why it tends to happen at some times and not at others. Only then can one explain why certain kinds of critical social accumulation sometimes occur and sometimes not.

We believe that a central internal institutional condition for social and economic development, underlying all of the other desirable institutional features such as education and life expectancy and democracy, is an acceptably fair and reasonably stable distribution of pay. While Barro expresses an interest in the relationship between inequality and democracy, serious discussion of this issue is missing entirely from his work, indeed from the entire corpus of the new growth theory that he represents.

The theoretical link between a reasonably egalitarian, reasonably stable pay structure and democratic development is not mysterious at all. The pay structure affects the capacity and the willingness to save and invest. In highly unequal societies, the poor have no savings and the middle class, exposed always to the image of lifestyles far more opulent than their own, consume their bottom dollar. That leaves only the wealthy with savings to spare. But the wealthy in such societies are rarely savers in the old Victorian sense; they are not the busy bees who accumulate, accumulate, but never consume for themselves. Rather, they provide for their own needs and decline to rely on the social security mechanisms of the state. They therefore resist taxation for social purposes, except (as in the case of public universities in many middle-income countries) where the benefits are narrowly focused on the elites themselves. Surplus funds are often moved overseas to escape the potential reach of the tax man. The result tends to be a chronic deficiency of public investment and of effective demand, strong alienation of the population from politics, and subversion of the forms of democracy by monied interests.

Conversely, egalitarian societies work on the basis of shared burden and shared benefit. They tend to work through large social institutions – trade unions and governments – and to rely heavily on collective measures of social security, on public education, and on public services for such functions as transportation and health. Because public institutions and budgets tend to be stable, the economies of egalitarian countries also tend to be more stable. With fewer internal disparities, they are less consumed by envy. Hence, savings may be higher and debt burdens less. And because a larger fraction of the citizenry has that modicum of time and energy left over for the pursuit of public purposes, stable and egalitarian societies also tend to be more democratic.

The empirical evidence behind this general proposition is remarkably strong. Consider the cluster diagram that appears as Figure 8.9 of this volume, which separates out the countries of the world by the stability and instability of their movements of inequality through time. The diagram divides the world in two. On the left side is the entire democratic world, including so large and poor a country as India (which, for most of the period under study, held its domestic capital inside through rigorous exchange controls).[1] These countries have, for the past fifty years, largely enjoyed peace on their own territory and, over the long haul, unprecedented prosperity. On the right side of the figure is virtually every half-developed, war-ravaged land in the world, each afflicted in its own way by economic, political, and military instabilities, which appear as inequality instabilities on this chart. From this and our closely related evidence on state violence and financial crises, we draw an inference. Instability and rising inequalities are almost always and almost everywhere a social evil. Stability in the structure of pay is a public and social good, particularly where inequality declines gradually over time.

There is indeed a global economy. But it is one that favors the strong, the rich, the stable, the industrially diverse, and the democratic. Smaller, poorer countries blow with the global winds, with the prices of their commodities, the demand for their exports, and the rate of interest. And the smaller and less balanced their economies, the more remote from the center of things, the more violently those winds can blow.

Thus, for the small and weak countries of the developing world, external conditions matter. Whether the general movement of inequality

---

[1] Also to be found here, interestingly enough, are the pseudodemocratic countries of the Second World – the "people's democracies" of the communist era. But this is hardly surprising: A major function of communism was to impose stability from above.

tends to be down (as it was in the 1970s) or up (as it was in the 1980s and 1990s), there is characteristically such a general movement. This itself suggests that economic conditions at the level of the world economy as a whole need to be considered, that one must go beyond the individual institutional traits of individual countries and consider how the world economy as a whole is governed. Indeed, as a rule, the smaller, more open, more unbalanced a country is, the more it depends on favorable global conditions.

Needless to say, under these circumstances the past several decades have been very bad for large parts of the developing world. For with liberalization and globalization, countries have become more exposed to global conditions just at the time when global conditions have themselves become dramatically worse. The commodity booms and oil bonanzas of the 1970s occurred at a time when many commodity-exporting developing countries were still following import substitution models: They could and did invest their export gains in internal development. The oil bust and the debt crisis heralded the age of globalization. The result was, in effect, a crisis of global coordination. It is obvious from the 1997 Asian crisis that we haven't even begun to work out the ways and means for establishing stable growth and declining inequality in a liberal world. Unless and until this problem is solved, it is reasonable to infer that in the long run the neoliberal world order cannot, will not, and probably should not endure.

PART IV
METHODS AND TECHNIQUES

CHAPTER 15

Constructing Long, Dense Time Series of Inequality Using the Theil Index

Pedro Conceição and James K. Galbraith

Wage and earnings data by industrial sectors are readily available for many countries over long time frames. This chapter explores the application of the between-group component of the Theil index to data on wages, earnings, and employment by industrial classification in order to measure the evolution of wage or earnings inequality through time. We provide formal criteria under which such a between-group Theil statistic can reasonably be assumed to give results that also track the (unobserved) evolution of inequality within industries. While the evolution of inequality in manufacturing earnings cannot be taken as indicating per se the larger movements of inequality in household incomes, including those outside the manufacturing sector, we argue on theoretical grounds that the two will rarely move in opposite directions. We conclude with an empirical application to the case of Brazil.

15.1 Introduction

Most empirical work on inequality uses measures that are based on household surveys. These measures aim to provide a comprehensive overview of income inequalities, covering all social strata and comparable both through time and between countries. The Gini coefficient is the index most commonly computed from these sources, though various quintile ratios are also frequently deployed. But, as Galbraith and Lu have discussed (see Chapter 8), there are many gaps as well as other deficiencies in this data.

Fortunately, the decomposability properties of the Theil measure make it possible to repair this gap in part, albeit in most cases only for the limited span of the manufacturing economy. In particular, one can compute between-group measure of inequality (T' hereafter) across industrial sectors, as delineated by national or international industrial classification schemes. Data on industrial wages, earnings, and employment are very easily found. The data are also reasonably reliable; there

263

is little reason to suspect that they are faked in any systematic way that would affect a Theil measure. Where gross errors do occasionally enter into the recording, the regularity and hierarchical structure of the data sets often mean that these can be detected.

15.2   Theil's Inequality Measure

Henri Theil (1967) first noted the possibility of using Claude Shannon's (1948) information theory to produce measures of income inequality. Shannon's theory was motivated by the need to measure the value of information. Shannon argued that the more unexpected an event is, the higher the yield of information it will produce. To formalize this idea, Shannon proposed to measure the information content of an event as a decreasing function of the probability of its occurrence. Adding some axiomatic principles, most importantly that independent events should yield information corresponding to the sum of the individual events' information, Shannon chose the logarithm of the inverse of the probability as the way to translate probabilities into information. The logarithm allows the decomposition of the multiplicative probabilities into additive information content.

If we have a set of n events, one of which we are certain is going to occur, and each with a probability x_i of occurring, then $\sum_{i=1}^{n} x_i = 1$ and the expected information content is given by Shannon's measure:

$$H = \sum_{i=1}^{n} x_i \log \frac{1}{x_i} \tag{1}$$

The information content is zero when one of the events has probability 1; we draw no information from the occurrence of an event we are sure is going to happen. The information content is maximum when $x_i = 1/n$, $i = 1, \ldots, n$; in this case, $H = \log n$. In other words, maximum information is derived from the occurrence of one event in a context of maximum uncertainty. To borrow from thermodynamics, maximum information is derived from a state of maximum disorder, or maximum entropy. This is the reason entropy is used as a synonym for expected information.

Theil was attracted to information theory because he believed it might lead toward a general partitioning theory. Beyond dividing certainty (probability 1) into various uncertain probabilities, information theory presented an opportunity to devise measures for the way in which some set is divided into subsets. Theil considered it natural to apply information theory to the partitioning of overall income across the taxpayers of a country. If we were to apply Shannon's measure directly to individual shares of income, we would have a measure of equality (recall that the maximum of Shannon's measure occurs when all the shares are equal). Therefore, Theil proposed to subtract Shannon's measure from $\log n$, leading to his well-known measure of *in*equality:

$$T = \frac{1}{n}\sum_{i=1}^{n} r_i \cdot \log r_i \qquad (2)$$

Where r_i is the ratio between individual income (y_i) and average income (μ_Y), $r_i = \frac{y_i}{\mu_Y}, \mu_Y = \frac{\sum_{i=1}^{n} y_i}{n}$. The value of the Theil index (T index) is a monotonically increasing measure of inequality in the distribution of income bounded by $T \in [0, \log n]$.

Theil argues that the fact that T does not have an upper bound but depends always on population size is desirable. Consider a society with only two individuals in which one earns all the income. In this case, $T = \log 2$. Next, consider another society in which all the income is again concentrated in one person, but the overall population is now 1,000. In this case, $T = \log 1,000$, a much higher value, as desired in a much more unequal society. Consider now a different situation: If the division of income in this larger society were in the same proportion as in the first (half of the population having all the income), then we would again have $T = \log 2$ for the larger society, as is to be expected. In general, Theil showed that $T = \log 1/\theta$, in which θ is the proportion of the population having all the income (1/2 in our last example). This is independent of the size of the population.

Theil's measure has all of the desirable properties of an inequality measure: It is symmetric (invariance under permutations of individuals), replication invariant (independent of population replications), mean independent (invariant under scalar multiplication of income), and satisfies the Pigou-Dalton property (inequality increases as a result of a regressive transfer). It is also Lorenz-consistent, meaning that it agrees with the quasi-ordering that can be derived from comparing Lorenz curves.

An important characteristic of entropy-based indexes such as the Theil index is that they are decomposable. If individuals are grouped in a mutually exclusive, completely exhaustive way, overall inequality can be separated into a between-group component and a within-group component. If we consider that the population is divided into m groups,

$g_1, g_2, \ldots, g_m$, each with n_j individuals, $j = 1, \ldots, m$, then the decomposition takes the self-similar form of a fractal:

$$\begin{cases} T = \sum_{j=1}^{m} p_j R_j \log R_j + \sum_{j=1}^{m} p_j R_j T_j \\ T_j = \frac{1}{n_j} \sum_{i \in g_j} r_i \log r_i \end{cases} \tag{3}$$

The population proportion in each group is represented by $p_j = n_j/n$ and the ratio of average group income to overall average income by $R_j = \mu_j/\mu_Y$.

There are several reasons why it may be of interest to have a decomposable measure of inequality. One might be interested in analyzing the functional distribution of income according to some criterion that divides the overall population into groups. Examples are race, gender (both of which were explored by Theil in 1967), education level, economic sector, and age, to name a few. Another reason might be associated with geography (different regions like, say, states or countries, which were also explored by Theil in 1967). Another possibility is to study differences in urban versus rural populations. Yet another reason may be related to the differentiation of sources of income.

A further important motivation, again recognized by Theil himself, is associated with data. Data on income are often reported in income brackets, which do not give information on the distribution of income *within* the income bracket. Theil explored how the decomposition properties of the T index might help in devising measures of inequality not based on percentiles.

In this chapter, we go beyond these efforts to explore the use of T to construct long, dense time series of inequality measures from industrial data. We are interested in looking at the time evolution of inequality to allow the study of the processes that drive and determine changes in inequality. Problems associated with data availability and with the choice of the instruments used to measure inequality have hindered the possibility of constructing long, dense time series, as we saw earlier.

Clearly, T' constructed across industrial sectors yields an incomplete picture of inequality at each point in time. T' is not a substitute for T. But, we argue, the potential for constructing long, dense time series outweighs this disadvantage. The question is, to what extent do changes in T' measure changes in T? Can we use the change in T' as a proxy for the evolution of inequality in the larger distribution from which T' is computed? Section 3 quantifies the "information loss" when one uses

T' instead of T. In Section 4, we discuss procedures for isolating income-change effects from population-shift effects so that we can reduce the range of uncertainty associated with inferring the change in T from the change in T'. Finally, in Section 5, we provide some empirical illustrations using data for Brazil.

15.3   Going from T to T': What Is Included and What Is Left Out?

The between-group component of Theil's T can be computed from wage or earnings data aggregated by industrial sectors in a very large number of countries. All that is required are measures of total payrolls or the wage bill, and measures of employment or hours, for consistently organized industrial categories. However, overall inequality also depends on the inequality *within* each group and on the change in population shares across groups as time passes. Therefore, it is of interest to examine these two effects and to assess how large their impact on inequality may be. In this section, we discuss how to account for the left-out inequality associated with the unobservable within-group inequality. A discussion of how to isolate population effects is presented in the next section.

We are primarily interested in a dynamic analysis of inequality, that is in how inequality changes over time. Therefore, we focus on the behavior of rates of change.

From (3) we can compute the change in inequality over time

$$\dot{T} = \sum_{j=1}^{m}[(R_j \log R_j + R_j T_j)\cdot \dot{p}_j + (p_j \log R_j + p_j + p_j T_j)\cdot \dot{R}_j + p_j R_j \dot{T}_j] \quad (4)$$

and the change over time associated exclusively with the between-group component:

$$\dot{T}' = \sum_{j=1}^{m}[R_j \log R_j \dot{p}_j + (p_j \log R_j + p_j)\cdot \dot{R}_j] \quad (5)$$

This means that (4) can be written as

$$\dot{T} = \dot{T}' + \sum_{j=1}^{m}\left[\frac{d(R_j \cdot p_j)}{dt}T_j + R_j p_j \dot{T}_j\right] \quad (6)$$

From (6), the only unobservable components T_j are $\dot{T}_j$.

Therefore, we can measure the first term on the right-hand side of (6), but we cannot measure the second term. This nonmeasurable component corresponds to the change unaccounted for by the between-group component change, which is given by (5). However, we can state conditions under which the effect of the within-group change is likely to be small.

The within-group change is the time derivative of the product $R_j \cdot p_j \cdot T_j$, and therefore, with broad generality, within-group changes will be small whenever changes in $R_j \cdot p_j \cdot T_j$ are small. Because

$$R_j = \frac{1}{p_j} \cdot \frac{Y_j}{Y} \tag{7}$$

where Y_j is group j's total income, the product $R_j \cdot p_j \cdot T_j$ can be reduced to $(Y_j/Y) \cdot T_j$, which is independent of p_j. Finally, we can do the following simplification:

$$\frac{d(R_j \cdot p_j)}{dt} T_j + R_j p_j \dot{T}_j = \frac{Y_j}{Y}[\dot{T}_j + T_j(g_j - g)] \tag{8}$$

where g and g_j are the proportionate changes in y and y_j, respectively.

Two features are immediately apparent from (8). First, the within-group Theil change is independent of the employment structure and depends exclusively on the *relative levels of average wages* and on the *relative rates of wage change*, in addition to the unobservable T_j and $\dot{T}_j$. Second, there are two contributions to the within-group change, one related to the obvious group endogenous change in the distribution over time, $\dot{T}_j$, and the other reflecting the effect of relative change in the wage structure. The term $(g_j - g)$ can be understood as the relative growth rate of average wages for group j.

How large is each of the terms given by (8)? We know that Y_j/Y_j is between 0 and 1. Moreover, if the number of groups, m, is relatively large, then $g_j = \dot{Y}_j/Y_j$ is likely to be small. Consequently, the impact of Y_j/Y on the expression will always be to reduce the effect of the within-group component on the time variation of the Theil index as a whole.

If $g_j \sim g$, for every j, then the effect associated with structural wage change is low. There is no reason why each group's rate of wage changes should be equal and close to g, but there is a trade-off. Because g is the overall growth rate, if one or a few group rates of growth are higher than g, then it must be that the remaining ones are lower. Therefore, the coefficients are likely to cancel out on average, and the overall contribution of relative wage change to within-group inequality is likely to be small.

The remaining problem is that we do not know the levels T_j, the extent of inequality within each group. Because the changes in T_j are also unknown, there is not much that one can do with generality from this point on. Nonetheless, we can estimate the *maximum* impact of this unobservable effect. We know that $T_j^{\mathrm{MAX}}(t) = \log[n_j(t)]$, that is, the maximum value of the inequality within each group is equal to the log of the population in that group. It is much more difficult to determine the maximum for the rate of change of the within-group inequality. In principle, $\dot{T}_j$ could be almost infinite, because we could go from any distribution of income to a situation in which all the income in the group is concentrated in one individual. However, this is not very likely to happen instantaneously. If we move from a continuous analysis to a discrete analysis across time, the highest change occurs when inequality moves from zero to $\log(n_j)$ from t to $t + 1$, or from $\log(n_j)$ to zero from one period to the other. Note that there is a duality here: The highest possible change implies that at one of the periods t or $t + 1$, within-group inequality is zero and the impact of the level component is therefore zero. For example, when the within-group inequality jumps from virtually zero to $T_j^{\mathrm{MAX}}(t) = \log[n_j(t)]$, the $T_j(t)$ terms would have contributed very little to overall inequality before the jump.

Taking first the issue of the maximum inequality level within group, consider that the upper bound for the summation on the right-hand side of (6) occurs when *all* groups have their maximum level of inequality (all the group's income is earned by one individual). And though this is an unlikely and unstable situation, we will assume that all groups will remain with their maximum level of inequality. In this situation, $\dot{T}_j = \dot{p}_j/p_j$. Introducing this last expression and $T_j^{\mathrm{MAX}}(t) = \log[n_j(t)]$ in (6), we find that when within-group inequality is kept at its maximum level, the maximum impact of the unobservable component is given by

$$d_{\mathrm{within}}^{\mathrm{MAX}} = \sum_{j=1}^{m} \left\{ \frac{Y_j}{Y} \left[\frac{\dot{p}_j}{p_j} + (g_j - g) \cdot \log n_j \right] \right\} \qquad (9)$$

From a formal point of view, it is worthwhile to note the dependency of this expression on the rate of change of the employment structure. The term in square brackets depends only on rates of change in employment and wages, with the weight for the relative wage growth now being given by the log of the groups' population. All the variables in (9) are observable, but expression (9) still cannot be used empirically, because it contains differential terms. Expressing the growth rates by logarithmic differences, as is standard practice, we obtain an expression that can be used with discrete data:

$$d_{\text{within}}^{\text{MAX}}(t,t+1) = \sum_{j=1}^{m}\left\{\frac{Y_j(t+1)}{Y(t+1)}\left[\log\left[\frac{p_j(t+1)}{p_j(t)}\right]\right.\right.$$
$$\left.\left. +\log\left[\frac{Y_j(t+1)}{Y(t+1)}\cdot\frac{Y(t)}{Y_j(t)}\right]\cdot\log n_j(t+1)\right]\right\} \tag{10}$$

We can thus express the maximum changes in the within-group Theil values exclusively with observable variables. First, we will assume that from t or $t + 1$ the within-group inequality will jump, for every group, from zero to the maximum level. In this case, again expressing the growth rates by logarithmic differences:

$$\Delta_{\text{within}}^{\text{MAX}^+}(t,t+1) = \sum_{j=1}^{m}\left\{\frac{Y_j(t+1)}{Y(t+1)}\cdot\log[n_j(t+1)]\cdot\left[1+\log\left[\frac{Y_j(t+1)}{Y(t+1)}\cdot\frac{Y(t)}{Y_j(t)}\right]\right]\right\} \tag{11}$$

The maximum change in the opposite direction, from the maximum level of within-group inequality to zero, is given by

$$d_{\text{within}}^{\text{MAX}^-}(t,t+1) = -\sum_{j=1}^{m}\left\{\frac{Y_j(t+1)}{Y(t+1)}\cdot\log[n_j(t)]\right\} \tag{12}$$

Expressions (9) through (11) include only measurable variables and can be computed from data on industrial wages. However, one must bear in mind that these estimates are certainly highly exaggerated. We are assuming the unrealistic situation under which either all income in each group is concentrated in a single individual, or else the change between consecutive periods goes from one extreme to the other of possible within-group Theil values, that is, from zero to $\log(n_j)$.

How big are the changes in within-group inequality likely to prove in practice? It is possible to consider this issue by reflecting on the nature of industrial classification schemes. Consider first the extreme, and once again unrealistic, case in which industrial classifications have no intrinsic economic meaning but are simply a random classification system whose only virtue, for our purposes, is that each factory retains its identifying label through time and is therefore recorded in the same category every year. In this case, the level of T' will be a stable lower-bound estimate of T. The value of T' in relation to T should simply reflect the depth of the group structure: The more disaggregated the groups, the more closely groups approach individuals and the more closely T' approaches T.

In this case, the fractal character of the distribution, and of the Theil index, assures us that any change in T' will be very close to the change in T. This result is obvious from the assumption of randomness. Changes within groups must also be happening across groups. There is no basis for within-group inequalities to be changing at a different rate from between-group inequalities, other than random differences that are likely in any event to be offsetting once groups are added together.

Now consider the more realistic case in which industrial classification schemes actually do, to some imperfect extent, distinguish between qualitatively differing types of economic activity. The effect of this is again obvious. Relative to the random taxonomy case, some within-group and unobservable variations must move to the between-group part of the expression, where they can now be observed. Why? Because industries now mean something, and if they mean anything at all, the effect must be to impose a measure of homogeneity on entities classified together and a measure of distinctiveness on entities classified as being in different groups.

Pursuing this line of thought further, consider that "industries" are in fact collections of similar factories, which operate from one year to the next with labor forces, internal wage structures, managerial hierarchies, and technologies that change fairly little and that, when they do change, tend to change in similar ways. It seems clear that while within-group inequalities may well be large relative to differences between group averages, the internal rigidity of the industrial structure tends to ensure that changes in within-group inequalities in an industrial classification will be small relative to changes between groups. Therefore, a measure of the change in T' is likely to be a robust estimate of the change in T, so long as changes in employment structures and the distribution of the workforce across categories are not too large.

15.4   Separating Out Employment Effects

We now turn to the effect of changes in the distribution of employment across industries on T'. Our strategy relies on Theil's own hypothetical question: What would have happened to inequality if employment shares had not changed? Taking the beginning of the time series as a starting point, then, if employment shares do not change, (5) simplifies to

$$\dot{T}'_F = \sum_{j=1}^{m} p_j (\log R_j + 1) \cdot \dot{R}_j \tag{13}$$

What are the implications of a fixed employment structure for our estimates of the maximum change in the within-group component of T? We established that the within-group component and its changes over time are independent of changes in employment across groups. However, when estimating the maximum impact of high levels of within-group inequality, expression (9) shows a dependency on employment changes. With the assumption of a fixed employment structure, (9) becomes

$$d_{\text{with},F}^{\text{MAX}} = \sum_{j=1}^{m} \cdot \left[\frac{Y_j}{Y} \cdot (g_j - g) \cdot \log n_j \right] \tag{14}$$

Expression (14) can easily be turned into a discrete form, amenable to empirical use, using the same procedure discussed earlier when moving from (9) to (10).

In short, isolating the effect of changes in employment structure on the Theil index is entirely straightforward and requires only observable data. In the next section, we illustrate the practical effect of changing employment structures on inequality in the case of Brazil.

15.5   Empirical Application to the Case of Brazil

We will now compute T' for the case of Brazil using monthly data on wages and employment for seventeen industrial sectors. Data are monthly for the period 1976–1995, leading to the long, dense, continuous time series of Figure 15.1.[1]

In Figure 15.2, we plot the series after smoothing, using a twelve-month moving average. Also plotted here are the "high-quality" Gini coefficients from Deininger and Squire's (1996a) data set for Brazil.

To determine how much of the change in inequality overall has not been accounted for, we begin with an informal discussion of the structure of the data. First, consider the wage structure. The proportion of total wages held by each industrial group is depicted in Figure 15.3, which shows the evolution of each industry wage's share. The highest positive rate of change is 7 percent, and the highest negative rate of change is −4.5 percent. Average rates of change, both negative and positive, are just over 1 percent. The mechanical sector has the highest share, which reaches just over 20 percent. Steel and transportation have shares above 10 percent, but the remaining fourteen sectors have shares below 8 percent.

---

[1] The economic and political aspects of this measure are analyzed in Chapter 12.

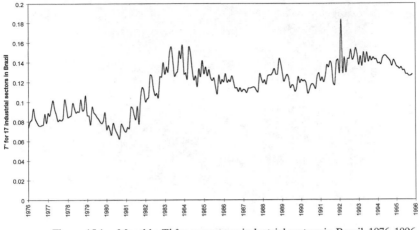

Figure 15.1.   Monthly T' for seventeen industrial sectors in Brazil, 1976–1996.

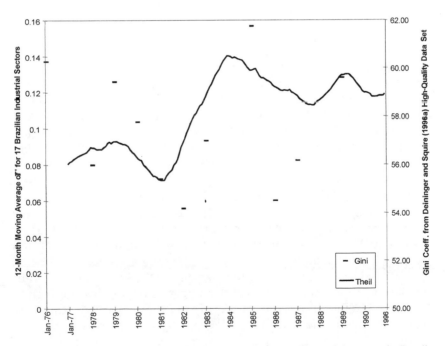

Figure 15.2.   Smoothed T' series for seventeen industrial sectors in Brazil, 1976–1996, and available high-quality Gini coefficients.

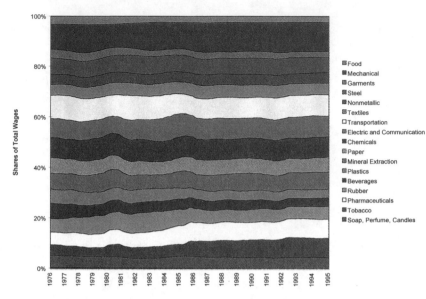

Figure 15.3.   Smoothed shares of wages for seventeen industrial sectors in Brazil.

Figure 15.4 shows the evolution of the employment structure. Despite being irrelevant to the estimate of the unobservable impact given by (8), this effect is important for the maximum potential impact estimate given by (9). Four groups have consistently more than 10 percent of employment, and one, food, reaches a high of 19 percent in 1992 and 1993. The next four industries in employment share – nonmetallic, textiles, transportation, and electric/communications – have shares that oscillate between 5 percent and less than 10 percent. More importantly, because (9) depends only on changes in employment, Figure 15.4 shows that there are no sharp transitions in population shares. In fact, the highest positive rate of change is 3 percent and the highest negative rate of change is –6 percent (average growth rates, both positive and negative, are about 1 percent). From this we infer that changing population shares will rarely affect T by very much.

Given what we know about the changes in the shares of wages and employment, we can explore what the outcomes of (10) through (12) are likely to be. Because the structure of wages changes little from one instant in time to the other, the following approximations are valid:

$$\frac{Y_j(t+1)}{Y(t+1)} \cdot \frac{Y(t)}{Y_j(t)} = \left(\frac{Y_j(t+1)}{Y(t+1)} \bigg/ \frac{Y_j(t)}{Y(t)} \right) \approx 1 \rightarrow \log\left[\frac{Y_j(t+1)}{Y(t+1)} \cdot \frac{Y(t)}{Y_j(t)} \right] \approx 0 \qquad (15)$$

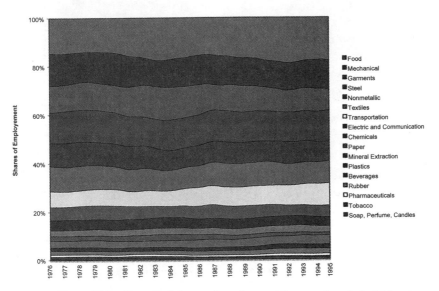

Figure 15.4. Smoothed shares of employment for seventeen industrial sectors in Brazil.

Therefore, expression (10) can be approximated by

$$d_{\text{within}}^{\text{MAX}}(t,t+1) \approx \sum_{j=1}^{m} \left\{ \frac{Y_j(t+1)}{Y(t+1)} \log\left[\frac{p_j(t+1)}{p_j(t)} \right] \right\}$$ (16)

and expression (11) by

$$d_{\text{within}}^{\text{MAX}^+}(t,t+1) = \sum_{j=1}^{m} \left\{ \frac{Y_j(t+1)}{Y(t+1)} \cdot \log[n_j(t+1)] \right\}$$ (17)

Expression (12) is unaffected by approximation (15). Note, however, that (17) is almost symmetric with (12); whenever $n_j(t) \approx n_j(t+1)$, we should expect $\Delta_{\text{within}}^{\text{MAX}^+}(t,t+1) \approx -\Delta_{\text{within}}^{\text{MAX}^-}(t,t+1)$.

In both (17) and (12) $\log[n_j(\bullet)]$ tends to smooth the differences across industries. Taking the extreme cases, employment in the food industries is around 500,000, and in the soap and perfume industries it is around 20,000; when logs are taken, the values are 13 for food and 10 for soap and perfume. Likewise, and in an even more dramatic way, the log smoothes the changes in employment within industries across time, which means that expressions (17) and (12) are almost constant, because we also saw that the change over time in wage shares was smooth.

Table 15.1. *Maximum Impact of the Maximum Changes over Time of Within-Industry Inequality*

	$\Delta_{\text{within}}^{\text{MAX}^+}(t,t+1)$	$\Delta_{\text{within}}^{\text{MAX}^-}(t,t+1)$
Average (n = 226)	12.51906	-12.52010
Standard deviation	0.11943	0.11883

Therefore, there is no need to compute a time series for either $\Delta_{\text{within}}^{\text{MAX}^+}(t,t+1)$ or $\Delta_{\text{within}}^{\text{MAX}^-}(t,t+1)$. Their values are likely to be almost constant over time. Furthermore, a time series of either (17) or (12) makes no sense, because, for example, the Theil value cannot jump from zero to the maximum from t to $t+1$ and then again from zero to the maximum from $t+1$ to $t+2$. What would be meaningful would be one time series in which (12) and (17) alternate from one period to the next. But because we know that the values are almost constant over time, we might as well compute averages over time.

Table 15.1 shows the average values for $\Delta_{\text{within}}^{\text{MAX}^+}(t,t+1)$ and $\Delta_{\text{within}}^{\text{MAX}^-}(t,t+1)$, in which the computation was made using the exact formulas (11) and (12), and the averages are of the monthly values over the entire period of time under consideration.

Table 15.1 confirms that (11) and (12) are symmetrical and also that their change over time is low (note the low levels of the standard deviation). Clearly, these values are far above the changes in between-group Theil index that we observe, which never surpass 0.00437 and are never below −0.00270. But it is also clear that the values in Table 15.1 are highly unlikely to correspond to a real evolution of the Theil index.

From expression (10) or its simplified form (16), it is not possible to make any further simplifications. In fact, the "strong" $\log[n_j(\bullet)]$ term is almost washed out in (16). In this case, then, it is of interest to know what is the time evolution of (10) and to compare it with the observed between-industry Theil. Figure 15.5 shows what the maximum change in the overall Theil index would be if the levels of the within-industry Theil index remain at their maximum.

Again, discrepancies exist, namely, when the observed change is different in sign from the maximum possible change, but the overall pattern of evolution of the two series looks quite similar.

In essence, we have built a framework of analysis to account for the "measure of our ignorance" whenever only the between-group component of a measure of inequality is used. Our aim was to show how this

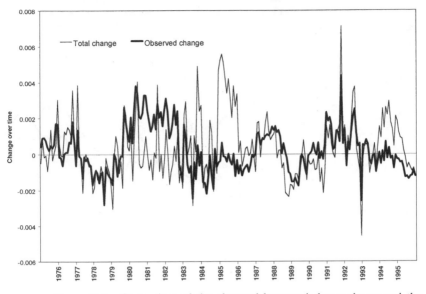

Figure 15.5. Comparison of the observed between-industry change and the maximum Theil change when the levels of within-group Theil are at their maximum.

framework could be implemented and to illustrate this with real data. Further refinements of our analysis should include explicit consideration of more plausible within-group distributions rather than the extreme cases we considered, which are unlikely ever to be found in practice.

From a conceptual point of view, how important is the within-group component in practice? We believe that when the underlying data set is drawn from industrial classification schemes, the answer will generally be "not very important." Industrial classification schemes, after all, are designed to group together entities that are composed of firms engaged in similar lines of work, and firms, like all bureaucracies, tend to keep their internal relative pay structures comparatively stable from one period to the next. Thus, the within-group variation in inequality will never approach the extreme case in which all the income moves from equal distribution to concentration in a single individual, the example of Michael Milken in the last years of Drexel Burnham Lambert to the contrary notwithstanding. For this reason, we remain convinced that, in practice, the effect of the unobservable component on the evolution of T will generally be very small. So long as the group structure is sufficiently disaggregated so that changing population shares and wage shares are not likely to dominate, the movement of T' will closely approximate the

Figure 15.6.   Fixed and variable T' for Brazil.

movement of T. And it is obvious that as one moves toward a finer classification scheme, T' must necessarily converge toward T.

To complete the analysis proposed in Section 4, we must isolate the population effects. This we will do by fixing the employment structure to the beginning of the period. This way, we will compute a T'_F, which gives the evolution of inequality under the hypothetical situation of no changes in the structure of employment. Figure 15.6 presents the results.

Figure 15.6 shows the power of this simple procedure. Changes in T'_F follow changes in T' during most of the period under analysis, showing that wage changes have driven most of the dynamic behavior of inequality. However, between 1981 and 1986 there is a clear discrepancy. T'_F rose steadily, at what looks like a constant rate of change, but our measured T' rose much more sharply between 1982 and 1984 and even decreased between 1984 and 1986. From then on, the changes are very similar. Therefore, we can argue that during the 1982–1986 period, but particularly between 1984 and 1986, changes in T' were driven by changes in the employment structure rather than by changes in wages.

We have shown how it is possible to study the dynamics of inequality using Theil indexes calculated from industrial wage data. The structure of the data required is extremely simple; basically, only employment and wages or earnings by sector are required. The wide availability of such data for many countries over long periods of time opens new possibilities for the analysis of inequality dynamics.

CHAPTER 16

Cluster and Discriminant Analysis of Time Series as a Research Tool

James K. Galbraith and Lu Jiaqing

This chapter presents a procedure for studying industrial performance and related issues, such as changes in the wage structure. This procedure combines cluster analysis and discriminant analysis as a package and applies this package to time-series data. This enables us to organize industrial data into groups with similar wage or performance histories and then to extract summary time series showing the main pattern of variation in performance between groups.

16.1   Introduction

This chapter presents a procedure for studying industrial performance and related issues, such as change in the wage structure. The procedure combines cluster and discriminant analysis and applies them to time series data to explore, first, the group pattern and, second, the forces that promote the formation of that group pattern. This procedure can be applied to many fields for which time-series data are available on a single key measure of behavior for a large number of related entities – for example, wages by industry or occupation or expenditure by account in a study of government budgets.

The use of dated information as a tool for classification is well established in disciplines such as geology, paleontology, archeology, and even biology and developmental psychology. For example, Chiodi (1989) uses time-series height and arm span data to classify children, and Hirsch and DuBois (1991) classify children based on the similarities in behavior through time. So far as we know, however, the present sequence of cluster and discriminant analysis on multivariate time-series data had not been done until Galbraith and Calmon's work on industrial wage rates (1990, 1994, 1996); the technique is used extensively in Galbraith (1998). Very recently, Kakizawa, Shumway, and Taniguchi (1998) published a full development and empirical application of closely related techniques to a problem in seismology, namely, that of distinguishing earthquakes from nuclear explosions.

A more formal presentation of our procedure is now needed. In Section 2, we will explain the theoretical linkage between wages or earnings and industrial performance underlying the use of the former as attribute variables in a cluster and discriminant analysis. Section 3 will present the method of cluster and discriminant analysis.

16.2   Wages and Industrial Performance

The first step in cluster and discriminant analysis is to choose characteristic or attribute variables for the objects to be clustered. For analyses of industrial performance, Galbraith and Calmon (1994, 1996) propose the year-to-year change in average wages by Standard Industrial Classification (SIC) category as a performance measure. The notion of industry-specific labor rents is helpful in motivating this choice. If capital markets clear but labor markets don't, we should expect that rates of return on investment will equalize across industries but that rates of pay will not. Hence, there will be industry-specific pay differentials. There is a persuasive body of information to this effect, summarized in Katz, and Summers (1989) and strongly seconded in an important paper by Blanchflower, Oswald, and Sanfey (1996). The burden of this analysis is that source factors, such as human skill, eventually capture the monopoly rents that an industry's market position may earn.

The Katz-Summers argument is essentially static, based on the degree of monopoly power enjoyed by an industry at a particular moment in time. But if degrees of monopoly change (and who would deny it?), then surely industry-specific labor rents will also change. And if that is so, the patterns of change through time can serve as markers of similarity and difference in economic performance among and between industries. When a pattern of wage changes is essentially identical in two separate industrial subclassifications over a long period of time, it becomes unlikely that this is accidental. Instead, similar effects result from structural characteristics that produce like reactions to common causes. That being so, patterns of similar effects can be used to classify industries according to structural similarity, even if one has no direct measure of what the structural similarities may be.[1]

---

[1] A drawback of the change in average wage rates by industrial group as a performance measure is that there may be intra-industry distributional shifts, such as from production

The use of percentage rates of change in our performance variable, rather than the level, has an economic justification and also technical advantages. From an economic standpoint, we are interested in the change in performance through time; this is a matter of rates of change rather than of initial levels. As a technical matter, because cluster analysis is sensitive to the units and scale of variables, a change in scale of one of the measures can change the implicit weight of the characteristic being measured and hence the group structure. But if we use annual percentage change, we are free of units and scale problems because each measurement is of the same form as any other and scale-altering forces such as inflation do not affect our analysis.

16.3   Cluster and Discriminant Analysis

Cluster analysis is a technique used to classify objects into homogeneous groups, or clusters, based on their similarities in some attribute or characteristic variables. For example, the technique may be used to group flowers by visual characteristics or students according to their pattern of scores on a series of tests. For details about cluster analysis, please refer to Lorr (1983), Anderberg (1973), and Aldenderfer and Blashfield (1984). Informative use of cluster analysis has recently been made by Hirschberg and Slottje (1994).

Suppose there are N industrial sectors or objects, such as those based on SIC codes at the three- or two-digit level. The attribute variables are percentage rates of change in our performance measure – wages or annual earnings, for the most part in this volume – for each year. Each element $\Delta L(i, t)$ in the matrix $\Delta \mathbf{L}$ of order $N \times (T - 1)$ can therefore represent the annual percentage change in earnings of industry i in year t. The complete row of values across variables (years) is called the industry's *profile*, and cluster analysis classifies industries into groups by the similarity between profiles. Geometric similarity can be measured by Euclidean distance, which is defined as

$$d_{ij} = \sqrt{\Sigma_t} \left(\Delta L_{it} - \Delta L_{jt} \right)^2 \tag{1}$$

where d_{ij} is an element of $\mathbf{D}$, the $N \times N$ matrix of distances between objects.

workers to salaried employees, and these may confound the use of wage change as a proxy for industrial performance. When data are available, we therefore suggest *total payroll per production worker hour*, a measure that Galbraith, 1998a, calls the *P-measure*, as a better measurement of industrial performance. However, this measure is not as readily available in the international statistics, so that this volume restricts itself largely to wage and earnings measures.

Deciding the structural model for the expected clusters, as well as the clustering method or algorithm that can generate this cluster structure, is the most important step. There are two kinds of cluster structure, chained and compact. According to Lorr (1983:18), a chained or serpentine cluster is a category of objects in which every member is more like *one* other member than it is like any object not in the category. The compact or ellipsoidal cluster is a category in which all members are more like *every* other member than they are like objects in any other subgroup; such clusters exhibit "high mutual similarity." For the comparison of industrial groupings, we have a strong preference for high mutual similarity and therefore for compact structure.

There are many available clustering algorithms, and still more are under development. All of these methods fall into two major categories, single-level cluster methods and multilevel hierarchical methods, with the choice typically depending on the problem. But according to Lorr (1983:20), hierarchical methods are often preferred. One of the reasons is that hierarchical methods tend to reflect a developmental or evolutionary pattern or sequence. For this reason, most biologists favor this method, and because our data are historical in character, so do we.

We choose Ward's method, a hierarchical method, also known as the *minimum-variance method* (Ward, 1963). This method begins by treating each object as a separate group, so that no information is missing. At each step afterward, group or cluster numbers are reduced from N to $N-1, N-2, \ldots, 2, 1$ in such a way that a specified objective function is minimized at each step. The objective function Ward chose is the increase in the total error sum of squares – or the geometric distance from each data point to the center of its cluster – due to the merger of two objects, clusters, or objects-and-clusters to form a new, more encompassing cluster. The details are presented in Anderberg (1973:147–148). In our case, the error sum of squares for cluster g is

$$E_g = R_g - \frac{1}{m_g} \sum_t T_{tg}^2 \qquad (2)$$

where

$$T_{tg} = \sum_i \Delta L_{itg} \qquad (3)$$

is the sum of changes of earning in year t for industries in the gth cluster and

$$R_g = \sum_t \sum_i \Delta L_{itg}^{\,2} \tag{4}$$

is the sum of squared changes of wages in all years for all industries in the gth cluster. Here m_g is the number of industries in cluster g and ΔL_{itg} is the change in earnings at time t for the ith of m_g industries in the gth cluster.

The increase in the total error sum of squares due to the merger of clusters g and h to form the new cluster k is

$$\Delta E_{gh} = E_k - (E_g + E_h) \tag{5}$$

By Ward's method, in each step, clusters g and h will be merged to form a new cluster, k, if they satisfy

$$\text{Min}(\Delta E_{gh}) \tag{6}$$

for all possible values of g and h, contingent on the clustering achieved at the previous step. The next question is when to stop, and this is essentially a matter of deciding when too much information is being lost by forcing dissimilar objects to associate, that is, when the minimum increase in the error sum of squares has become too large. The semipartial R^2 criterion can be used to choose this point (Lorr, 1983:99). There is an element of judgment in applying this criterion.

Discriminant analysis is a multivariate technique that is used to examine the differences between two or more groups of objects with respect to several variables. The basic elements of a discriminant analysis are objects, group membership of objects, and a set of attribute or characteristic variables. The goal of the analysis is to find discriminant function(s) that can differentiate groups, that is, can make group means on the function(s) differ widely. For those who are interested in the more technical details of discriminant analysis, please refer to Tatsuoka (1988) and Klecka (1980).

Because we derive cluster membership from cluster analysis, which classifies industries by annual changes in wages or earnings, an intuitive way to construct a discriminant function is to combine these annual changes linearly, that is,

$$F = a_1 \Delta L_1 + a_2 \Delta L_2 + a_3 \Delta L_3 + \ldots + a_{t-1} \Delta L_{t-1} \tag{7}$$

where ΔL_t is the change of the earnings measure in year t, $i = 1, 2, \ldots,$ $T - 1$.

To get the coefficients $a_1, a_2, \ldots a_{T-1}$, or simply the $(t - 1)$ vector $\mathbf{a}$, consider the $(T - 1)$ dimensional matrices $\mathbf{W}$ and $\mathbf{B}$, where the diagonal elements of $\mathbf{W}$ are the sums of squared deviations of each observation from its group mean (for each year) and the diagonal element of **B** is the difference between this value and the sum of squared deviations of each observation from the *global* mean. Off-diagonals are sums of cross-products of deviations for the pairs of years corresponding to each row and column. The problem is to find **a** so that F differentiates group means in a way that minimizes within-group differences (**W**) and simultaneously maximizes between-group differences (**B**). This can be done by solving a maximization problem:

$$\text{Max}[(\mathbf{a'Ba})/(\mathbf{a'Wa})] \tag{8}$$

Applying differential calculus to (8), we get

$$\partial/\partial a[a'\mathbf{B}a/a'\mathbf{W}a] = 0 \tag{9}$$

or

$$[\mathbf{W}^{-1}\mathbf{B} - \lambda\mathbf{I}]a = 0 \tag{10}$$

Here, λ is the vector of eigenvalues associated with matrix $\mathbf{W}^{-1}\mathbf{B}$. Because **W** and **B** can be calculated from our data set, we can solve (10) to get eigenvalues and associated eigenvectors **a**. In the literature of discriminant analysis, **a** are often called *canonical roots of the discriminant functions*. Suppose that there are G groups from cluster analysis; the number of eigenvalues and eigenvectors is determined by the rank of $\mathbf{W}^{-1}\mathbf{B}$ (Klecka, 1980):

$$\text{Min}[(G-1), (T-1)] \tag{11}$$

Because in most cases, if not all, we run discriminant analysis with more years than the number of clusters, we can use $(G - 1)$ as the number of eigenvalues and eigenvectors safely. The discriminant function associated with a bigger eigenvalue should more powerfully explain the differences among groups than those with smaller eigenvalues; the eigenvalue λ is therefore called the *discriminant criterion* (Tatsuoka, 1988:213).

How many eigenvectors one should actually use depends on how many are needed to account for the between-group variations. If, for example, the first three functions associated with the three biggest eigenvalues can account for a large fraction of all discriminatory power, we are confident that three functions are sufficient. In practice, the acceptable proportion, as well as the optimum number of functions, depends on the problem at hand.

If we derive $G - 1$ discriminant functions, they are

$$F_1 = a_{11}\Delta L_1 + a_{12}\Delta L_2 + \ldots + a_{1(t-1)}\Delta L_{t-1}$$
$$F_2 = a_{21}\Delta L_1 + a_{22}\Delta L_2 + \ldots + a_{2(t-1)}\Delta L_{t-1}$$
$$\ldots$$ \hfill (12)
$$F_{G-1} = a_{(G-1)1}\Delta L_1 + a_{(G-1)2}\Delta L_2 + \ldots + a_{(G-1)(t-1)}\Delta L_{t-1}$$

in which the **a** values are known. Obviously, the **a** values are actually a set of weights on annual changes of the earnings measures. The weights, which are components of an eigenvector, form a $(T-1)$ dimension vector in space. *But if we assume that the weight associated with a specified annual change is that-year-specific, we can reasonably assume that the sequence of weights for each year also form a time series. By doing so, a $(T-1)$ dimension vector in space is converted into a one-dimensional time series with $(T-1)$ values at $(T-1)$ different time points.* This is the beauty of the present procedure and the one feature that we claim to have pioneered.

Based on the theoretical and empirical background of the problem at hand, we can next try to use historical economic data to match and identify these eigenvectoral time series. For example, we might match the weights of F_1 with a gross national product time series, F_2 with the interest rate, and so on. If we are successful in making such a match for some subset of our $G-1$ eigenvectors, we can infer that in those cases we have identified the economic forces underlying the differentiation of group behavior, and because we have the eigenvalues, we also know the relative contribution of each force.

An intuitive way to show how discriminant functions i and j differentiate clusters is to plot their scores on functions i and j on a Root i – Root j coordinate. The scores for each group can be calculated by simply substituting each year's group mean of the earnings change of each group into (7). To show how discriminant functions differentiate each industry, follow a similar procedure using the annual values of change in average earnings for each industry. The resulting scores, which are the vector inner products of the weighting function **a** and the vector of rates of change in our performance measures, are scalars that can be plotted against a variety of variables to reveal cross-sectional relationships.

In our repeated experience, this technique is useful for many social science problems in which the essential problem is to identify the principal patterns of movement in time-series data sets involving blocks of observations on similar entities, such as firms or industries, where the appropriate group structure must be derived from the data themselves.

DATA APPENDIX

Data Appendix I: The UTIP World Data Set, 1970–1995

Year	Algeria	Argentina	Australia	Austria	Bangladesh	Belgium	Bolivia	Brazil	Bulgaria	Canada	Chile	China	Colombia	Cuba
1970	100		100	100	100	100	100	100	100	100	100		100	
1971	92	100	99	89	144	102	132	87	114	99	77		111	
1972	88	102	105	84	149	105	160	84	419	100	51		119	
1973	108	94	100	82	245	61	65	78	378	99	48		111	
1974	92	93	99	90	160	61	60	72	357	95	61		107	
1975	98	92	84	91	196	63	80	78	421	92	64		127	
1976	75	76	71	90	276	62	96	67	421	94	88		116	
1977	62	88	72	88	348	65	107	76	442	94	102	100	139	100
1978	68	111	71	86	247	64	72	81	486	93	103		104	90
1979	40	117	72	87	195	68	49	84	589	87	115	79	93	107
1980	42	115	81	87	166	69	73	117	579	88	118		84	139
1981	29	115	80	95	213	68	82	106	560	95	126		92	133
1982	25	128	87	92	259	71	114	117	557	106	134		95	148
1983	31	97	84	77	287	73	120	122	563	115	185		111	134
1984	49	84	94	84	248	76	254	124	549	119	210		108	115
1985	42	91	77	81	321	74	344	145	552	121	224	71	121	108
1986	72	112	100	80	393	77	174	134	611	123	259	56	114	103
1987	70	110	107	84	400	76	170	143	584	118	231	53	120	83
1988	94	130	102	73	442	75	177	165	568	113	206	75	105	75
1989	67	155	111	78	710	72	143	131	452	110	183	85	114	98
1990	56	190	99	74	637	75	143	144	408	104	179	88	121	
1991	48	160	140	69	818	74	171	158	1,047	112	178	94	136	
1992	68	163	145	64	854		211	144	1,615	134	130	120	70	
1993	48	123					172	192	1,044		197	159	122	
1994	48						235	180	226		201	138		
1995									216					

Year	Czechoslovak	Denmark	Ecuador	Egypt	Finland	France	Germany	Ghana	Greece	Guatemala	Hong Kong	Hungary	India	Indonesia
1970	100	100	100		100	100	100	100	100			100	100	100
1971	108	103	102	100	81	98	97	86	97	100		96	106	107
1972	110	102	89	99	88	88	93	129	95	138		76	107	92
1973	106	87	68	77	91	93	96	98	95	99	100	76	129	72
1974	103	87	48	81	84	98	104	73	108	99	133	69	163	97
1975	98	103	48	84	81	86	106	62	107	80	113	76	161	97
1976	102	87	50	75	79	96	108	78	98	76	94	42	182	110
1977	101	77	45	77	73	136	110	94	100	75	61	45	180	106
1978	100	78	32	82	73	137	104	111	113	68	51	42	168	104
1979	98	71	59	93	84	147	110	96	125	88	50	41	161	101
1980	99	67	73	99	75	150	110	104	130	110	59	43	188	100
1981	95	68	64	98	72	165	108	85	136	68	71	42	197	88
1982	97	74	75	96	67	162	111	94	147	90	66	41	163	85
1983	98	67	78	94	69	154	115	140	110	96	59	47	138	86
1984	96	64	87	93	77	148	123	50	116	93	45	53	137	89
1985	88	59	87	103	77	160	118	108	106	99	55	60	131	102
1986	96	60	99	95	81	156	113	172	90	135	55	57	141	102
1987	91	63	96	96	76	156	120	120	93	135	56	69	143	105
1988	80	67	116	98	65	157	115		98	123	56	107	136	91
1989	76	61	111	98	74	157	116		109		72	123	146	86
1990	74	64	113	100	79	157	115		121		95	129	139	59
1991	104	66	141	98	89	154	110		129		107	144	132	58
1992			156	97	85	156	114	236	136		58	214	149	65
1993			168	93	92			236	141		289	292	158	47
1994			206	101								317		54
1995				107								278		51

Data Appendix I: The UTIP World Data Set, 1970–1995 *(continued)*

Year	Iran	Iraq	Ireland	Israel	Italy	Jamaica	Japan	Jordan	Kenya	Korea, South	Kuwait	Macau	Madagascar	Malaysia
1970	100	100	100	100	100		100	100	100	100	100		100	100
1971	87	122	106	103	82	100	93		97	82	120		69	107
1972	75	140	106	138	77	86	92		75	94	135		76	94
1973	67	102	84	121	76	82	94		84	95	172		119	88
1974	86	73	80	121	72	84	91	100	97	90	172		100	68
1975	91	80	83	140	76	77	92	118	90	89	172		70	67
1976	80	85	96	200	73	98	95	125	90	102	131		58	62
1977	85	55	95	179	62	90	99	127	78	96	125		109	68
1978	85	58	95	187	63	67	106	65	78	69	126	100	101	65
1979	85	95	99	290	60	71	100	49	94	57	108	102	77	49
1980	33	54	93	316	62	106	89	72	74	60	119	83	56	45
1981	20	51	89	272	63	102	90	91	82	80	119	162	22	46
1982	17	56	98	221	64	47	91	106	79	98	119	115	14	54
1983	14	58	105	270	64	40	94	104	71	114	98	176	41	71
1984	14	68	118	378	62	42	88	106	96	105	126	107	54	67
1985	10	62	117	355	67	50	85	121	98	98	126	80	36	84
1986	12	60	132	329	69	82	87	121	93	84	169	105	24	100
1987	20	52	131	313	71	173	79	117	89	75	168	92	33	102
1988	13	52	132	321	80	193	81	101	76	70	183	92	33	105
1989	17	52	126	299	81	207	87	63	85	68	175	92		85
1990	24	52	125	337	80	193	87	61	77	75	392	79		75
1991	26	52	116	391	80	223	81	61	78	88	429	71		72
1992	50	86	133	400	85	151	83	67	66	104	253	89		63
1993	57	86	146	378	89	149	77	61	58	113	244	234		60
1994		86	179	388					60		294	213		62
1995		61	248						48		570			65

290

Year	Mexico	Netherlands	New Zealand	Nicaragua	Nigeria	Norway	Pakistan	Peru	Philippines	Poland	Portugal	Singapore
1970	100	100	100	100	100	100	100	100	100	100		100
1971	101	100	97	102	117	100	216	98	77	101		96
1972	94	95	94	114	133	89	218	99	59	100		86
1973	92	96	91	106	139	91	193	99	84	118		69
1974	86	100	68	178	156	92	160	108	99	111	100	62
1975	85	92	78	168	120	94	139	118	76	126	99	48
1976	84	80	111	261	118	89	128	89	101	127	61	52
1977	91	78	63	151	113	84	174	70	120	108	66	53
1978	94	78	117	97	93	80	203	99	99	106	64	51
1979	86	78	63	109	93	83	245	110	77	110	51	47
1980	84	75	73	74	93	85	191	104	54	110	49	44
1981	87	77	80	67	66	87	175	104	68	65	49	42
1982	94	75	78	80	71	83	229	130	71	53	53	38
1983	92	84	106	155	146	86	236	177	91	56	57	37
1984	90	87	98	110	91	94	268	235	81	67	54	33
1985	96	81	111	116	124	100	225	331	85	75	57	35
1986	100	75	119	167		94	213	366	102	91	66	35
1987	117	74	140	144		95	236	236	110	74	58	34
1988	136	80	154	118		99	219	226	120	63	56	33
1989	137	82	132		124	95	250	574	114	71	58	31
1990	137	82	197		120	87	291	790	136	160	56	29
1991	129	74	172			89	243	591	135	114	59	29
1992	148	71	169			86	243	312	122	150		26
1993	139	76						333	131	181		27
1994								510	141			23
1995								491	184			61

Data Appendix I: The UTIP World Data Set, 1970–1995 (continued)

Year	South Africa	Spain	Sri Lanka	Sweden	Taiwan	Tanzania	Turkey	United Kingdom	United States	Uruguay	USSR/Russia	Venezuela	Zimbabwe
1970	100			100		100	100	100	100	100	100	100	100
1971	104			86		83	122	92	108		106	76	106
1972	93			85		52	144	96	115	59	108	60	113
1973	96			88	100	52	100	97	120	58	105	61	108
1974	101			85	127	52	105	87	119	87	102	50	105
1975	115			80	136	52	117	99	122	135	97	49	93
1976	123			73	128	52	100	81	133	175	85	46	91
1977	121			68	81	42	117	85	140	269	84	38	95
1978	118	100		61	109	32	149	87	139	296	75	38	97
1979	116	102	100	67	127	34	254	85	138	297	73	41	109
1980	115	96	130	66	98	32	186	90	143	122	77	53	94
1981	128	95	121	71	84	50	172	90	148	78	78	70	71
1982	118	93	81	75	79	38	144	94	150	68	81	58	73
1983	120	93	108	75	102	39	123	94	151	97	77	54	76
1984	122	99	106	81	86	88	125	91	149	48	93	58	91
1985	121	101	62	96	91	86	123	90	146	48	92	76	80
1986	124	99	113	99	90	94	124	92	146	59	95	71	75
1987	122	100	99	95	85	94	140	91	157	45	89	71	74
1988	120	104	79	77	96	94	144	93	170	74	78	92	92
1989	0	108	96	80	118	160	215	95	171	77	78	152	85
1990	0	102	70	85	125		246	96	170		72	110	97
1991	0	100	48	70	128		266	104	171		392	148	90
1992	120	84	73	75	137		336	97	181		711	0	92
1993	115			72	94		318		177		1,030	0	94
1994	125				103		316				1,361	0	106
1995	147				103						630		80

Notes: Values are interindustry Theil statistics computed from UNIDO, Industrial Statistics, OECD, the Structural Analysis Data Set, and the China State Statistical Yearbook.

The data measure changes in the dispersion of earnings in the manufacturing sector.

Calculations by the authors, set as index values with 1970 or first available year = 100.

Additional data are available on the website of the University of Texas Inequality Project: http://utip.gov.utexas.edu.

Data Appendix II: Inequality in U.S. Manufacturing Pay, 1920–1997: A Continuous Series

1920	100	1940	329	1960	307	1980	408
1921	211	1941	288	1961	309	1981	413
1922	187	1942	235	1962	313	1982	411
1923	167	1943	174	1963	301	1983	405
1924	170	1944	138	1964	299	1984	403
1925	165	1945	117	1965	294	1985	393
1926	167	1946	122	1966	259	1986	387
1927	172	1947	137	1967	244	1987	379
1928	176	1948	164	1968	247	1988	366
1929	175	1949	160	1969	245	1989	360
1930	198	1950	163	1970	280	1990	376
1931	264	1951	184	1971	310	1991	379
1932	313	1952	211	1972	308	1992	383
1933	343	1953	226	1973	307	1993	388
1934	334	1954	257	1974	336	1994	365
1935	318	1955	238	1975	358	1995	347
1936	306	1956	252	1976	370	1996	332
1937	302	1957	282	1977	377	1997	303
1938	326	1958	301	1978	376		
1939	330	1959	303	1979	382		

Notes: Calculations by Vidal Garza Cantú, Tom Ferguson, and James K. Galbraith.
Between-Industries Theil ututistic indexed, 1920 = 100.
Figures for 1920–1947 weighted by 1940 employment, including agriculture.
Figures after 1947 weighted by current employment, agriculture excluded.

References and Selected Bibliography

Abramovitz, M. "Catching Up, Forging Ahead, and Falling Behind." *Journal of Economic History*, 46(2), 1986: pp. 385–406.

Adelman, Irma, and S. Robinson. "Income Distribution and Development," in H. Chenery and T. N. Srinivasan (eds.), *Handbook of Development Economics*, vol. 1. Amsterdam: Elsevier Science, North Holland, 1989.

Aghion, Phillipe, and Patrick Bolton. "A Trickle-Down Theory of Growth and Development with Debt-Overhang." Working paper, London School of Economics, 1994.

Aghion, Phillipe, and Peter Howitt. "A Model of Growth Through Creative Destruction." *Econometrica*, 60(2), March 1992: pp. 323–352.

Endogenous Growth Theory. Cambridge, MA: MIT Press, 1998.

Ahluwalia, Montek S. "Inequality, Poverty and Development." *Journal of Development Economics*, vol. 6, 1976: pp. 307–342.

Albin, Peter S. *Barriers and Bounds to Rationality: Essays on Economic Complexity and Dynamics in Interactive Systems*. Cambridge: Cambridge University Press, 1998.

Aldenderfer, M., and R. Blashfield. *Cluster Analysis*. London: Sage, 1984.

Alesina, A., and R. Perotti. "The Political Economy of Growth: A Critical Survey of the Recent Literature." *World Bank Economic Review*, 8(3), 1994: pp. 351–371.

Alesina, A., and D. Rodrik. "Distributive Politics and Economic Growth." *Quarterly Journal of Economics*, 109(2), 1994: pp. 465–490.

Alston, Lee, and Joseph Ferrie. "Labor Costs, Paternalism, and Loyalty in Southern Agriculture: A Constraint on the Growth of the Welfare State." *Journal of Economic History*, 55, 1985: pp. 95–117.

Altimir, Oscar. "Income Distribution Statistics in Latin America and Their Reliability." *The Review of Income and Wealth*, Series 33, no. 3, June 1987.

Amadeo, Edward, and José Camargo. "Mercado de Trabalho e Dança Distributiva." *Distribuição de Renda no Brasil*. Rio de Janeiro: Paz e Terra, 1991.

"Instituiçoes e Mercado de Trabalho no Brasil," in José Márcio Camargo (ed.), *Flexibilidade do Mercado de Trabalho no Brasil*. Rio de Janeiro: FGV, 1996.

Amott, Teresa, and Julie Matthaei. *Race, Gender and Work*. Boston: South End Press, 1991.

Amsden, A. *Asia's Next Giant: South Korea and Late Industrialization*. New York, London: Oxford University Press, 1989.

Anand, Sudhir, and S. M. R. Kanbur. "Inequality and Development: A Critique." *Journal of Development Economics*, 41(1), 1993: pp. 19–43.

Anchordoguy, M. "Mastering the Market: Japanese Government Targeting of the Computer Industry." *International Organization*, 42(3), Summer 1988: 509–543.

Anderberg, M. R. *Cluster Analysis for Applications*. New York: Sage, 1973.

Archibald, R., M. Ritter, and David H. Pollock. *Latin American Prospects for the 1980's: Equity, Democratization and Development*. New York: Praeger, 1983.

Arco, J., E. Margain, and R. Cherol. *The Economic Integration Process of Latin America in the 1980's*. Washington, DC: Inter-American Development Bank, 1982.

Arrow, K. "The Economic Implications of Learning by Doing." *Review of Economic Studies*, 28, 1962: pp. 155–173.

Aspe, Pedro, and Javier Beristain. "Toward a First Estimate of the Evolution of Inequality in Mexico," in Pedro Aspe and Paul E. Sigmunds (eds.), op. cit.

Aspe, Pedro, and Paul E. Sigmund. "The Political Economy of Income Distribution in Mexico," from the series *The Political Economy of Income Distribution in Developing Countries*, ed. Henry Bienen. New York: Holmes and Meier, 1984.

Atkinson, A. B. "On the Measurement of Inequality." *Journal of Economic Theory*, 2(3), September 1970: pp. 244–263.

"Bringing Income Distribution in from the Cold." *The Economic Journal*, 107, March 1997: pp. 297–231.

Atkinson, A. B., L. Rainwater, and T. Smeeding. *Income Distribution in OECD Countries: The Evidence from the Luxembourg Income Survey*. Paris: Organization for Economic Cooperation and Development, 1995.

Autor, D., L. Katz, and A. Krueger. "Computing Inequality: Have Computers Changed the Labor Market?" NBER Working Paper 5956, 1997.

Auty, R. M. "The Macro Impacts of Korea's Heavy Industry Drive Re-evaluated." *The Journal of Development Studies*, 29(1), October 1992: pp. 24–49. *Economic Development and Industrial Policy*. New York: Mansel Publishing.

Backman, Jules, and M. R. Gainsbrugh. *Behavior of Wages*. New York: National Industrial Conference Board, 1948.

Balke, Nathan S., and Daniel J. Slottje. "A Macroeconometric Model of Income Inequality in the United States," in J. H. Bergstrand and T. F. Cosimano (eds.), *The Changing Distribution of Income in an Open U.S. Economy*. New York: North Holland, 1994.

Bank of Korea. *Economic Statistics Yearbook*. Seoul: Bank of Korea, 1971, 1984, 1995.

Barro, R. J. *Determinants of Economic Growth – A Cross-Country Empirical Study*. Cambridge, MA, and London: MIT Press, 1997.

Barro, R. J., and X. Sala-i-Martin. *Economic Growth*. New York: McGraw-Hill, 1995.

Baumol, W. "Productivity Growth, Convergence, and Welfare: What the Long-Run Data Show." *American Economic Review*, 76(5), 1986: pp. 1072–1085.

Becker, G. S. *Human Capital – A Theoretical and Empirical Analysis with Special Reference to Education*, 3rd ed. Chicago: University of Chicago Press, 1993.

Bell, Philip W. "Cyclical Variations and Trend in Occupational Wage Differentials in American Industry Since 1914." *Review of Economics and Statistics*, 33, 1951: pp. 329–337.

Bénabou, R. "Inequality and Growth." NBER Working Paper 5658, 1996.

Beney, M. Ada. *Wages, Hours, and Employment in the United States, 1914–36.* New York: National Industrial Conference Board, 1937.

Berman, E., John Bound, and Zvi Griliches. "Changes in the Demand for Skilled Labor within U.S. Manufacturing: Evidence from the Annual Survey of Manufactures." *Quarterly Journal of Economics*, 109, May 1994: pp. 367–397.

Berman, E., John Bound, and S. Machin. "Implications of Skill-Biased Technological Change: International Evidence." Centre for Economic Performance Discussion Paper 367. London: London School of Economics, 1997.

Bernstein, Irving. *The Turbulent Years*. Boston: Houghton Mifflin, 1970.

Berry, A. "Predicting Income Distribution in Latin America During the 1980's," in Archibald R. M. Ritter and David H. Pollock (eds.), *Latin American Prospects for the 1980's: Equity, Democratization and Development*. New York: Praeger, 1983.

"Poverty and Inequality in Latin America." *Latin American Research Review*, 22(2), 1987: pp. 202–214.

Blackburn, M., D. Bloom, and R. Freeman. "The Declining Economic Position of Less Skilled American Men," in G. Burtless (ed.), *A Future of Lousy Jobs? The Changing Structure of U.S. Wages*. Washington, DC: Brookings Institution, 1990.

"Changes in Earnings Differentials in the 1980s: Concordance, Convergence, Causes, and Consequences," in D. Papadimitriou and E. Wolff (eds.), *Poverty and Prosperity in the USA in the Late Twentieth Century*. New York: St. Martin's Press, 1993.

Blanchflower, David G., and Andrew J. Oswald. *The Wage Curve*. Cambridge, MA: MIT Press, 1994.

Blanchflower, David G., Andrew J. Oswald, and P. Sanfey. "Wages, Profits and Rent-Sharing." *Quarterly Journal of Economics*, 111(1), 1996: pp. 227–251.

Blau, F., and L. Kahn. "International Differences in Male Wage Inequality: Institutions versus Market Forces." *Journal of Political Economy*, 104(4), 1996: pp. 791–837.

Board of Governors of the Federal Reserve System. *Banking and Monetary Statistics, 1914–41*. Washington, DC: 1943.

Banking and Monetary Statistics, 1941–70. Washington, DC: 1976.

Bonelli, Regis, and Lauro Ramos. "Income Distribution in Brazil: An Evaluation of Long Term Trends and Changes in Inequality since the Mid-1970s," in Rosane Mendonça and Andre Urani (eds.), *Estudos Sociais e do Trabalho*. Brasilia: IPEA.

Borchardt, K. *Perspectives on Modern German Economic History and Policy*. Cambridge: Cambridge University Press, 1991.

Borjas, G., R. Freeman, and L. Katz. "On the Labor Market Effects of Immigration and Trade," in G. Borjas and R. Freeman (eds.), *The Economic Effects of Immigration in Source and Receiving Countries*. Chicago: Chicago University Press, 1992.

"Searching for the Effect of Immigration on the Labor Market." *American Economic Review*, 86(2), 1996: pp. 246–251.

Borjas, G., and Valerie A. Ramey. "The Relationship Between Wage Inequality and International Trade," in J. H. Bergstrand and T. F. Cosimano (eds.), *The Changing Distribution of Income in an Open U.S. Economy*. New York: North Holland, 1994.

Bortz, Jeff. *Los Salarios Industriales en la Ciudad de Mexico, 1939–1975*. Mexico, DF: Fondo de Cultura Economica, 1988.

Boudon, R. *L'Inegalité des Chances*. Paris: Libraire Armand Collin, 1973.

Bound, J., and G. Johnson. "Changes in the Structure of Wages in the 1980s: An Evaluation of Alternative Explanations." *American Economic Review*, 82(3), 1992: pp. 371–392.

Bourdieu, P., and J. C. Passeron. *La Réproduction. Éléments pour une Théorie du Système d'Enesignement*. Paris: Éditions du Minuit, 1970.

Bowles, B., and H. Gintis. *Schooling in Capitalist America*. London: Routledge, 1976.

Brandolini, A., and N. Rossi. "Income Distribution and Growth in Industrial Countries," in V. Tanzi and K. Chu (eds.), *Income Distribution and High-Quality Growth*. Cambridge, MA: MIT Press, 1998.

Braverman, H. "The Degradation of Work in the Twentieth Century." *Monthly Review*, 41(5), 1989: pp. 35–48.

Brenner, Y. S., Hartmut Kaelbe, and Mark Thomas. *Income Distribution in Historical Perspective*. Cambridge: Cambridge University Press, 1991.

Bresser Pereira, Luiz Carlos, and Yoskiaki Nakano. "Hyperinflation and Stabilization in Brazil: The First Collor Plan." Paper presented to the workshop on Economic Problems of the 1990s, Knoxville, University of Tennessee, June 28–July 4, 1990.

Bruno, M., and S. Fischer. *The Aftermath of Stabilization*. Cambridge, MA: MIT Press, 1991.

Burch, Philip. "The NAM as an Interest Group." *Politics and Society*, 4, 1973: pp. 97–130.

Burnlaux, J. M., T. T. Dang, D. Fore, M. Forster, M. d'Ercole, and H. Oxley. "Income Distribution and Poverty in Selected OECD Countries." OECD Economics Department Working Paper 189. Paris: OECD, 1998.

Calmon, P., P. Conceição, J. K. Galbraith, V. Garza Cantú, and A. Hibert. "The Evolution of Industrial Wage Inequality in Mexico and Brazil: A Comparative Study." *Review of Development Economics*, 4(2), June 2000: pp. 194–203.

Card, D., and A. Krueger. "Minimum Wages and Employment: A Case Study of the Fast-Food Industry in New Jersey and Pennsylvania." *American Economic Review*, 84(4), 1994: pp. 772–793.

"Time-Series Minimum-Wage Studies: A Meta-Analysis." *American Economic Review*, 85(2), 1995: pp. 238–243.

"The Economic Return to School Quality," in W. Becker and W. Baumol (eds.), *Assessing Educational Practices: The Contribution of Economics*. Cambridges, MA: MIT Press, 1996a.

"*Myth and Measurement: The New Economics of the Minimum Wage*. Princeton, NJ: Princeton University Press, 1996b.

Cardoso, E. "Inflation and Poverty." NBER Working Paper No. 4006, 1992.

Cardoso, E., and E. Faletto. *Dependency and Development in Latin America*. Berkeley: University of California Press, 1979.

Cardoso, E., and A. Helwege. "Below the Line: Poverty in Latin America." *World Development*, 20(1), 1995: pp. 19–38.

Latin America's Economy: Diversity, Trends and Conflicts. Cambridge, MA: MIT Press, 1996.

Carnoy, Martin. *Faded Dreams: The Politics and Economics of Race in America*. New York: Cambridge University Press, 1994.

Carruth, Alan A., and Andrew Oswald. *Pay Determination and Industrial Prosperity*. Oxford: Oxford University Press, 1989.

Caselli, F. "Technological Revolutions." *American Economic Review*, 89(1), 1999: pp. 78–102.

Chandler, Alfred D. *Strategy and Structure*. Cambridge, MA: MIT Press, 1962.

Chenery, H., and T. N. Srinivasan (eds.). *Handbook of Development Economics*, vol. 1. Amsterdam and New York: Elsevier Science, North Holland, 1988.

Chiodi, M. "The Clustering of Longitudinal Multivariate Data When Time Series Data Are Short," in R. Coppi and S. Bolasco (eds.), *Multiway Data Analysis*. Amsterdam: North Holland, 1989.

Cho, Y. J. "The Effects of Financial Liberalization on the Efficiency of Credit Allocation: Some Evidence from Korea." *Journal of Development Economics*, 29, 1988: pp. 101–110.

Cho Y. J., and D. Cole. "The Role of the Financial Sector in Financial Adjustment," in C. Vittirio and S. M. Suh (eds.), *Structural Adjustment in a Newly Industrializing Country: The Korean Experience*. Washington, DC: World Bank, 1992.

Cohen, D. *The Wealth of the World and the Poverty of Nations*. Cambridge, MA: MIT Press, 1998.

Collins, Robert. *Business Response to Keynes*. New York: Columbia University Press, 1981.

Cook, Phillip J., and Robert D. Frank. *The Winner-Take-All Society: How More and More Americans Compete for Ever Fewer and Bigger Prizes, Encouraging Economic Waste, Income Inequality, and an Impoverished Cultural Life*. New York: Free Press, 1995.

Cullen, Donald, "The Interindustry Wage Structure, 1899–1950." *American Economic Review*, 46, 1956: pp. 353–369.

Cutler, D., and L. Katz. "Rising Inequality? Changes in the Distribution of Income and Consumption in the 1980's." *American Economic Review*, 82(2), 1992: pp. 546–551.

Danziger, Sheldon, and Peter Gottschalk. *America Unequal*. Cambridge, MA: Harvard University Press, 1995.

D'Arista, Jane. *The Evolution of US Finance*, vol. I. Armonk, NY: M. E. Sharpe, 1994.

Dasgupta, P., and P. David. "Toward a New Economics of Science." *Research Policy*, 23, 1994: pp. 487–521.

David, P. "Clio and the Economics of QWERTY." *American Economic Review*, 75(2), 1986: pp. 332–337.

"Knowledge, Property, and the System Dynamics of Technological Change," in L. H. Summers and S. Shah (eds.), *Proceedings of the World Bank Annual Conference on Development Economics 1992, Supplement to the World Bank Economic Review, 1993*. Washington, DC: World Bank, 1993.

Deininger, K., and L. Squire. "A New Data Set Measuring Income Inequality." *The World Bank Economic Review*, 10(3), 1996a: pp. 565–591.

"New Ways of Looking at Old Issues: Inequality and Growth." Mimeo, World Bank, 1996b.

Denslow, David, Jr., and William G. Tyler. "Perspectives on Poverty and Income Distribution in Brazil." *World Development*, 11, 1984: pp. 1019–1028.

Devlin, R. *Debt and Crisis in Latin America: The Supply Side of the Story.* Princeton, NJ: Princeton University Press.

Dickens, W., and L. F. Katz. "Inter-Industry Wage Differences and Industry Characteristics," in K. Lang and J. Leonard (eds.), *Unemployment and the Structure of Labor Markets.* Oxford: Basil Blackwell, 1987.

Dietz, J., and J. Street. *Latin America's Economic Development: Institutionalist and Structuralist Perspectives.* Boulder, CO: Lynne Rienner, 1987.

Di Nardo, J., and J. Pischke. "The Returns to Computer Use Revisited: Have Pencils Changed the Wage Structure Too?" *Quarterly Journal of Economics*, 112(1), 1997: pp. 291–303.

do Valle Silva, Nelson. "Updating the Cost of Not Being White in Brazil," in Pierre-Michel Fontaine (ed.), *Race, Class and Power in Brazil.* Los Angeles: UCLA, Center for Afro-American Studies, 1985.

Dogan, Mattei, and John Higley. *Elites, Crises and Origins of Regimes.* Lantham, MD: Bowman, 1998.

Dore, R. *The Diploma Disease – Education, Qualification, and Development.* Berkeley: University of California Press, 1976.

Dornbusch, R. "Mexico: Stabilization, Debt and Growth." Mimeo, MIT, 1988.

The Road to Economic Recovery. New York: Twentieth Century, 1989.

"From Stabilization to Growth." NBER Working Paper No. 3302, March 1990.

Dornbusch, R., and Mario Henrique Simonsen. *Inflation Stabilization with Incomes Policy Support.* New York: Group of 30, 1986.

Dornbusch, R., Federico Sturzenegger, and Holger Wolf. "Extreme Inflation: Dynamics and Stabilization." *Brookings Papers on Economic Activity*, no. 2, 1991: pp. 1–84.

Douglas, Paul H. *Real Wages in the United States, 1890–1926.* Boston: Houghton Mifflin, 1930.

Dubofsky, Melvyn, and Warren Van Tine. *John L. Lewi: A Biography.* New York: Quadrangle, 1977.

Dunlop, John T. "The Wage Structure: Job Clusters and Wage Contours," in G. W. Taylor and F. C. Pierson (eds.), *New Concepts in Wage Determination.* New York: McGraw-Hill, 1957.

"Labor Markets and Wage Determination: Then And Now," in B. Kaufman (ed.), *How Labor Markets Work.* Lexington, MA: D. C. Heath, 1988.

Earle, Carville. "Divisions of Labor and the Splintered Geography of Labor Markets and Movements in Industrializing America, 1790–1930." *International Review of Social History*, 38, 1993: pp. 5–37.

Eckstein, Otto, and Thomas A. Wilson. "The Determination of Money Wages in American Industry." *Quarterly Journal of Economics*, 76, 1962: pp. 379–414.

Eckstein, S., G. Donald, D. Horton, and T. Carroll. *Land Reform in Latin America: Bolivia, Chile, Mexico, Peru and Venezuela.* Staff Working Paper No. 275. Washington, DC: World Bank, 1987.

Edin, P., and B. Holmlund. "The Swedish Wage Structure: The Rise and Fall of Solidarity Wage Policy?" in R. Freeman and L. Katz (eds.), *Differences and Changes in Wage Structures.* Chicago: University of Chicago Press, 1995.

Edwards, P. K. *Strikes in the United States 1886–1974.* New York: St. Martin's Press, 1981.

Edwards, S., and M. S. Khan. "Interest Rate Determination in Developing Countries: A Conceptual Framework. *IMF Staff Paper*, 32, September 1985: pp. 377–403.

Eichengreen, Barry. "The Origins and Nature of the Great Slump." *Economic History Review*, 45(2), 1992: pp. 213–239.

Eichengreen, Barry, and T. J. Hatton. *Interwar Unemployment in International Perspective*. Dordrecht The Netherlands: 1988.

Enos, J. L., and W. H. Park. *The Adoption and Diffusion of Imported Technology: The Case of Korea*. London, Croom Helm, 1987.

Erikson, Christopher L., and Andrea Ichino. "Wage Differentials in Italy: Market Forces, Institutions, and Inflation." NBER Working Paper No. 4922, 1994.

Ezekiel, Mordecai. "European Competition in Agricultural Production, with Special Reference to Russia." *Journal of Farm Economics*, 14, 1932: pp. 267–281.

Feenstra, Robert C., and Gordon Hanson. "Foreign Direct Investment and Relative Wages: Evidence from Mexican Maquiladoras." NBER Working Paper No. 5122, 1995.

Ferguson, Thomas. *Golden Rule: The Investment Theory of Party Competition and the Logic of Money-Driven Political Systems*. Chicago: University of Chicago Press, 1995a.

"From Boiling Pot to Melting Pot: The Real Lessons of the American Experience of Immigration and 'Assimilation,' in R. Benjamin, C. R. Neu, and D. Quigley (eds.), *Between States and Markets: The Limits of the Transatlantic Alliance*. New York: St. Martin's Press, 1995b.

Fields, G. *Poverty, Inequality and Development*. New York: Cambridge University Press, 1980.

"Who Benefits from Economic Development?" *American Economic Review*, no. 67, 1997: pp. 570–582.

Fishlow, A. "Brazilian Size Distribution of Income." *American Economic Review*, 2(62), 1972: pp. 391–402.

"Lessons of the 1890's for the 1980's," in R. Findlay (ed.), *Debt, Stabilization and Development*. New York: Basil Blackwell, 1988.

Foner, Philip S. *Women and the American Labor Movement*. London: Macmillan, 1980.

Foxley, A. *Latin American Experiments in Neoconservative Economics*. Berkeley: University of California Press, 1976.

Freeman, R. "How Much Has De-unionization Contributed to the Rise in Male Earnings Inequality?" in S. Danziger and P. Gottschalk (eds.), *Uneven Tides: Rising Inequality in America*. New York: Russell Sage Foundation, 1993.

"The Minimum Wage as a Redistributive Tool." *Economic Journal*, 106(436), 1996: pp. 639–649.

Friedman, Milton, and Anna Jacobson Schwartz. *A Monetary History of the United States, 1867–1960*. Princeton, NJ: Princeton University Press, 1963.

Frischtak, C. R. "Competition Policies for Industrializing Economies." *Policy and Research Series* No. 7. Washington, DC: World Bank, 1989.

Fuhrer, J. C., and J. S. Little. *Technology and Growth: Conference Proceedings*. Boston: Federal Reserve Bank of Boston, 1996.

Furtado, C. *Economic Development of Latin America*. Cambridge: Cambridge University Press, 1976.

Gabin, Nancy. *Feminism in the Labor Movement.* Ithaca, NY: Cornell University Press, 1990.

Galambos, Louis. *Competition and Cooperation: The Emergence of a National Trade Association.* Baltimore, MD: Johns Hopkins University Press, 1966.

Galbraith, James K. "Uneven Development and the Destabilization of the North." *International Review of Applied Economics*, 10(1), 1996: pp. 107–120.

Created Unequal: The Crisis in American Pay. New York: Free Press, 1998a.

"The Ethical Rate of Unemployment: A Technical Note." *Journal of Economic Issues*, 32(2), June 1998b: pp. 531–537.

"Inequality and Unemployment: An Analysis Across Time and Countries," in David Slottje (Series ed.), *Research on Economic Inequality*, vol. 8. Stamford, CT: JAI Press, 1998c.

Galbraith, James K., and Paulo Calmon. "Industries, Trade, and Wages," in M. Bernstein and D. Adler (eds.), *Understanding American Economic Decline.* Cambridge: Cambridge University Press, 1994.

"Wage Change and Trade Performance in U.S. Manufacturing Industries." *Cambridge Journal of Economics*, 20, 1996: pp. 433–450.

Galbraith, James K., and W. Darity. *Macroeconomics.* Boston: Houghton Mifflin, 1994.

Galbraith, James K., and Paulo Du Pin Calmon. "Relative Wages and International Competitiveness in U.S. Industry." Austin, TX: L. B. J. School of Public Affairs Working Paper No. 56, 1990.

"Industries, Trade and Wages," in Michael Bernstein and David Adler (eds.), *Understanding American Economic Decline.* New York: Cambridge University Press, 1994.

"Wage Change and Trade Performance in U.S. Manufacturing Industries." *Cambridge Journal of Economics*, 20(4), 1996: pp. 433–450.

Galbraith, J. K., and Junmo Kim. "The Legacy of the HCI: An Empirical Analysis of the Korean Industrial Policy." *Journal of Economic Development* 23(1), 1998: pp. 1–20.

Galenson, Walter. *The CIO Challenge to the AFL.* Cambridge: Harvard University Press, 1960.

Galor, O., and Daniel Tsiddon. "Income Distribution and Growth: The Kuznets Hypothesis Revisited." *Economica*, 63, 1996: s103–s117.

Galor, O., and Joseph Zeira. "Income Distribution and Macroeconomics." *Review of Economic Studies*, 60, 1993: pp. 35–52.

Garcia Rocha, Adelberto. *La Desigualidad Económica.* Mexico, DF: El Colegio de Mexico, Centro de Estudios Económicos, 1986.

Gardiner, K. "A Survey of Income Inequality – the UK," in P. Gottschalk, B. Gustafsson and E. Palmer (eds.), *Changing Patterns in the Distribution of Economic Welfare – An International Perspective.* Cambridge and New York: Cambridge University Press, 1997.

Gerschenkron, A. *Economic Backwardness in Historical Perspective.* Cambridge, MA: Harvard University Press, 1962.

Glick, R., and M. Hutchison. "Financial Liberalization in the Pacific Basin: Implications for Real Interest Rate Linkage." *Journal of Japanese and International Economies*, 4, 1990: pp. 36–48.

Glyn, Andrew, and Wiemer Salverda. "Employment Inequalities." Manuscript, Corpus Christi College, Oxford and Groningen University, May 1999.

Goldin, Claudia. *Understanding the Gender Gap.* New York: Oxford University Press, 1990.

Goldin, Claudia, and Lawrence F. Katz. "The Decline of Non-competing Groups: Changes in the Premium to Education, 1890 to 1940." National Bureau of Economic Research, Cambridge, MA, 1995.

"The Origins of Technology – Skill Complementarity." *Quarterly Journal of Economics*, 113(3), 1998: pp. 693–732.

Goldin, Claudia, and Robert A. Margo. "The Great Compression: The Wage Strucuture in the United States at Mid-Century." National Bureau of Economic Research, Cambridge, MA, 1991.

Goldstein, M. "Commentary: The Causes and Propagation of Financial Instability: Lessons for Policy Makers," in *Maintaining Financial Stability in a Global Economy.* Kansas City: Federal Reserve Bank of Kansas City, 1998.

Goldstein, Robert. *Political Repression in Modern America.* New York: Schenkman, 1978.

Gollas, Manuel. *"La Economia Desigual: Empleo y Distribucíon en México.* Mexico, DF: Consejo Nacional de Ciencia y Tecnologia, México, 1982.

Gordon, Robert J. *The American Business Cycle: Continuity and Change.* Chicago: University of Chicago Press, 1986.

Gourevitch, P. *Politics in Hard Times: Comparative Responses to International Economic Crises.* Ithaca, NY, and London: Cornell University Press, 1986.

Government of the Republic of Korea. *The Fourth Fifth Year Economic Development Plan 1977–1981.* Seoul, 1976.

Griffin, J. *Strikes.* New York: Columbia University Press, 1939.

Grossman, G. M., and E. Helpman. *Innovation and Growth in the Global Economy.* Cambridge, MA: MIT Press, 1991.

Grubb, W. N., and R. H. Wilson. "Sources of Increasing Inequality in Wages and Salaries, 1960–80." *Monthly Labor Review*, 112(4), 1989: pp. 3–13.

"Trends in Wage and Salary Inequality, 1967–1988." *Monthly Labor Review*, 115(6), 1992: pp. 23–39.

Gustafsson, B., and E. Palmer. "Changes in Swedish Inequality: A Study of Equivalent Income," in P. Gottschalk, B. Gustafsson and E. Palmer (eds.), *Changing Patterns in the Distribution of Economic Welfare – An International Perspective.* Cambridge and New York: Cambridge University Press, 1997.

Haddy, Pamela, and Melville R. Currell. "British Inter-Industrial Earnings Differentials, 1924–55." *Economic Journal*, 104(11), 1958: pp. 104–111.

Haddy, Pamela, and N. Arnold Tolles. "British and American Changes in Interindustry Wage Structure Under Full Employment." *Review of Economics and Statistics*, 39, 1957: pp. 408–414.

Haggard, S., R. N. Cooper, S. Collins, and Choongsoo Kim. *Macroeconomic Policy and Adjustment in Korea 1970–1990.* Cambridge, MA: Harvard University Press, 1994.

Hall, P. *Governing the Economy: The Politics of the State Intervention in Britain and France.* Oxford and New York: Oxford University Press, 1986.

Hanson, Gordon, and Ann Harrison. "Trade, Technology and Wage Inequality." NBER Working Paper No. 5110, May 1995.

Harrington, Michael. *The Other America: Poverty in the United States.* Baltimore: Penguin Books, 1971. First published 1963.

Harrison, B., and B. Bluestone. *The Great U-turn: Corporate Restructuring and the Polarizing of America.* New York: Basic Books, 1988.

Hicks, John. "Real and Monetary Factors in Economic Fluctuations." *Scottish Journal of Political Economy*, 21(3), 1974: 205–14.

Hinojosa-Ojeda, Raul, and Sherman Robinson. "Labor Issues in a North American Free Trade Area." Paper presented at the Brookings Institution Conference "NAFTA: An Assessment of the Research," Washington, April 9–10, 1992.

Hirsch, B., and D. DuBois. "Self-Esteem in Early Adolescence: The Identification and Prediction of Contrasting Longitudinal Trajectories." *Journal of Youth and Adolescence*, 20(1), 1991: pp. 53–72.

Hirschberg, J., and D. Slottje. "An Empirical Bayes Approach to Analyzing Earnings Functions for Various Occupations and Industries." *Journal of Econometrics*, 61, March 1994: pp. 65–79.

Hirschman, Albert. *The Strategy of Economic Development*. New Haven, CT: Yale University Press, 1964.

"The Political Economy of Latin American Development: Seven Exercises in Retrospection." *Latin American Research Review*, 22(3), 1987: pp. 7–36.

Hoffman, H. "Poverty and Prosperity: What Is Changing?", in E. Bacha and H. Klien (eds.), *The Social Change in Brazil: The Incomplete Transition*. Albuquerque: University of New Mexico Press, 1989.

Howell, David R. "Information Technology, Skill Mismatch and the Wage Collapse: A Perspective on the U.S. Experience," in *Employment and Growth in the Knowledge-Based Economy*. Paris: OECD, 1996.

Howell, David R., Margaret Duncan, and Bennett Harison. "Low Wages in the U.S. and High Unemployment in Europe: A Critical Assessment of the Conventional Wisdom." CEPA Working Paper No. 5, New School for Social Research, February 5, 1998.

Howell, David R., and Maury B. Gittleman. "Job, Labor Market Segmentation in the 1980's: A New Perspective on the Effects of Employment Restructuring by Ruce and Gender," New York: Mimeo, New School for Social Research, 1993.

Hugh, H. "Policy Lessons of the Development Experience." Occasional Paper No. 16, Group of the Thirty New York, 1985.

Achieving Industrialization in East Asia. New York: Cambridge University Press, 1988.

Jacoby, Sanford. *Employing Bureaucracy*. New York: Columbia University Press, 1985.

Jantti, M., and V. Ritakallio. "Income Inequality and Poverty in Finland in the 1980s," in P. Gottschalk, B. Gustafsson and E. Palmer (eds.), *Changing Patterns in the Distribution of Economic Welfare – An International Perspective*. Cambridge and New York: Cambridge University Press, 1997.

Jencks, C. *Inequality*, New York: Basic Books, 1972.

Jenkins, S. P. "Accounting for Inequality Trends: Decomposition Analysis for the UK, 1971–86." *Economica* 62(1), 1995: pp. 29–63.

Johnson, C. *MITI and the Japanese Miracle: The Growth of Industrial Policy, 1925–1975*. Stanford, CA: Stanford University Press, 1982.

"Political Institutions and Economic Performance: The Government–Business Relationship in Japan, South Korea, and Taiwan," in Frederick Deyo (ed.), *The Political Economy of the New Asian Industrialization*. Itaca, NY: Cornell University Press, 1987.

Juhn, C. *Relative Wage Trends, Women's Work, and Family Income*. Washington, DC: AEI Press, 1996.

Juhn, C., and K. Murphy. "Wage Inequality and Family Labor Supply." *Journal of Labor Economics*, 15(1), 1997: pp. 72–97.

Juhn, C., K. Murphy, and B. Pierce. "Wage Inequality and the Rise in Returns to Skill." *Journal of Political Economy*, 101(3), 1993: pp. 410–442.

Juhn, C., Kevin M. Murphy, and Brooks Pierce. "Wage Inequality and the Rise in Returns to Skill." *Journal of Political Economy*, 101(3), 1993: pp. 410–442.

Jwa, Sung-Hee. "Korea's Interest Rate and Capital Controls Deregulation: Implications for Monetary Policy and Financial Structure." *Joint Korea–U.S. Academic Symposium*, 3, 1993: pp. 65–84.

Kakizawa, Yoshihide, Robert H. Shumway, and Masanobu Taniguchi. "Discrimination and Clustering for Multivariate Time Series." *Journal of the American Statistical Association*, 93(441), 1998: pp. 328–340.

Kakwani, Manek. *Income Inequality and Poverty: Methods of Estimation and Policy Implications*. New York: Oxford University Press, 1980.

Kaldor, N. "Alternative Theories of Distribution." *The Review of Economic Studies*, 23, 1956: pp. 83–100.

Kaminsky, G., and C. M. Reinhart. *The Twin Crises: The Causes of Banking and Balance of Payment Problems*. Mimeo, Board of Governors for the Federal Reserve System, Washington, DC, 1996.

Katz, L., G. Loveman, and D. Blanchflower. "A Comparison of Changes in the Structure of Wages in Four OECD Countries." NBER Working Paper 4297, 1993.

Katz, L., and K. Murphy. "Changes in Relative Wages, 1963–1987: Supply and Demand Factors." *Quarterly Journal of Economics*, 107(1), 1992: pp. 35–78.

Katz, L., and Lawrence H. Summers. "Industry Rents: Evidence and Implications." *Brookings Papers on Economic Activity: Microeconomics*, 1, 1989: pp. 209–290.

Katzenstein, P. *Between Power and Plenty*. Madison: University of Wisconsin Press, 1978.

Small States in the World Market: Industrial Policy in Europe. Ithaca, NY, and London: Cornell University Press, 1985.

Keat, Paul. "Long-Run Changes in Occupational Wage Structure, 1900–1956." *Journal of Political Economy*, 68, 1960: pp. 584–600.

Keely, L., and D. Quah. "Technology in Growth." Centre for Economic Performance Discussion Paper 391. London: London School of Economics, 1998.

Kenneally, James J. *Women and American Trade Unions*. Montreal: Eden Press, 1981. Koskoff, David. *Andrew Mellon*. New York: Crowell, 1978.

Kessler, D., and A. Masson (eds.). *Modeling the Accumulation and Distribution of Wealth*. Oxford: Clarendon Press, 1988.

Keynes, J. M. *The General Theory of Employment, Interest and Money*. London: Macmillan, 1936.

Kim, Dae-Il, and Robert H. Topel. "Labor Markets and Economic Growth: Korea's Industrialization," in Richard Freeman and Lawrence Katz (eds.), *Differences and Changes in Wage Structures*. Chicago: University of Chicago Press, 1995.

Kim, Ji-Hong. "Korean Industrial Policy in the 1970s: Heavy and Chemical Industrialization Drive." Korea Development Institute Working Paper, July 1990.

Kim, Jung-Ryum. *Thirty Years of Economic Policy in Korea*. Seoul: Joong Ang Ilbo, 1992.

Kim, Tae-Joon. "Perspectives on Korea's Financial Liberalization." *Joint Korea–U.S. Academic Symposium*, 3, 1993: pp. 29–39.

Klaren, P. F., and T. J. Bossert, *Promise of Development: Theories of Change in Latin America*. Bouldes, CO: Westured Press, 1986.

Klecka, C. O. *Discriminant Analysis*. Beverly Hills, CA: Sage, 1980.

Kotlikoff, L., and L. Summers. "The Contribution of Intergenerational Transfers to Total Wealth: A Reply," in D. Kesser and A. Masson (eds.), *Modeling the Accumulation and Distribution of Wealth*. Oxford: Clarendon Press, 1988.

Krueger, Alan B. "How Computers Have Changed the Wage Structure: Evidence from Micro Data." *Quarterly Journal of Economics*, 108(1), 1993: pp. 33–60.

Krueger, Alan B., and Lawrence H. Summers. "Reflections on the Inter-Industry Wage Structure," in Kevin Lang and Jonathan Leonard (eds.), *Unemployment and the Structure of Labor Markets*. Oxford: Basil Blackwell, 1987.

"Efficiency Wages and the Inter-Industry Wage Structure." *Econometrica*, 56(2), 1988: pp. 259–293.

Krueger, Anne O., and Baran Tuncer. "An Empirical Test of the Infant Industry Argument: Reply." *American Economic Review*, 84(4), 1994: p. 1096.

Kuznets, S. "Economic Growth and Income Inequality." *American Economic Review*, 65(1), 1955: pp. 1–28.

Modern Economic Growth. New Haven, CT: Yale University Press, 1966.

Kwack, T. "Industrial Restructuring Experience and Policies in Korea in the 1970s." Korea Development Institute Working Paper 8408, 1984.

Landes, D. *The Unbound Prometheus – Technological Change and Industrial Development in Western Europe from 1750 to the Present*. Cambridge and New York: Cambridge University Press, 1969.

The Wealth and Poverty of Nations: Why Some Are So Rich and Some So Poor. New York: W. W. Norton, 1998.

Langoni, Carlos. *Distribuição de Renda e Crescimento no Brasil*. Rio de Janeiro: Editora Expressão e Cultura, 1973.

Lawrence, Robert Z. *Single World, Divided Nations? International Trade and OECD Labor Markets*. Paris: Brookings Institution Press/OECD Development Centre, 1996.

Lawrence, Robert Z., and Matthew Slaughter. "Trade and American Wages in the 1980s: Giant Sucking Sound or Small Hiccup?" *Brookings Papers on Economic Activity: Microeconomics*, 2, 1993: pp. 161–210.

Lazonick, William. *Business Organization and the Myth of the Market Economy*. Cambridge: Cambridge University Press, 1991.

Leal, Carlos Simonsen, and Sergio Werlang. "Educação e Distribuição de Renda," José Marcio Camargo and Fabio Giambiagi (eds.), *Distribuição de Renda no Brasil*. Rio de Janeiro: Paz e Terra, 1991.

Lebergott, Stanley. "Wage Structures." *Review of Economics and Statistics*, 29, 1947: pp. 274–284.

Lecaillon, J., *Income Distribution and Economic Development: An Analytical Survey*. Geneva: International Labor Office, 1984.

Leamer, Edward E. "Wage Effects of a U.S.–Mexican Free Trade Agreement." Cambridge: National Bureau of Economic Research Working Paper No. 3991, January 20, 1992.

"A Trade Economist's View of U.S. Wages and Globalization." Mimeo, 1995.

"In Search of Stolper–Samuelson Effects on U.S. Wages." NBER Working Paper No. 5427, January 1996.

Lee, Hyung-Koo. *The Korean Economy: Perspectives for the Twenty-First Century*. Albany: State University of New York Press, 1996.

Leipziger, D. M. "Recent Korean Trade and Industrial Policies: Is Korea Coping with Industrial Change Better Than Its Trade Partners?" Paper presented at the 8th annual research conference of the Association for Policy Analysis and Management, L. B. J. School of Public Affairs, Austin, Texas, October 30–November 1, 1986.

Korea: Managing the Industrial Transition. A World Bank Country Study, vols. I and II. Washington, DC: World Bank, 1987.

Leontief, W. *The Structure of the American Economy*. New York: Oxford University Press, 1951.

Lester, Richard A. "A Range Theory of Wage Differentials." *Industrial and Labor Relations Review*, 5, 1952: pp. 483–500.

Leuven, E., H. Oosterbeek, and H. Ophem. "Explaining Differences in Male Wage Inequality by Differences in Demand and Supply of Skill." Centre for Economic Performance Discussion Paper 392, London School of Economics, 1998.

Levy, F., and R. Murnane. "U.S. Earnings Levels and Earnings Inequality: A Review of Recent Trends and Proposed Explanations." *Journal of Economic Literature*, 30(3), 1992: pp. 1333–1381.

Lewis, H. G. *Unionism and Relative Wages in the United States*. Chicago: University of Chicago Press, 1963.

Li, Hongyi, Lyn Squire, and Heng-Fu Zou. "Explaining International and Intertemporal Variations in Income Inequality." Working paper, Policy Research Department, the World Bank, 1996.

Lorr, M. *Cluster Analysis for Social Scientists*. San Francisco: Jossey-Bass, 1983.

Lovell, Peggy. "The Geography of Economic Development and Racial Discrimination in Brazil." *Development and Change*, 24(1), 1993: pp. 83–101.

Lucas, R. E. "On the Mechanics of Economic Development." *Journal of Monetary Economics*, 22, 1988: pp. 3–42.

Maddison, A. *Two Crises: Latin America and Asia, 1929–38 and 1973–83*. Paris: OECD, 1985.

Maher, John E. "An Index of Wage Rates for Selected Industries." *Review of Economics and Statistics*, 43, 1961a: pp. 277–282.

"The Wage Pattern in the United States, 1946–57." *Industrial and Labor Relations Review*, 15, 1961b: pp. 3–20.

Matsui, Kiyoshi. *Essays in International Trade*. Tokyo: Science Council of Japan, 1958.

McLeod, Darryl, and John Welch. "Real Exchange Rates and Investment Booms in Mexico." *North American Free Trade: Proceedings of a Conference*. Dallas: Federal Reserve Bank of Dallas, 1991.

Meade, J. E. *Efficiency, Equality and the Ownership of Property*. London: Allen and Unwin, 1964.

Mehra, Y. P. "Spillovers in Wage Determination in U.S. Manufacturing Industries." *Review of Economics and Statistics*, 58, 1976: pp. 300–312.

Meller, Patricio. "Economic Adjustment and Its Distributive Impact: Chile in the 1980's." Mimeo. Santiago, Chile: CIEPLAN, 1989.

Minsky, Hyman P. "The Financial Instability Hypothesis: A Clarification," in Martin Feldstein (ed.), *The Risk of Economic Crisis*. Chicago: University of Chicago Press, 1991.

Mitchell, D. "Shifting Norms in Wage Determination." *Brookings Papers on Economic Activity*, 2, 1985: pp. 575–599.

"Wage Pressures and Labor Shortages: The 1960s and 1980s." *Brookings Papers on Economic Activity*, 2, 1989: pp. 191–231.

Modigliani, F. "Measuring the Contribution of Intergenerational Transfers to Total Wealth: Conceptual Issues and Empirical Findings," in D. Kesser and A. Masson (eds.), *Modeling the Accumulation and Distribution of Wealth*. Oxford: Clarendon Press, 1988.

Modigliani, F., and R. Brumberg. "Utility Analysis and Aggregate Consumption Functions: an Attempt at Integration," in K. Kurihara (ed.), *Post-Keynesian Economics*. New Brunswick, NJ: Rutgers University Press, 1954.

Mokyr, J. *The Lever of Riches – Technological Creativity and Economic Progress*. Oxford: Oxford University Press, 1990.

Montgomery, David. "Labor and the Political Leadership of New Deal America." *International Review of Social History*, 39, 1994: pp. 335–360.

Morley, S. *Labor Markets and Inequitable Growth*. Cambridge: Cambridge University Press, 1982.

Morrison, D. G. "On the Interpretation of Discriminant Analysis." *Journal of Marketing Research*, 6, 1969: pp. 156–163.

Murphy, K., C. Riddell, and P. Romer. "Wages and Technology in the United States and Canada," in E. Helpman (ed.), *General Purpose Technologies and Economic Growth*. Cambridge, MA: MIT Press, 1998.

Murphy, K., and F. Welch. "The Role of Industrial Trade in Wage Differentials," in M. Kosters (ed.), *Workers and Their Wages*. Washington, DC: AEI Press, 1991.

Musgrove, P. "Food Need and Absolute Poverty in Urban South America." *Review of Income and Wealth*, no. 31, 1985: pp. 63–84.

National Industrial Conference Board. "Wages, Hours, and Employment in the United States July, 1936–December, 1937." New York: National Industrial Conference Board, 1938.

Wartime Pay of Women in Industry. New York: National Industrial Conference Board, 1943.

The Economic Almanac for 1948. New York: National Industrial Conference Board, 1948.

The Economic Almanac 1953–54. New York: Crowell, 1954.

Nelson, R. R., and S. Phelps. "Investment in Humans, Technological Diffusion and Economic Growth." *American Economic Review*, 56(2), 1966: pp. 69–75.

Nelson, R. R., and P. Romer. "Science, Economic Growth, and Public Policy," in B. L. R. Smith and C. E. Barfield (eds.), *Technology, R&D, and the Economy*. Washington, DC: Brookings Institution, 1996.

Nelson, R. R., and S. G. Winter. *An Evolutionary Theory of Economic Change*. Cambridge, MA: Belknap Press of Harvard University Press, 1982.

Nickell, Stephen. "Unemployment and Labor Market Rigidities: Europe versus North America." *Journal of Economic Perspectives*, 11(3), 1997: pp. 55–74.

Ober, Harry. "Occupational Wage Differentials, 1907–47." *Monthly Labor Review*, 67, 1948: pp. 127–132.

OECD. *The Future of Social Protection*. Paris: OECD, 1988.

The OECD Jobs Study: Facts, Analysis, Strategies. Paris: OECD, 1994.

Office of the Prime Minister, Republic of Korea. *Evaluation Report of the First Year Program: The Fourth Year Economic Development Plan 1978*.

Okimoto, D. *Between MITI and Market: Japanese Industrial Policy for High Technology*. Stanford, CA: Stanford University Press, 1989.

Pack, H. "Endogenous Growth Theory: Intellectual Appeal and Empirical Shortcomings." *Journal of Economic Perspectives*, (8)1, 1994: pp. 55–72.

Pack, H., and L. E. Westpal. "Industrial Strategy and Technological Change." *Journal of Development Economics*, 27, 1986: pp. 87–128.

Pasinetti, L. L. "Rate of Profit and Income Distribution in Relation to the Rate of Economic Growth." *Review of Economic Studies*, 29(4), 1962: pp. 267–279.

Structural Economic Dynamics: A Theory of the Economic Consequences of Human Learning. Cambridge and New York: Cambridge University Press, 1993.

Patrick, H., and H. Rosovsky. *Asia's New Giant*. Washington, DC: Brookings Institution, 1976.

Paukert, F. "Income Distribution at Different Levels of Development: A Survey of Evidence." *International Labor Review*, 68, 1973: pp. 97–125.

Perotti, R. "Fiscal Policy, Income Distribution, and Growth." *American Economic Review*, 82, 1992: pp. 311–316.

"Political Equilibrium, Income Distribution and Growth: Theory and Evidence." *Review of Economic Studies*, 60, 1993: pp. 755–766.

"Income Distribution and Investment." *European Economic Review*, 38, 1994: pp. 827–835.

"Growth, Income Distribution and Democracy." *Journal of Economic Growth*, 1, 1996: pp. 147–187.

Persson, T., and G. Tabellini. "Is Inequality Harmful for Growth? Theory and Evidence." *American Economic Review*, 84, 1994: pp. 600–621.

Petit, P. "Technology and Employment," in P. Stoneman (ed.), *Handbook of the Economics of Innovation and Technological Change*. Oxford and Cambridge, MA: Blackwell, 1995.

Pritchett, L. "Divergence, Big Time." *Journal of Economics Perspectives*, 11(3), 1997: pp. 3–17.

Ram, R. "Level of Economic Development and Income Inequality: Evidence from the Post-War Developed World." *Southern Economic Journal*, 64(2), 1997: pp. 576–578.

Ramos, Lauro, and José Almeida Reis. *A Distribuição de Rendimentos no Brasil 1976/85*. Série IPEA, 141. Rio de Janeiro: IPEA, 1993.

"Interindustry Wage Differentials." Discussion Paper No. 374. Rio de Janeiro: IPEA, 1995a.

"Salário Mínimo, Distribuição de Renda e Pobreza no Brasil." *Pesquisa e Planejamento Econômico*, 25(1), April 1995b: pp. 99–114.

Rawls, J. *A Theory of Justice*. Cambridge, MA: Belknap Press of Harvard University Press, 1971.

Reder, M. W. "The Theory of Occupational Wage Differentials." *American Economic Review*, 45, 1955: pp. 833–852.

"Wage Differentials: Theory and Measurement," in National Bureau of Economic Research, *Aspects of Labor Economics*. Princeton: Princeton University Press, 1962.

Reich, R. *The Work of Nations: Preparing Ourselves for 21st Century Capitalism.* New York: Alfred A. Knopf, 1991.

Reis, José Almeida, and Ricardo Barros. "Distribuição da Educação e Desigualdade Salarial." Discussion Paper No. 178. Rio de Janeiro: Instituto de Pesquisa Economica Aplicada, Brasilia, 1989.

Rencher, Alvin C. "Interpretation of Canonical Discriminant Functions, Canonical Variates, and Principal Components." *The American Statistician*, 46, 1992: pp. 217–225.

Reyes-Heroles, Jesus F. "The Distribution of Labor Income in Mexico," in Pedro Aspe and Paul E. Sigmund (eds.), *The Political Economy of Income Distribution in Mexico*. New York: Holmes and Meier, 1984.

Rhee, S. "Policy Reforms of the 80s and the Industrial Adjustments in Korean Economy." Working Paper No. 8708, Korea Development Institute, Seoul, 1987.

Romer, P. "Increasing Returns and Long-Run Growth." *Journal of Political Economy*, 98(5), 1986: pp. 1002–1037.

"Endogenous Technological Growth." *Journal of Political Economy*, 98(5), 1990: pp. 71–102.

"The Origins of Endogenous Growth." *Journal of Economic Perspectives*, 8(1), 1994: pp. 3–22.

Rosenberg, N. *Inside the Black Box: Technology and Economics.* Cambridge and New York: Cambridge University Press, 1982.

Exploring the Black Box: Technology, Economics and History, Cambridge and New York: Cambridge University Press, 1994.

Ross, Arthur M. "The External Wage Structure," in G. W. Taylor and F. C. Pierson (eds.), *New Concepts in Wage Determination.* New York: McGraw-Hill, 1957.

Rowthorn, Robert, and Richard Kozul-Wright. *Exploring the Black Box: Technology, Economics and History.* Cambridge and New York: Cambridge University Press, 1994.

"Globalization and Economic Convergence: An Assessment." United Nations Conference on Trade and Development, Discussion Paper No. 131, February 1998.

Russell, R. "Comments on Chapter 10," in D. Kessler and A. Masson (eds.), *Modeling the Accumulation and Distribution of Wealth.* Oxford: Clarendon Press, 1988.

Saboia, João. "Politica Salarial e Distribuição de Renda: 25 anos de Desencontros," in José Marcio Camargo and Fabio Giambiagi (eds.), *Distribuição de Renda no Brasil.* Rio de Janeiro: Paz e Terra, 1991.

Sachs, J. "External Debt and Macroeconomic Performance in Latin America and East Asia." *Brookings Papers on Economic Activity*, no. 2, 1985: pp. 523–573.

Developing Country Debt and Economic Performance, vol. 2. Chicago: University of Chicago Press, 1990.

Samuels, R. *The Business of the Japanese State: Energy Markets in Comparative and Historical Perspective.* Ithaca, NY, and London: Cornell University Press, 1987.

Samuelson, P. A. *Economics: An Introductory Analysis.* New York: McGraw-Hill, 1964.

Sanchez, Carlos. "Labor Markets in an Era of Adjustment: Argentina." Cordoba: IEERAL, Fundacion Mediterranea 1989.

Sawyer, Malcolm. *The Economics of Michal Kalecki.* London: Macmillan, 1985.

Schmitt, J. "The Changing Structure of Male Earnings in Britain 1974–1988," in R. Freeman and L. Katz (eds.), *Differences and Changes in Wage Structures.* Chicago: University of Chicago Press, 1995.

Schultz, T. "Capital Formation by Education." *Journal of Political Economy,* 68(6), 1960: pp. 571–583.

Schumpeter, J. *The Theory of Economic Development.* Cambridge, MA: Harvard University Press, 1934.

Capitalism, Socialism and Democracy, New York: Harper Row, 1950.

Sebastiani, Mario. *Kalecki and Unemployment Equilibrium.* New York: St. Martin's Press, 1994.

Sen, A. *Resources, Values and Development.* Cambridge, MA: Harvard University Press, 1984.

On Economic Inequality. Oxford: Clarendon Press, 1997.

Sen, A. *Development as Freedom.* Oxford: Oxford University Press, 1999.

Shannon, C. E. "A Mathematical Theory of Communication." *Bell System Technical Journal,* 27, 1948: pp. 379–423.

Sheahan J. *Patterns of Development in Latin America: Poverty, Repression and Economic Strategy.* Princeton, NJ: Princeton University Press, 1987.

Shorrocks, Daniel. "The Class of Additively Decomposable Inequality Measures." *Econometrica,* 48(3), 1980: pp. 613–625.

"Inequality Decomposition by Population Subgroups." *Econometrica,* 52(6), 1984: pp. 1369–1385.

Silva, Salomão. "Sistema Financeiro, Participação na Renda, Funções e Disfunções," in José Marcio Camargo and Fabio Giambiagi (eds.), *Distribuição de Renda no Brasil.* Rio de Janeiro: Paz e Terra, 1991.

Simonsen, M. "The Developing Country Debt Problem," in G. Smith and J. Cuddingston (eds.), *International Debt and the Developing Countries.* Washington, DC: World Bank, 1985.

Singer, David J., and Melvin Small. "Alliance Aggregation and the Onset of War, 1816–1965," in J. David Singer (ed.), *Quantitative International Politics: Insights and Evidence.* New York: Free Press, 1968.

Slichter, Sumner. "Notes on the Structure of Wages." *Review of Economics and Statistics,* 32, 1950: pp. 80–91.

Smith, A. *An Inquiry into the Nature and Causes of the Wealth of Nations.* Edinburgh, 1776.

Soffer, Benson. "On Union Rivalries and the Minimum Differentiation of Wage Patterns." *Review of Economics and Statistics,* 41, 1959: pp. 53–60.

Sola, Lourdes. "Heterodox Shock in Brazil: *Tecnicos,* Politicians and Democracy." *Journal of Latin American Studies,* 22, February 1991: pp. 163–180.

Solow, R. M. "A Contribution to the Theory of Economic Growth." *Quarterly Journal of Economics,* 70(1), 1956: pp. 65–94.

"Technical Change and the Aggregate Production Function." *Review of Economics and Statistics,* 39, August 1957: pp. 312–320.

Learning from Learning by Doing. Stanford: Stanford University Press, 1997.

Sraffa, Piero. *Production of Commodities by Means of Commodities: Prelude to a Critique of Economic Theory.* Cambridge: Cambridge University Press, 1960.

Steinmo, S., K. Thelen, and F. Longstreth. *Structuring Politics: Historical Institutionalism in Comparative Analysis*. New York: Cambridge University Press, 1992.

Stern, J., J. H. Kim, and D. H. Perkins. *Industrialization and the State: The Korean Heavy and Chemical Industry Drive*. Cambridge, MA: Harvard University Press, 1995.

Stiglitz, J. "Distribution of Income and Wealth Among Individuals." *Econometrica*, 37(3), 1969: pp. 382–397.

Stoneman, Paul. *Handbook of the Economics of Innovations and Technological Change*. Blackwell Handbooks in Economics. Oxford: Blackwell, 1995.

Strackbein, O. R. *The Prevailing Minimum Wage Standard*. Washington, DC: Graphic Arts Press, 1939.

Sundstrom, William. "Down the Down Staircase: Changes in the Employment and Occupational Status of Urban Black Men During the Depression." Santa Clara, Department of Economics, Santa Clara University, 1993.

Tatsuola, M. *Multivariate Analysis*. New York: Macmillan, 1988.

Taylor, Lance. "Varieties of Stabilization Experience." Marshall Lectures at Cambridge University, May 6–7, 1987.

Temporary National Economic Committee: "Concentration and Composition of Individual Incomes, 1918–37." Washington, DC: 76th Congress, 3d Session, Senate Committee Print, 1940.

Theil, Henry. *Economics and Information Theory*. Amsterdam: North-Holland, 1967.

Statistical Decomposition Analysis: With Applications in the Social and Administrative Sciences. Amsterdam and London: North Holland, 1972.

Thiesenhusen, W. *Searching for Agrarian Reform in Latin America*. Winchester, MA: Unwin Hyman, 1989.

Tinbergen, J. *Income Distribution*, Amsterdam: North Holland, 1975.

Thurow, Lester C. *Generating Inequality*. New York: Basic Books, 1975.

"Wage Dispersion: 'Who Done It?'" *Journal of Post Keynesian Economics*, 21(1), Fall 1998: pp. 25–38.

Troy, Leo. *Distribution of Union Membership Among the States, 1939 and 1953*. New York: National Bureau of Economic Research, 1956.

Trade Union Membership, 1897–1962. New York: National Bureau of Economic Research, 1965.

U.S. Department of Commerce. *Survey of Current Business – 1936 Supplement*. Washington, DC: U.S. Government Printing Office, 1936.

U.S. Department of Commerce, Bureau of the Census. *Statistical Abstract of the United States*. Washington, DC: U.S. Government Printing Office, 1951.

U.S. Department of Commerce. *Survey of Current Business – 1942 Supplement*. Washington, DC: U.S. Government Printing Office, 1942.

Historical Statistics of the United States – Colonial Times to 1970. Washington, DC: U.S. Bureau of the Census, 1975.

U.S. Department of Labor, Bureau of Labor Statistics. *Handbook of Labor Statistics 1950 Edition*. Washington, DC: U.S. Government Printing Office, 1950.

Union Wages and Hours: Printing Industry, Vol. Bulletin No. 1592. Washington, DC: U.S. Government Printing Office, 1968.

Van Ginneken, Wouter. *Socio-Economic Groups and Income Distribution in Mexico*. London: Croom Helm, 1980.

Vanhoudt, P. "Do Labor Market Policies and Income Fundamentals Matter for Income Inequality in OECD Countries? Some Empirical Evidence." IMF Working Paper. Washington, DC: IMF, 1997.

"An Assessment of the Macroeconomic Determinants of Inequality." Stockholm School of Economics, Stockholm School of Economic Working Paper 271, 1998.

Wade, R. *Governing the Market: Economic Theory and the Role of Government in East Asian Industrialization*. Princeton, NJ: Princeton University Press, 1990.

Wallis, John J. "Employment in the Great Depression." *Explorations in Economic History*, 26, 1989: pp. 45–72.

Ward, J. H., Jr. "Hierarchical Grouping to Optimize an Objective Function." *Journal of the American Statistical Association*, 58, 1963: pp. 236–244.

Weiss, A. *Efficiency Wages – Models of Unemployment, Layoffs, and Wage Dispersion*. Princeton, NJ: Princeton University Press, 1990.

Westphal, L. E. "The Republic of Korea's Experience with Export Led Industrial Development. *World Development*, 6(3), 1978: pp. 347–382.

Williamson, J. *The Progress of Policy Reform in Latin America*. Washington, DC: Institute for International Economics, 1990.

Williamson, J., and P. Lindert. *American Inequality: A Macroeconomic History*. Academic Press, 1980.

Wilson, W. J. *The Truly Disadvantaged – The Inner City, the Underclass, and Public Policy*. Chicago: University of Chicago Press, 1986.

Witte, E. E. *The Government in Labor Disputes*. New York: McGraw-Hill, 1932.

Wolff, E. N. "Life-Cycle Savings and the Individual Distribution of Wealth by Class," in D. Kesser and A. Masson (eds.), *Modeling the Accumulation and Distribution of Wealth*. Oxford: Clarendon Press, 1988.

Wood, A. *North–South Trade, Employment and Inequality*. Oxford: Clarendon Press, 1994.

World Bank. World Debt Tables. Baltimore: Johns Hopkins University Press, 1988–1989.

World Development Report, 1990. New York: Oxford University Press, 1990.

World Development Report, 1991. New York: Oxford University Press, 1991.

Woytinsky, W. S. *Three Aspects of Labor Dynamics*. New York: Social Science Research Council, 1942.

Woytinsky, W. S., and E. S. Woytinsky. *World Commerce and Governments*. New York: Twentieth Century Fund, 1955.

Wright, Annette C. "Strategy and Structure in the Textile Industry: Spencer Love and Burlington Mills, 1923–62." *Business History Review*, 69(1), 1995: 42–79.

Wyckoff, Viola. *The Public Works Wage Rate and Some of Its Economic Effects*. New York: Columbia University Press, 1946.

Yotopoulos, Pan. *Exchange Rate for Trade and Development: Theory, Tests and Case Studies*. Cambridge: Cambridge University Press, 1996.

Zieger, Robert H. *The CIO 1935–55*. Chapel Hill: University of North Carolina Press, 1995.

Index

313